Diplomacy

Date Due

Previous books by the author:

Economic Power in Anglo-South African Diplomacy: Simonstown, Sharpeville and After (Macmillan: London, 1981)

Diplomacy at the UN (ed) with A. Jennings (Macmillan: London; St. Martin's Press, New York, 1985)

The Politics of the South Africa Run: European Shipping and Pretoria (Clarendon Press: Oxford, 1987)

Return to the UN: UN Diplomacy in Regional Conflicts (Macmillan: London, 1991)

International Politics: States, Power and Conflict since 1945, 2nd ed (Harvester Wheatsheaf: Hemel Hempstead, 1992)

South Africa, the Colonial Powers and 'African Defence': The Rise and Fall of the White Entente, 1948–60 (Macmillan: London, 1992)

An Introduction to International Relations, with D. Heater (Harvester Wheatsheaf: Hemel Hempstead, 1993)

Talking to the Enemy: How States without 'Diplomatic Relations' Communicate (Macmillan: London, 1994)

Diplomacy
Theory and Practice

G. R. BERRIDGE

*Professor of International Politics and
Director of the Centre for the Study of Diplomacy,
University of Leicester*

PRENTICE HALL
HARVESTER WHEATSHEAF

London   New York   Toronto   Sydney   Tokyo   Singapore
Madrid   Mexico City   Munich

First published 1995 by
Prentice Hall/Harvester Wheatsheaf
Campus 400, Maylands Avenue
Hemel Hempstead
Hertfordshire, HP2 7EZ
A division of
Simon & Schuster International Group

Typeset in 10/12pt Sabon
by Hands Fotoset, Leicester

Printed and bound in Great Britain by
Biddles Ltd, Guildford and King's Lynn

Library of Congress Cataloging in Publication Data

Available from the publisher

British Library Cataloguing in Publication Data

A catalogue record for this book is available from
the British Library

ISBN 0-13-433889-8

---

1 2 3 4 5   99 98 97 96 95

For my children, Cathy and William

CONTENTS

viii   *Contents*

PREFACE

This book on diplomacy is based on the course which I have taught on the MA in Diplomatic Studies at Leicester University over the last four years. The chapter on mediation has appeared previously in *Talking to the Enemy* (Macmillan: London, 1994), and I am grateful to Macmillan for permission to reprint it here. I have employed the Harvard referencing system and, for the sake of consistency, also used this style in listing 'Further reading' at the end of each chapter. However, the reader wishing to track a reference from the text should consult 'References' at the end of the book rather than 'Further reading'. I should also add that the reader with an interest in bilateral diplomacy but no taste for legal commentary can proceed with reasonable safety directly from the Introduction to Chapter 2. Chapter 1, in other words, carries an author's health warning.

I would like to record here my gratitude to those of my colleagues at Leicester and elsewhere who have stimulated me with their ideas (most recently at the LSE and Bristol), and I am particularly grateful to David H. Dunn, Alan James, Helen Leigh-Phippard, Jan Melissen and John Young for taking the trouble to comment on all or part of this manuscript. I am, as always, grateful, too, to Clare Grist of Prentice Hall/Harvester Wheatsheaf for her guidance on editorial matters.

G. R. B., Leicester, October 1994

LIST OF ABBREVIATIONS

ANC	African National Congress
ASEAN	Association of South-East Asian Nations
CHOGMs	Commonwealth Heads of Government Meetings
EU	European Union
EC	European Community
GATT	General Agreement on Tariffs and Trade
IAEA	International Atomic Energy Agency
IMF	International Monetary Fund
ILC	International Law Commission
MIRV	Multiple Independently Targetable Re-entry Vehicle
OAU	Organization of African Unity
OECD	Organization of Economic Cooperation and Development
P5	Permanent 5 [on the UN Security Council]
PLO	Palestine Liberation Organization
SAARC	South Asian Association for Regional Cooperation
SALT	Strategic Arms Limitation Talks
SWAPO	South-West African People's Organization
UNITA	National Union for the Total Independence of Angola

INTRODUCTION

Diplomacy is the conduct of international relations by negotiation rather than by force, propaganda, or recourse to law, and by other peaceful means (such as gathering information or engendering goodwill) which are either directly or indirectly designed to promote negotiation. Despite suffering ideological assaults in the first half of the twentieth century, diplomacy survived and it now flourishes. This is because the circumstances which first encouraged its development as the key institution of the system of states themselves remain commanding: the balance of power together with a weak international legal regime. Diplomacy is an activity which is regulated by custom and by law, though flexibility remains one of its vital features.[1] It is also a professionalised activity, though non-professionals now play an important part in it – and it does not cease to be diplomacy for this reason (Bull, 1977, p. 163).

There was a time, before the First World War, when this activity was conducted almost entirely on a bilateral basis, generally by means of the exchange of permanent diplomatic missions. It is true, of course, that today diplomacy is conducted by other means as well, notably in multilateral settings and via the special envoy. Nevertheless, since the present world diplomatic system had its origins in the resident mission, and since this mission is still – despite repeated pronouncements of its death – the foundation on which the system rests, it is appropriate to begin this study with an examination of its early features, including its early and continuing drawbacks.

The basis of the present world diplomatic system has its roots in fifteenth century Italy, where permanent embassies were first

1

established (Mattingly, 1965). Nevertheless, Harold Nicolson, perhaps the most well known twentieth century writer on diplomacy in the English language, describes this kind of diplomacy not as the 'Italian' but as the 'French system of diplomacy' (Nicolson, 1954). This seems reasonable. Why?

To begin with, it was the French, during the seventeenth and eighteenth centuries, who were chiefly responsible for cleaning up and professionalising the Italian inheritance and giving us the system which we have today. Secondly, the most important writers on diplomacy were French, notably François de Callières, described as the first writer to move the discussion of diplomacy away from jurisprudence and homilies on the ideal ambassador towards considerations of political reality (Callières, 1983, p. 23). Thirdly, the French language itself – 'better adapted than any other to an intercourse requiring the perfect fusion of courtesy with precision' (Nicolson, 1954, p. 57) – had replaced Latin as the accepted medium through which different states conducted their business, the *lingua franca* of diplomacy (Latin lost its general predominance in Western Europe at the end of the thirteenth century but not in Italy until the fifteenth) (Queller, 1967, p. 32). Thirdly, if not self-evidently the best diplomatic service in Europe (Roosen, 1985), the French service was certainly the most extensive.

As it evolved from the diplomatic system which originated in Italy in the middle of the fifteenth century, the French system of diplomacy naturally embodied some of its central features. These included permanent diplomatic representation, secrecy in negotiation, and elaborate ceremonial. These will be described first and the modifications introduced by the French later.

PERMANENCE

In the middle ages, diplomacy conducted other than by princes themselves and what might be called part-timers (lawyers, merchants, consuls, and so on) had been placed in the hands of *nuncii* and, with growing frequency after the late twelfth century, plenipotentiaries. While the two differed in that the former was no more than a 'living letter' whereas the latter had 'full powers' – *plena potestas* – to negotiate on behalf of and bind his principal, both were alike in that they were temporary envoys with narrowly focused tasks[2] who were required to return home when those tasks were completed (Queller, 1967, chs 1 and 2). It was the mark of the French system that these ad hoc envoys were replaced or, more accurately, supplemented by permanent embassies with broad responsibilities. Why did this occur?

The invention of the resident mission was above all a function of the intensification of diplomatic activity in the fifteenth century, especially on the part of the nervous, vulnerable and yet frequently ambitious Italian city states. As envoys were having to be despatched more and more often on journeys which did not become more and more safe, and as the duration of their stays had to be increasingly extended, 'it was discovered to be more practical and more economical to appoint an ambassador to remain at a much frequented court' (Queller, 1967, p. 82). In any case, in the new conditions it had also become difficult to find enough suitable persons to act as envoys, a role which was even less popular than modern-day jury service. However, apart from its practical and economic advantages, the institutionalisation of the resident ambassador also signalled an increasing awareness that diplomacy itself worked most efficiently when it was a continuous, rather than episodic, process.

For one thing, continuing representation in a foreign country produced maximum familiarity with conditions and personalities in the country concerned and was thus likely to produce a more regular and reliable flow of information for any number of purposes considered important back home; it would also be more likely to produce the kind of intelligence, personal contacts, and sheer experience which would prove particularly invaluable when an important negotiation had to be undertaken, even if this should not be undertaken by the ambassador himself. Secondly, continuing representation made it easier to launch a diplomatic initiative without attracting the attention which would probably accompany the arrival of a special envoy (Queller, 1967, p. 83). Thirdly, it was likely to reinforce continuity in policy, whatever that policy was. And finally, it fostered as well as expressed the notion – so well articulated by Richelieu – that states had certain permanent interests which might not be overridden by considerations of a sentimental, ideological, or personal kind (Nicolson, 1954, p. 51). Permanent diplomatic missions were the most obvious feature of the French system, though the more powerful and thus relatively more relaxed states – including France itself – were slower to despatch than to receive them (Hale, 1957, pp. 267–8; Anderson, 1993, pp. 8–10). The China of the Manchu Emperors, which first had to be encouraged to view foreign governments as sovereign equals rather than as barbarous vassals whose representatives must acknowledge this status by the delivery of tribute and performance of the kow-tow (Peyrefitte, 1993), did not entertain foreign relations on this basis until 1861 (Moser and Moser, 1993, p. 2ff).

SECRECY

A second feature of the French system – and in the eyes of radical critics of this 'old diplomacy' after the First World War a baleful one – was secret negotiation. In current usage this can mean all or any of the following: keeping the contents of a negotiation secret, keeping knowledge that negotiations are going on at all secret, keeping the content of any agreement issuing from negotiations secret, or keeping secret the fact that any agreement at all has been reached. When the pleonasm 'secret diplomacy' is carelessly employed, it is not normally clear which of these meanings is involved. However, in the French system, and certainly in the hands of its publicists, secret negotiation normally meant keeping either the fact or the content of negotiations secret. Why was this considered important?

Two very excellent reasons are normally advanced for secret negotiation. The first is that serious discussion between states, often on matters vital to national security or economic prosperity, unavoidably involves the revelation of weaknesses and habits of negotiating tactics. It is bad enough having to reveal these to the other side; having to reveal them to the whole world might prove damaging in subsequent negotiations with different parties. The second reason is that secrecy (here, concerning the fact that negotiations are going on at all) protects the negotiators from the clamour of those demanding a settlement at almost any price, thus enabling them to walk away from the talks if a decision which they consider acceptable cannot be reached. The third, and generally more important reason, is that a successful negotiation means, by definition, that each side will have to settle for less than its ideal requirements. This means that certain parties – radical supporters of the governments concerned, some other domestic constituency, or a foreign friend – will have to be in some measure 'sold out'. If such parties are aware of what is afoot at the time, they might well be able, and will certainly try, to sabotage the talks. In some cases this may even involve attempted assassination. Henry Kissinger, National Security Advisor to the US President and then Secretary of State in the Republican administrations from 1969 until 1974, sums up this point well when he remarks in his memoirs that 'The sequence in which concessions are made becomes crucial; it [the negotiation] can be aborted if each move has to be defended individually rather than as part of a mosaic before the reciprocal move is clear' (Kissinger, 1979, p. 803). He could have added, however, that a negotiation might have to be aborted even when the other side's concessions are apparent, since there will always be some who regard these as inadequate. As a general rule, therefore, the more radical the departure in policy which a negotiation implies, the greater the need for secrecy. This was demonstrated no more clearly than by the long secret negotiations between Israel and the Palestine Liberation Organization (PLO), which only began to leak out in the weeks prior to the historic agreement between them which was sealed in Washington in September 1993. The nature of the Israeli concessions did not prevent the issuance of death threats against Yasser Arafat from diehard Palestinian factions.

CEREMONIAL AND PROTOCOL

Protocol is the term given to the procedural rules of diplomacy, some but not all of which concern elaborate ceremonial. Ceremonial procedures, not least religious ones, were an important feature of diplomatic relations before the Renaissance and were developed even more fully in the following centuries to become an important feature of the French system. Ceremonial was used to burnish a prince's prestige, flatter his allies, and solemnise agreements reached by negotiation. 'Negotiations were often begun with prayers, agreements signed in a church or abbey and holy relics displayed to add greater solemnity to the occasion' (Anderson, 1993, p. 15). Ratification of agreements concluded by plenipotentiaries, which was juridically unnecessary, was also often accompanied by high ceremony in order to reinforce the compact (Queller, 1967, pp. 219–20). Ambassadors, like the earlier *nuncii* (though unlike plenipotentiaries), were of great value in ceremonial because they were held to represent their principals so completely that anyone who killed an ambassador was held to be guilty of *lesé majesté* (p. 100). The greater the nobility, or clerical or – with the advent of the Renaissance – scholarly authority of an ambassador, the greater his value in ceremonial (pp. 154–5).

While the rules of ceremony were developed with precise ends in view, protocol in general – including its less ostentatious aspects – has always had the less obvious function of enabling states to concentrate more on the substantive issues which divide them and not have to argue afresh about procedure each time they meet. In this regard, diplomatic protocol fulfils exactly the same function as the rules of procedure governing any activity. As Cohen says,

the substantive causes for abrasion between states are real enough without adding unnecessary disagreement about the external forms of intercourse. Knowing that issues of procedure and prerogative have been decided in advance on an invariant and impersonal basis, no participant need feel that he is being snubbed or discriminated against. (1987, p. 142)

The regulation of diplomatic precedence, that is, the order in which diplomats are received and seated at official functions, or append their signatures to treaties, for example, has always been particularly important. This is because of the sensitivities of princes to their prestige, which is such a valuable currency in international relations (Morgenthau, 1978, ch. 6). It was a major achievement of the French system to overturn, at the Congress of Vienna in 1815, the controversial scheme of precedence laid down by the Pope in 1504.[3] Henceforward, diplomats would take rank according to the date of the official notification of their arrival in the capital concerned, the longest serving being accorded the highest seniority. It also became customary that plenipotentiaries at a conference would sign treaties in alphabetical order (Nicolson, 1963, p. 100).

The importance of protocol is seen no more clearly than during a war between two states. Every war must end some time and even while it continues there may well be need for limited communication between the parties, for example on prisoner exchange or on measures to prevent the fighting getting out of hand. In such circumstances it is doubly important that diplomacy should be rule-governed. Callières saw this early:

The ministers of Princes who are at war, and who happen to be in the same court, do not visit one another so long as the war lasts, but they pay to one another mutual civilities when they chance to meet in a third place. War does not destroy the rules of civility, nor those of generosity; nay, it even affords frequent opportunities of practising them with greater glory, both for the minister who puts them in practice, and the Prince who approves them. (1983, p. 129)

HONESTY

According to Nicolson, what really marked off the French system from its Italian precursor – which he characterised as cynical, duplicitous, corrupt and opportunistic (Nicolson, 1954, p. 46) – was its adoption of the critical principle that deceit had no place in diplomacy. It is likely that Nicolson exaggerated the depravity of the diplomatic methods popularised by Machiavelli (Hale, 1957, pp. 272–5; Queller, 1967, p. 109). Nevertheless, it does seem that as the resident ambassador became more accepted, achieved a higher social standing, and gradually became part of a profession (see below), he – and his prince – attached more importance to honesty in diplomacy. Callières emphasised, indeed, that the purpose of negotiation was not to trick the other side but to reconcile states on the basis of a true estimate of their enduring interests (1983, p. 33, 110). This was right; it was also prudent. For only if agreements are made on this basis are they likely to endure, and if they are unlikely to endure they are unlikely to be worth concluding in the first place. By contrast, if a state secures an agreement by deceit or subsequently throws over an agreement immediately it becomes inconvenient, it is not only likely to breed a desire for revenge in the breast of its victim (p. 83) but find other states disinclined to enter negotiations with it in the future. Greater honesty in diplomacy was a sign of the maturing of the diplomatic system.

PROFESSIONALISM

A second original feature of the French system was the professionalisation of diplomacy. For Callières in particular diplomacy was too important, and too much in need of extensive knowledge and technical expertise to be entrusted to anyone who had not served a proper apprenticeship and was not provided with suitable rewards (1983, pp. 99–100). Despite the repeated use of certain individuals as envoys as far back as the middle ages (Queller, 1967, pp. 157–8) and the experiment with the French Political Academy in the early eighteenth century, the professionalisation of diplomacy (with clear ranks, regular payment, and controlled entry) was a slow and fitful process and was not seriously underway, not even in France itself, until well into the nineteenth century (Anderson, 1993, pp. 80–96, 119–28).

Nevertheless, diplomacy was a fairly well established profession by the outbreak of the First World War and an equally interesting development was associated with this: the appearance of the *corps diplomatique* or diplomatic body. The 'diplomatic corps', as it was corrupted in English, were the community of diplomats representing different states who are resident in the same capital.[4] The evolution of this institution, with its own rules of procedure, such as the rule that the longest-serving ambassador should be the spokesman of the corps on matters of common interest (its *doyen*), was clear evidence of an emerging sense of professional solidarity among diplomats. Diplomats under the French system, in other words, had come to recognise that they had professional interests which united them as diplomats, as well as political and commercial interests which divided them as, say, Englishmen, Frenchmen, or Austro-Hungarians. This institution perhaps reached its apogée in late nineteenth century China, where the diplomatic corps was physically restricted to an enclave within the city of Peking, the better to 'facilitate surveillance and control of the barbarians' by the Manchu Court (Fleming, 1959, p. 17). Under the International Protocol of 1901, which was imposed on Peking by the foreign powers following their relief of the siege of the legations by the Boxers in 1900, the Legation Quarter, as it had come to be known, was removed altogether from the control of the Chinese government. Protected by detachments of their own armed forces, the foreign diplomats effectively administered life within the Quarter until it was wrested back by the Communists in 1949 (Moser and Moser, 1993, chs 6–8).[5]

The emergence of the diplomatic corps was important for at least two reasons. First, it helped to fortify the position of all diplomats by defending their rights against host governments. This was more necessary in some states than in others[6] but unnecessary in none.

Secondly, this 'professional freemasonry', as Nicolson called it, often reinforced by personal acquaintanceships developed in shared postings at earlier stages in their careers, could prove of great value in negotiations. As Nicolson says of the ambassadors who, under Sir Edward Grey's chairmanship, managed to settle the Balkan crisis of 1913, they 'each represented national rivalries that were dangerous and acute. Yet they possessed complete confidence in each other's probity and discretion, had a common standard of professional conduct, and desired above all else to prevent a general conflagration' (Nicolson, 1954, p. 75). Antoine Pecquet, writing 20 years after Callières, was the first to give clear expression to the idea of the diplomatic corps (Callières, 1983, pp. 38–9).

THE DRAWBACKS OF THE FRENCH SYSTEM

In his elegant lectures, Nicolson remarked that the French method was 'that best adapted to the conduct of relations between civilised States' (Nicolson, 1954, p. 72). Nevertheless, he was aware of weaknesses and drawbacks, and others were less charitable. Indeed, though Nicolson vigorously disputed this, some held the old diplomacy to have been one of the causes of the First World War. Among the deficiencies of the French system were 'the habit of secretiveness' (Nicolson, 1954, p. 77), the tendency of the resident diplomat to 'go native', the stranglehold on the profession of the traditional aristocracy, and excessive leisureliness.

The habit of secretiveness

It was one thing to conduct negotiations in secret, even to conceal the fact that negotiations were going on at all; it was quite another to keep from public view the agreements which might issue from such negotiations. This was not only inconsistent with the increasingly democratic circumstances of the late nineteenth and early twentieth centuries, but it intensified the atmosphere of suspicion and fear then prevailing in the system of states and coloured the French system with the very duplicitousness which Nicolson held to be the hallmark of the earlier Italian model of diplomacy. But such was the emphasis given to the importance of secrecy in negotiations that, according to Nicolson, the habit became undiscriminating, even on the part of 'men of the highest respectability' (Nicolson, 1954, p. 77). The 'secret treaties' of the First World War were subsequently held up to savage criticism, not least by American president Woodrow Wilson, and used to smear the entire system of the old diplomacy. In future, insisted Wilson, covenants between states would not only have to be open but 'openly arrived at'. This heralded the transition to the new, or American, system of diplomacy.

The tendency to 'go native'

As well as being naturally inclined to excessive secrecy, the professional diplomat, especially one who had been abroad for a very long time and operated in only one part of the world, ran an occupational hazard which has been long recognised, not least in the United States (Eban, 1983, p. 342). At best the diplomat would lose touch with sentiments at home (however precise the directives which continued to be received from the foreign ministry); at worst become a mouthpiece for the receiving rather than the sending government. In the latter case, the diplomat was said (at any rate in Britain) to have 'gone native'. It seems generally to be as a result of this process, rather than of any abstract professional attachment to 'peaceful solutions', that resident diplomats are sometimes to be found supporting policies of 'appeasement' towards the governments to which they are accredited, which is now understood to mean urging concessions to belligerent governments in an effort to preserve peace.

Examples of diplomats going native, or being suspected to have gone native, are not difficult to find. Writing of Renaissance diplomacy, Hale comments that the dispatches of resident ambassadors were not always believed at home: 'Venice, for instance, was kept from enjoying all the benefits of her own diplomats by suspecting them of becoming corrupted by life abroad' (1957, p, 272). More than three centuries later, Britain's ambassadors to Nazi Germany and Fascist Italy in the late 1930s were both very effective spokesmen for the governments to which they were accredited. This was particularly true of the ambassador in Berlin, Sir Neville Henderson, who also resisted instructions from London which he thought would harm Britain's relations with Hitler (Gilbert, 1953).

It is not difficult to understand why this process should occur. In order to be effective in his or her foreign posting a diplomat would have to learn at least something of the local culture, perhaps even – despite the widespread use of French in court and diplomatic circles – the language. This would not in itself lead to sympathy for the local point of view but it would present the opportunity, especially if the culture in question prized values and personal attributes which were also important to the nation and social class from which the diplomat was drawn. This was certainly a part of the explanation of the fascination exerted over British diplomats by the desert tribes of Arabia (Monroe, 1963, pp. 116–17; Seale and McConville, 1978, p. 22). Diplomats could also, of course, be won over by gifts and decorations. A common feature of mediaeval diplomacy, this is not unknown in the twentieth century.[7] It was, of course, the reason why Queen Elizabeth I of England is said to have remarked, with her ambassadors in mind: 'I would not have my sheep branded with any other mark than my own' (Satow, 1922, I, p. 369).

Without doubt generally more important, however, was the fact that the resident diplomat was at the sharp end, in constant touch with local officials and other influentials and of necessity required to show a certain sympathy for their point of view if he was to command their respect and their attention. (This would obviously vary in some degree, however, with the discrepancy in power between the states concerned and perhaps also with the kinds of state involved.)[8] Gilbert adds an acute observation to this when he remarks that 'this tendency [to adopt the other side's point of view] grows in direct proportion to the resistance of the home office to such persuasion' (Gilbert, 1953, p. 547). As Valentine Lawford, a junior member of the British Embassy in Paris in the 1930s, says in his memoirs: 'Naturally, being on the spot and having to put the British case, we were inclined to treat the opposing side's point of view rather less cavalierly than our colleagues in Whitehall. But perhaps, too,' he adds, 'the thought of them safely scoffing from the far side of the Channel did sometimes tend to prejudice one a little perversely in favour of a French thesis' (1963, p. 360). An even more striking case was provided by the tension which developed between the Foreign Office and the beleaguered British mission in Peking during the Cultural Revolution. In order to alleviate their own difficulties and reduce the clear threat to themselves and their families, the mission repeatedly begged the Foreign Office to make a gesture to the Chinese by taking the first step in lifting some restrictions on China's own mission in London. It was a long time before the Foreign Office relented, which led Percy Cradock, Political Counsellor and Head of Chancery at the British mission, to formulate 'Cradock's First Law of Diplomacy, namely that it is not the other side you need to worry about, but your own' (1994, p. 78).

It was substantially because of recognition of the possibility that the resident diplomat might 'go native' that it became normal to rotate diplomats between postings, despite the sacrifice of hard-won area expertise which this involved. Even in the early nineteenth century, US president John Quincy Adams, himself a former ambassador, expressed the view that American diplomats should always be recalled after a few years 'to be renovated by the wholesome republican atmosphere of their own country' (Eban, 1983, p. 342).

Aristocratic character

Though the earliest resident diplomats were not generally of the highest social standing, special envoys normally had considerable status. This was necessary to maintain the prestige of the prince and flatter the party with whom he was dealing, as well as to make it easy for the diplomat to move in circles of influence. As the French system matured with the institutionalisation of resident diplomacy, permanent ambassadorships – at least in the important capitals – attracted leading notables and the emerging foreign services of the various European states became the province of the traditional aristocracy (Anderson, 1993, pp. 119–21).

Aristocratic dominance of diplomacy was significant because of the considerable uniformity of outlook which it fostered across the diplomatic services of different states. As Anderson says,

The aristocracies which ruled so much of Europe could still see themselves even in 1914 as in some sense parts of a social order which transcended national boundaries . . . A diplomat who spent most of his working life in foreign capitals could easily feel himself part of an aristocratic international to which national feeling was hardly more than a vulgar plebeian prejudice. (p. 121)

For one thing, they often had foreign wives. (p. 121) Nicolson supports this, admitting that the diplomat 'often becomes denationalised, internationalised, and therefore dehydrated, an elegant empty husk' (Nicolson, 1954, pp. 78–9).

The cosmopolitanism of these aristocratic diplomats had the advantage of reinforcing the solidity of the diplomatic corps in each capital, the importance of which was noted earlier. On the downside, however, as the Nicolson quote suggests, it could have the effect of making them less than enthusiastic servants of a strong national policy. Similarly, it made them uncomfortable with the growing trend towards more democratic control of foreign policy in Europe in the early twentieth century, and attracted hostility – generally unwarranted – towards their methods, such as secret negotiation. Since the traditional aristocracy was also contemptuous of 'trade', its dominance of diplomacy made this a poor instrument for promoting the commercial and financial interests of the state abroad (Platt, 1968), though whether this was in fact a bad thing is debatable. Nevertheless, this, along with other menial tasks, was left to 'consuls', who were generally recruited from the lower classes and treated correspondingly badly (Platt, 1971). This was unfortunate, since the consuls did important work and were often in a position to provide vital political information from outlying regions.

An excessively leisurely pace

Finally, it has to be said that as the number of states increased, the complexity of the problems confronting them multiplied, and the urgency attending them grew, the French system became too slow to cope. 'Ordinary diplomatic channels', namely communication between individual governments via resident ambassadors and even special envoys, were no longer adequate. This was realised during the First World War and was demonstrated by the huge rash of conferences, many of them achieving permanent status, which were hurriedly organised to cope with the crisis (Nicolson, 1963, pp. 84–5). After the First World War, 'multilateral diplomacy' was properly inaugurated with the creation of the League of Nations, and it was widely believed that the old diplomacy had been replaced by a 'new diplomacy'. This was an exaggeration but some things clearly had changed, and these changes will be discussed at length in chapters 2 and 3. Nevertheless, since the French system remained at the core of the world diplomatic system after the First World War, and remains – albeit sometimes disguised – at its core today, an examination of its modern manifestation will be the first item on the agenda of Part I of this book.

NOTES

1. This is the principal theme of my *Talking to the Enemy* (Berridge, 1994).
2. Plenipotentiaries with general responsibilities did exist but were rare (Queller, 1967, pp. 35–6).
3. 'The Pope, not unnaturally, placed himself first among the monarchs of the earth. The Emperor came second and after him his heir-apparent, "The King of the Romans". Then followed the Kings of France, Spain, Aragon and Portugal. Great Britain came sixth on the list and the King of Denmark last. This papal class-list was not accepted without demur by the sovereigns concerned' (Nicolson, 1963, pp. 98–9).
4. The 'diplomatic corps' is commonly confused with the 'diplomatic service', which is a serious error since the whole point of the former is that it is multinational while the latter is definitely not: the London diplomatic corps but the British diplomatic service.
5. In 1958 the Communist government began to remove the foreign diplomats to a new embassy district in a quite different part of Peking (Moser and Moser, 1993, p. 145).
6. During the Cultural Revolution of 1966–7 the Peking diplomatic corps had an experience which was almost as alarming as that during the Boxer uprising (Cradock, 1994, chs 5–9).
7. Hayter laments distribution to foreigners of the *Légion d'Honneur* by the French government, together with its willingness to allow its own officials to compete for foreign decorations. 'It is curious', he continues, 'that in these days, when the occasions for wearing decorations are constantly diminishing, the hunger for them continues unabated. The desire to obtain them may distract a diplomat from attending to his real duties, and may put him at a disadvantage *vis-à-vis* the foreign Government on whom he places his hopes' (Hayter, 1960, p. 35).
8. Gilbert maintains that the risk of adopting the standpoint of the host government is particularly great for diplomats from democracies who find themselves in totalitarian states: first, because the propaganda to which they are subjected is so relentless; and secondly, because the sheer oddity of the regime to which they are accredited requires unusual explanatory exertions – 'The person who explains glides easily into the role of the person who justifies and advocates' (Gilbert, 1953, p. 547).

FURTHER READING

Anderson, M. S. (1993), *The Rise of Modern Diplomacy* (Longman: London and New York)

Bull, H. (1977), *The Anarchical Society: A Study of Order in World Politics* (Macmillan: London), ch. 7

Callières, F. de (1983), *The Art of Diplomacy*, ed. by H. M. A. Keens-Soper and K. Schweizer (Leicester University Press: Leicester)

Cohen, R. (1987), *Theatre of Power: The Art of Diplomatic Signalling* (Longman: London and New York)

Gilbert, F. (1953), 'Two British ambassadors: Perth and Henderson', in Craig, G. and F. Gilbert (eds), *The Diplomats 1919–1939* (Princeton University Press: Princeton, New Jersey)

Hale, J. B. (1957), 'International relations in the West: diplomacy and war', in Potter, G. R. (ed), *The New Cambridge Modern History*, I (Cambridge University Press: Cambridge)

Hayter, Sir W. (1960), *The Diplomacy of the Great Powers* (Hamish Hamilton: London)

Mattingly, G. (1965), *Renaissance Diplomacy* (Penguin: Harmondsworth)

Mayer, A. J. (1959), *Political Origins of the New Diplomacy, 1917–1918* (Yale University Press: New Haven)

Moser, M. J. and Y. W.-C. Moser (1993), *Foreigners within the Gates: The Legations at Peking* (Oxford University Press: Hong Kong, Oxford and New York)

Nicolson, H. (1954), *The Evolution of Diplomatic Method* (Constable: London)

Nicolson, H. (1963), *Diplomacy*, 3rd ed (Oxford University Press: London)

Peyrefitte, A. (1993), trsl. by J. Rothschild, *The Collision of Two Civilizations: The British Expedition to China in 1792–4* (Harvill: London)

Platt, D. C. M. (1971), *The Cinderella Service: British Consuls since 1825* (Longman: London)

Queller, D. E. (1967), *The Office of Ambassador in the Middle Ages* (Princeton University Press: Princeton, New Jersey)

I

THE MODES OF DIPLOMACY

1

BILATERAL DIPLOMACY I:
THE RESIDENT AMBASSADOR
IN LAW

It is now rare to find the conduct of diplomacy via resident ambassadors described as 'the French system of diplomacy'. The more usual term of description today is 'bilateral diplomacy', though it is important to note that this usually has a broader connotation than the term employed by Harold Nicolson. This is because 'bilateral diplomacy' does nothing more than signify communication limited to two parties at any one time; it signifies nothing about how they communicate. Thus bilateral diplomacy certainly occurs when, say, the British ambassador in Moscow is instructed by the Foreign Office to raise a question with the Russian government. However, while we would speak of 'multilateral diplomacy' in the event of British and Russian diplomats being present at a discussion involving other parties as well, for example on the UN Security Council, we would also describe as 'bilateral diplomacy' any conversations between British and Russian diplomats at the UN on matters of exclusive interest to Anglo-Russian relations. We would, for that matter, use the same term to categorise, say, a telephone conversation between the British and Russian foreign ministers. Nevertheless, while bearing all this in mind, for the purpose of this chapter and the following one 'bilateral diplomacy' will signify the conduct of relations on a state-to-state basis via resident missions.

When states enjoy 'diplomatic relations' they are in principle prepared to conduct any necessary business by direct communication through official representatives. These representatives may be located in permanent diplomatic missions. However, it should be emphasised that if states do not take this opportunity to establish such missions, perhaps because their bilateral agenda is insufficiently important, it does not follow that they do not enjoy 'diplomatic relations' (James, 1992). In other circumstances, only one state may have a mission on the territory of the other. Generally speaking, nevertheless, most international relationships of some mutual importance in which the states concerned are in diplomatic relations are characterised by the exchange of permanent missions. In the age of jet planes, fax machines, and electronic mail, not to mention the rambling architecture of 'multilateral diplomacy' which will be discussed in chapter 3, why this should be so is the chief question which the following chapter will address. First, however, it is necessary to look at the work of the Conference on Diplomatic Intercourse and Immunities which was held in Vienna beween 2 March and 14 April 1961, for this not only occasioned a re-examination of the role of the resident mission but placed it on the legal basis which it enjoys to this day. What was the background to this conference? What was its upshot? Why was it successful?

THE VIENNA CONVENTION ON
DIPLOMATIC RELATIONS, 1961

From the time of the origins of modern diplomacy in the middle ages, its international regulation ('diplomatic law') was concerned chiefly with the immunities and other privileges of diplomats while abroad, their obligations to foreign states, and – in the Regulation of Vienna of 1815 – the classification of heads of mission and their precedence (Nicolson, 1963, p. 100). Until 1961, however, this law was located chiefly in customary rules and a code of courtesy.

In the late nineteenth and early twentieth centuries lawyers in Europe and the United States took an interest in the codification of diplomatic law, prompted by the belief that this would improve the practical conduct of international affairs. They took an interest, in other words, in its clarification, reaffirmation, and formalisation (*Yearbook of the ILC*, 1956, vol. II, pp. 148–52; Langhorne, 1992, pp. 6–8). The League of Nations was also seized with the question between 1925 and 1928 but subsequently abandoned it, the great powers at least feeling that the subject was insufficiently important, and that agreement would in any case be difficult to reach (*Yearbook of the ILC*, 1956, vol. II, p. 136; Langhorne, 1992, pp. 10–11). Some progress was made at the sixth International Conference of

American States held in Havana, which actually produced a convention on diplomatic agents on 20 February 1928.[1] However, this was not well drafted and applied only to certain states in the Western hemisphere (Cahier, 1961, pp. 5–6). In retrospect, the real breakthrough came in 1949, when the International Law Commission (ILC) of the new United Nations decided to inscribe the codification of diplomatic law on its own agenda. Though not initially treated with any urgency, this changed in late 1952 when the General Assembly requested priority for the subject. This was a result of strong complaints from the Yugoslav government concerning the activities of the Soviet embassy in Belgrade. The Yugoslav case may have been the occasion for giving new priority to this subject but there were important underlying reasons of a more general nature.

First, a few changes of substance to the law of diplomacy were now clearly needed. Circumstances had changed considerably from the period when the extant rules had evolved, and as a result these rules required modernising. Many that did not, needed clarification. For example, not only were some embassies exploiting the looseness of existing rules on privileges to engage in flagrant intervention in the domestic affairs of receiving states, but others were increasingly being subjected to severe harassment – even to the point of mob attack – with the toleration and even, occasionally, with the encouragement of governments. Shortly before the conference assembled in Vienna, the Belgian embassy in Cairo was burned and ransacked. Moreover, with the substantial increase in the number of states which decolonisation had already produced, and the further increase which was in clear prospect, disquiet was increasing in some countries that the rules on diplomatic immunity were inadequate to cope with 'the armies of privileged persons in their capitals who by sheer numbers as well as occasional irresponsibility threatened to bring into disrepute the entire system of diplomatic immunity' (Denza, 1976, p. 5).[2]

Secondly, as well as changes of substance, a change in the form of the rules was required. Rules based merely on custom and courtesy could not change fast enough; nor did they have sufficient 'sanction of law'. Putting them in the form of a treaty (albeit one which in practice was designated as a 'convention')[3] would meet both of these objections.

Last but not least, there was a strong feeling among the established states that the international law on diplomacy needed the formal acceptance of the new states of Asia and Africa. For there were clear signs that they were threatening to dismiss the 'French system of diplomacy' as an imperialist conspiracy hatched by their ex-colonial masters to perpetuate their subservience. It was thus no accident that the Indian jurist on the ILC, Radhabinod Pal, was elected chairman of the Commission's drafting committee in May 1957 and that another Indian, Arthur Lall, was subsequently elected (by acclamation) to be chairman of the Committee of the Whole when the conference itself assembled – albeit in one of the oldest of European capitals. Nor was it any accident that the preamble to the convention subsequently agreed, which had not been included in the original ILC draft, should have been based on a document of the Asian–African Legal Consultative Committee.

By 1958 the ILC had adopted 45 draft articles, and on 7 December 1959 the General Assembly decided that an international conference should be held in order to conclude a convention using these drafts as the basis for discussion.

The choice of Vienna as the venue for this conference was not an arbitrary one. The cold war was still in a dangerous phase and Austria, which stood mid-way between East and West in central Europe and was not a colonial power, had been legally recognised as permanently neutral since 1955. Furthermore, as already noted, it was in Vienna, almost a century and a half earlier, that the last major act in the development of diplomatic law had been executed. Invitations were extended to states members of the United Nations, specialised agencies, and to parties to the Statute of the International Court of Justice.

Unfortunately, the criteria employed for issuing invitations to the conference in Vienna ensured that Communist China was excluded, together with other Communist states such as East Germany, North Korea and North Vietnam, and the conference started with this being protested by the Soviet Union. Nevertheless, it was attended by the representatives of 81 states and the work proceeded in general quite harmoniously.

The hallmark of the Vienna Convention on Diplomatic Relations, which was the title given to the legal instrument adopted at the conference and which is reproduced in full in the Appendix, was the unambiguously 'functional approach' to diplomatic privileges and immunities adopted by its framers. This meant simply that a resident mission's privileges were justified only by the need to ensure its most efficient functioning (Denza, 1976, p. 5). (A decade and a half earlier, the UN Charter had justified diplomatic privileges in connection with the work of the UN in identical terms.[4]) They were certainly not justified, in other words, by reference to the private interests of individual members of a mission (for example, in smuggling drugs in the 'diplomatic bag'); nor were they justified by reference either to the 'extraterritoriality' of the diplomat and embassy premises, or even entirely to the ancient notion that an ambassador was a direct representative of a sovereign prince. Since these latter ideas still have a certain popular currency, however, and since at least some part of the 'representative theory' finds important echoes in the Vienna Convention, it will be as well at this stage to say a little more about them.

As Cahier notes, the theory of extraterritoriality justified diplomatic privileges 'either on the ground of the fiction that the diplomat was not supposed to have left his own soil, or on the ground that the diplomatic mission was considered part of the territory of the sending state' (1961, p. 19). The key word here, of course, is 'fiction', for it is precisely on such a basis that this theory rested. Apart from this obvious weakness,[5] the notion of extra-territoriality had the serious disadvantage that it gave diplomats the impression that – even when outside the embassy premises – they could be judged only by their own sovereign's law and were thus entirely immune from local law, which was politically inconceivable. For example, a diplomat from a country where driving on the left-hand side of the road is the rule cannot expect to get away with maintaining this practice in a country where the opposite rule prevails. The League of Nations expert committee had itself thrown out extraterritoriality as a suitable explanation of diplomatic privileges and immunity and, as Hardy suggests, its similar rejection by the Vienna Convention 'may be taken as conclusive' (1968, p. 10).

As for the theory of personal representation, this held that diplomatic immunity rested on the character of a diplomat as a direct substitute for a sovereign prince: standing in the stead of a prince, he or she was – by definition – no more legally constrainable than the prince himself. There are, however, two problems with this view. In the first place, and as a matter of fact, the development of customary diplomatic law provided diplomats with privileges which were not identical with, and were sometimes even more extensive than, those customarily extended to individual rulers on visits abroad (Hardy, 1968, p. 10). In the second place, the theory falls down over the problem of equal sovereignties: 'if both receiving and sending States are sovereign, why should one yield to the other?' (p. 11). Nevertheless, the functional theory alone does not answer the question 'functional for whom?'; in principle it also opens up to daily reassessment the practical needs of the diplomat since in practice these may vary on a daily basis. It appears to have been for these reasons that it was felt necessary to add the reminder that diplomats exercise their functions as representatives of sovereign states – sensitive, dangerous, and juridically equal – and thus needing to be treated with some indulgence. Hence the Vienna Convention linked both theories in its preamble.

The functions of missions

The Vienna Convention, then, signified a fundamental shift 'away from the assumption that immunities might be demanded automatically on a plea of "sovereignty", to the notion that the question whether or not privileges are to be accorded is one which is subject to re-assessment in the light of practical needs' (Hardy, 1968, pp. 11–12). In light of this, it is not surprising that the Convention gave priority to enumerating, chiefly in Article 3 (see Appendix), the proper functions of a diplomatic mission, the first time that this had ever been done in a formal legal instrument (Denza, 1976, p. 20). These consisted, among others, of representation, the protection of interests, negotiation, information gathering and reporting, the promotion of friendly relations, and the development of economic, cultural, and scientific relations.

This list of functions provided no surprises, though that concerning the promotion of friendly relations and developing economic, cultural, and scientific relations had not appeared in traditional textbooks. 'Representing the sending State in the receiving State' was added at the suggestion of the ILC, apparently in somewhat coy reference to the traditional role of the embassy as *symbolic representative* of the power and wealth of the sending state in diplomatic ceremonial, a role of great importance to a state's prestige but – at least in the liberal democracies – by this time politically incorrect (Morgenthau, 1978, pp. 78–83, 532–3).

The privileges required

In view of the relentlessly functional approach of the Convention-makers, privileges which were clearly important to the functioning of diplomatic missions were generally strengthened by the Vienna Convention, while those which were less so were reduced – as were the categories of those by whom they could be invoked. As Denza points out, 'the reduction of privileges and immunities to what is essential makes that minimum easier to defend to public opinion' (Denza, 1976, p. 6).

The most important functional privilege required by a diplomatic mission has always been the inviolability of its premises, that is, its right to operate without constraint either from the receiving state's government (for example, by forced police entry) or from other elements (for example, by mob attacks), against which the receiving state is obliged to provide it with 'special protection' (Cahier, 1961, p. 20). In these regards, and in light of modern circumstances, the Vienna Convention made very strong statements indeed. It stated starkly that 'The premises of the mission shall be inviolable' (Article 22, 1) and ruled out any exceptions to this whatever.[6] This also applied, of course, in the event of a breach in diplomatic relations or of armed conflict. The Convention also elaborated on the importance of inviolability by singling out for particular emphasis certain of the facilities of a mission which are essential to its efficient functioning.

Thus it was stressed that inviolability of the mission extended to its contents, to bank accounts, and also to moveable property. In the last regard, means of transport and 'archives and documents' were emphasised. The inviolability of the mission's communications (couriers, correspondence, the diplomatic bag, and so on) was the subject of a long Article (Article 27) in the Vienna Convention, so important is free and confidential communication between a mission and its home government, as well as with other missions and consulates of the sending state, to the negotiating and reporting functions of the resident mission. However, there was one important qualification to the provisions on free communication, and this was that 'the mission may install and use a wireless transmitter only with the consent of the receiving State' (Article 27, 1). This was a concession to the developing states, which feared that unrestricted diplomatic wireless would, first, compromise their responsibilities under the International Telecommunication Convention, secondly, provide an unfair advantage to the diplomacy of the richer states who alone would be able to avail themselves of this facility[7] and, thirdly, permit inadmissible forms of intervention in their internal affairs (Kerley, 1962, pp. 111–16; Denza, 1976, p. 121).

As for the inviolability of the person of the diplomat himself – 'the oldest established and the most fundamental rule of diplomatic law' (Denza, 1976, p. 135) – the Vienna Convention also made a particularly strong statement of the customary position (Article 29). Diplomatic agents would remain immune from the criminal jurisdiction of the receiving state, and from its civil and administrative jurisdiction as well – except in some matters where they are involved in an entirely private capacity (Denza, 1976, p. 4). Of course, as was customary, the Convention reiterated the right of receiving states to expel, rather than subject to court proceedings, diplomats whose actions were regarded as pernicious. Inviolability also implies the duty of the receiving state to provide special protection for the person of the diplomat as well as for the premises of his mission, and this, too, is made clear in the Vienna Convention. Finally, it is worth noting here that the Convention also underwrote the freedom of movement of the diplomatic agent, so vital to a number of his or her functions, not least that of information gathering. Affirmation of this right had been made necessary by the policy of the Soviet Union and its East European satellites, introduced following the Second World War, of limiting the travel of foreign diplomats to 50 kilometres from the capital in the absence of special permission to the contrary, a limitation to which a number of Western states, notably the United States, had retaliated in kind (Denza, 1976, pp. 115–16). However, Article 26 also qualified freedom of movement by permitting receiving states to bar a diplomat from certain zones on grounds of national security, and the result was that state practice did not change a great deal (Denza, 1976, p. 117).

In these and other ways, then, informed by the doctrine of functional necessity, the Vienna Convention elaborated on the privileges of the diplomat and mission premises. Cahier, however, makes the reasonable point that in doctrine and practice the inviolability of the diplomatic agent – despite the longevity of the rule – is now somewhat less sacrosanct than the inviolability of the mission premises (1961, pp. 25–6). The first reason for this is that constraints on an individual agent endanger the efficient functioning of a mission less than constraints on its premises, moveable property, and communications. The second is that the diplomat moves about and may with justice regard the attempted provision of police protection at every moment of the day as a clumsily disguised strategy of professional emasculation.

The fear of intervention

The Vienna Convention also detailed the duties towards the receiving state which missions must observe in carrying out their tasks. Indeed, although these are not explicitly broached until Article 41, the emphasis in Article 3 on the need for missions to fulfil their duties within the limits imposed by international law was already a clear indication that the Convention would not be silent on this question. Since their inception in the fifteenth century, resident missions had always run the risk of being not only suspected (often with good reason) of espionage but also of subversive activities within the state to which they were accredited (*Yearbook of the ILC*, 1956, vol. II, pp. 154–6). Against the background of the cold war, in which the Soviet Union and the United States were openly vying for influence in the non-aligned world, Article 3 thus reflected a heightened sensitivity of states to intervention in what they regarded as purely domestic affairs (Berridge, 1992b, pp. 162–5). (This had, of course, been behind the Yugoslav case which had raised the profile of this whole question earlier in the 1950s.) Article 3, paragraph 1(d), was, as Cahier points out, 'an outright condemnation of all forms of espionage' (1961, p. 10). When, therefore, Article 41,1 stated that diplomats must 'respect the laws and regulations of the receiving State' and 'have a duty not to interfere in the internal affairs of that State', it was merely making explicit what was implicit in Article 3.

However, in order to reduce further the risk of domestic interference, the Convention made five practical stipulations: first, that diplomatic missions must confine their conduct of official business to 'the Ministry for Foreign Affairs of the receiving State or such other ministry as may be agreed' (Article 41,2); secondly, that 'offices forming part of the mission' may not be established 'in localities other than those in which the mission itself is established', unless prior permission is obtained (Article 12); thirdly, that *agrément* may be required for defence attachés (Article 7); fourthly, that receiving states have a right to insist that missions which it believes to be too large must be reduced in size (Article 11); and finally, as noted earlier, that radio facilities could only be installed in missions with the consent of the receiving state.

SUMMARY: THE SUCCESS OF THE CONFERENCE

The Convention was signed in Vienna on 18 April 1961 and came into force three years later when, on 24 April 1964, it had been ratified by 22 states, the minimum number required under its terms. By the end of the 1960s 90 states had either ratified or acceded to the Convention; when Communist China acceded to the Convention in November 1975 it enjoyed the support of the entire Permanent Five (P5) on the UN Security Council; and by the end of 1992 it had been either ratified or acceded to by 165 states (*Multilateral Treaties*, 1993). Practice subsequently revealed certain gaps and ambiguities in the Convention. Nevertheless, it remains 'without doubt one of the surest and most widely based multilateral regimes in the field of international relations' (Brown, 1988, p. 54). Why had the Vienna Conference proved so successful?

In the first place, the subject matter was reasonably technical, and a large part of the work had consisted of the codification of rules which had, as already noted, been widely accepted for centuries. The potential for controversy had been further reduced by the decision to exclude from the agenda certain issues over which serious disagreement was likely to occur, notably diplomatic asylum and specific instances of attacks on embassies (Kerley, 1962, p. 106). Secondly, the focus of the work was relatively narrow: it dealt only with traditional bilateral diplomacy, and thus excluded both rela- tions with international organisations and special missions.[8] Thirdly, the draft articles produced by the ILC had already taken account of governmental views, with the result – as is normal in the work of the ILC – that there was considerable prior agreement on them between the states represented at the conference (Denza, 1976, pp. 1–2). Fourthly, the Secretariat and the conference officers were also highly effective; according to Kerley, the Secretariat had 'matured and improved perceptibly' since the first Geneva Conference on the

Law of the Sea, which had been only partially successful; while the Chairman of the Commitee of the Whole, Arthur Lall, 'proved to be a parliamentarian of outstanding skill, both on the dais and in the corridors' (1962, pp. 128–9). Alfred Verdross,[9] the conference president, was also an extremely eminent and highly regarded jurist. Last but certainly not least, the delegations generally shared a strong interest in the success of the conference. As Kerley points out, and in strong contrast to the position in regard to missions to international organisations, 'all states are both sending and receiving states'; furthermore, where there were serious disagreements, as for example over diplomatic wireless, the major powers – whether East or West – had tended to be on the same side (1962, p. 128).

NOTES

1. The text of this interesting document can be found in *League of Nations Treaty Series*, vol. CLV, p. 261, and also in J. B. Scott (1931, pp. 420–4).
2. According to the Yugoslav jurist, Milan Bartos, 'Whereas in the past the diplomatic corps in an average capital had numbered only 200, there might now be 4000 on the diplomatic list and four or five times as many subordinate mission staff' (*Yearbook of the ILC*, 1957, vol. I, p. 124).
3. For discussion of the different forms of presenting agreements, see chapter 9.
4. In Articles 104 and 105.
5. For legal argument against extraterritoriality, see Hardy, p. 10 and *Yearbook of the ILC*, 1956, vol. II, pp. 157–8.
6. Cahier regrets this, and draws attention to the fact that the draft text submitted to the ILC by its Special Rapporteur in 1955 included provision for exceptions to the inviolablity rule in 'extreme emergencies' (1961, pp. 20–1). However, it is reasonable to assume that if an emergency is extreme and therefore as self-evident as all that, then the local authorities would probably have little difficulty in securing the permission of the head of the mission to enter his premises (Kerley, 1962, pp. 102–3).
7. In 1977 the Berrill Report noted that diplomatic radio was the primary means of communication of 59 British overseas missions, mainly in the Soviet bloc, Africa, the Middle East, and the Far East. It confirmed that, compared to the public telex network, radio was an expensive system for sending telegrams and noted that none of the countries (including West Germany and France) which the investigators employed as analogues used diplomatic radio as a primary method for sending telegrams.

However, it also acknowledged that there were strong arguments for retaining radio at missions in countries where Britain might be involved in military operations or where a breakdown in communications as a result of war, revolution or public disorder could jeopardise important British interests. This was because radio was less vulnerable than telex, private wire or telephones to interruption as a result of loss of power, natural causes, labour disputes, or political action: 'At the time of the 1956 Hungarian uprising the UK's diplomatic radio was initially the only contact with Western Embassies in Budapest' (Central Policy Review Staff, 1977, pp. 266, 271). Since then, however, radio communication has been phased out by the Foreign Office and replaced by satellite telephones and, for non-confidential messages, fax machines (Edwards, 1994, p. 62).

8. Among the reasons for avoiding consideration of representation at international organisations was the relative absence of customary law in this area and the danger of producing conflicts of law by attempting to codify the conventions which dominated. (On the unhappy attempt to grapple with this in 1975, see Fennessy, 1976.) By contrast, the ILC had from the beginning thought it important to consider special missions (*Yearbook of the ILC*, 1957, vol. I, pp. 2–6, 46–8) and, indeed, submitted a short draft on them. However, this was postponed by the conference for later consideration.

9. Verdross, an Austrian Professor of International Law, was former Rector of the University of Vienna, eminent member of the ILC, and President of the Institute of International Law.

FURTHER READING

Brown, J. (1988), 'Diplomatic immunity – state practice under the Vienna Convention', *International and Comparative Law Quarterly*, vol. 37

Cahier, P. (1961), 'Vienna Convention on Diplomatic Relations', *International Conciliation*, no. 571

Denza, E. (1976), *Diplomatic Law: Commentary on the Vienna Convention on Diplomatic Relations* (Oceana: Dobbs Ferry, New York; The British Institute of International and Comparative Law: London)

Fennessy, J. G. (1976), 'The 1975 Convention on the Representation of States in their Relations with International Organizations of a Universal Character', *American Journal of International Law*, vol. 70, no. 1

Hardy, M. (1968), *Modern Diplomatic Law* (Manchester University Press: Manchester; Oceana: Dobbs Ferry, New York)

Kerley, E. L. (1962), 'Some aspects of the Vienna Conference on Diplomatic Intercourse and Immunities', *American Journal of International Law*, vol. 56

Langhorne, R. (1992), 'The regulation of diplomatic practice: the beginnings to the Vienna Convention on Diplomatic Relations, 1961', *Review of International Studies*, vol. 18, no. 1

2

BILATERAL DIPLOMACY II:
THE RESIDENT AMBASSADOR
IN PRACTICE

It is one of the ironies of the history of diplomacy that not long after the Vienna Convention had placed its institutional cornerstone, the resident mission, on a surer legal foundation voices began to be heard – at least in the West – claiming that the resident mission had become an anachronism. Prominent among these was that of Zbigniew Brzezinski, a former member of the US State Department's Policy Planning Council (Brzezinski, 1970; Watson, 1982, p. 145). By the early 1980s these voices even included those of a senior ambassador, Roberto Ducci, the retiring Italian ambassador to Britain (Ducci) and George Ball, that eloquent defender of traditional diplomacy who turned down Jimmy Carter's offer of a choice of major diplomatic assignments on the grounds that he did not wish to end his days as 'an innkeeper for itinerant Congressmen' (Ball, 1982, p. 452).[1]

THE CASE FOR EUTHANASIA

The arguments for quietly putting the resident ambassador out of his or her misery are well known and can be briefly stated. First, the technology of travel and communications had advanced to such a degree that it had become easy for the political leaders and home-based officials of different countries – especially friendly ones – to establish direct contact, thereby bypassing their ambassadors (Ducci, 1980; Watson, 1982, p. 145). Secondly, there were diplomatic as well as economic advantages to this since certain diplomatic functions, in particular symbolic representation and negotiation, were actually better executed via direct contact, not least where experts were needed to deal with technical business (Watson, 1982, p. 133; Eban, 1983, pp. 361–2, 367). Thirdly, the opportunities for direct international dealing had also multiplied with the growth of international organisations and regional integration, notably in the European Union: the bilateral diplomacy in a multilateral context mentioned at the beginning of Chapter 1. Fourthly, it was alleged, information gathering and political reporting were at a discount as a result of the huge growth in the international mass media, an argument reinforced in recent years by the dramatic broadcasting from Baghdad of CNN (Cable News Network) reports during the Gulf War. And finally, serious ideological tensions and deepening cultural divisions across the world meant that the exchange of resident missions by hostile states provided – quite literally – dangerous hostages to fortune, the recently signed Vienna Convention notwithstanding.

The Iranian crisis at the end of the 1970s, during which the Shah's regime was replaced by a revolutionary theocratic government under the Ayatollah Khomeini, seemed to confirm that the resident embassy was both an anachronism and a liability in particularly spectacular fashion. The US ambassador in Teheran, William Sullivan (at the time the most senior member of the US Foreign Service on active duty), was repeatedly bypassed by direct communication between the White House and the Shah, and subsequently took early retirement (Sullivan, 1981, pp. 199–287). As for the embassy which he had left on 6 April 1979, nine months later this was seized by militant supporters of the new Islamic government and its staff held hostage for 444 days.[2] This humiliated the Carter administration and provoked a crisis which dominated its last year in office.

Against this background of misfortune, reinforced – it should be added – by the premium attaching to force and propaganda during the cold war (Sofer, 1988), it is hardly surprising that supporters of the resident mission should have been on the defensive throughout most of the post-war period. This was particularly true in Britain, where traditional diplomacy came under increasingly hostile official scrutiny three times between the early 1960s and the middle of the 1970s. Nevertheless, although an obvious result of this pressure was greatly increased emphasis in the work of diplomatic services such as that of Britain on commercial and economic work, the missions themselves comprehensively survived. In 1994 Britain had missions

– albeit varying greatly in size – in at least three-quarters of all states in the world. This was even true in neighbouring France, which has often been singled out as a country where a British ambassador was unnecessary because of ease of travel and communication and the communications networks of the European Union. Indeed, in 1994 the Paris embassy retained a diplomatic staff of 43, three-quarters of whom were first secretaries or above (Foreign & Commonwealth Office, 1994, p. 30). Why were the pronouncements of the death of the resident mission so obviously premature? The best way to explain this is probably to go back to the functions of the resident mission – an incomplete list of which was contained in the Vienna Convention on Diplomatic Relations – and show how it is often difficult to see how this work could be done as well, if in some cases at all, in its absence.

REASONS FOR REPRIEVE

The range and emphasis of the work done by embassies naturally varies with the national diplomatic services of which they are part, and with country of location within the same national diplomatic service. This is particularly true of the variety of functions within the consular services category and the numerous non-core embassy functions, and it will be necessary to return to this point in the conclusion as well as refer to it in passing. Nevertheless, many important tasks are performed in some degree by almost all well-run embassies of at least medium size, and it is these of which account must first be taken and to which most space must be given.

Representation

Representation, that often overlooked or naively minimised[3] function of diplomacy, which is chiefly concerned with prestige, certainly can be conducted by ministers and officials in direct contact with their foreign opposites; indeed, it can perhaps be conducted by them best of all. When General de Gaulle, president of the French Republic, towered over other mourners at the funeral of John F. Kennedy in 1963, he was representing France in the United States in a way that could have been done by no French ambassador. The trouble is, first, that while he was in the United States he could hardly be representing France in the many other countries which were important to Paris at that time (West Germany, for example); and secondly, he could not remain in Washington for very long. Permanent embassies – centrally located and impressively housed – are a permanent reminder of the importance and traditions of a state, as well as a symbol of the understanding that diplomacy is a continuous rather than episodic process (Jackson, 1981, pp. 165– 8). Besides, when government leaders or important officials go abroad on representative duties, it is generally indispensable for the security of their communications (and sometimes for their health) that they should enjoy the support of a local embassy. It is worth adding, too, that the existence of a permanent embassy broadens a state's representative options and thus its repertoire of non-verbal signals. For example, while at the funeral of Soviet leader Leonid Brezhnev in Moscow in 1982 most foreign delegations were headed by dignitaries flown in for the occasion, three countries – Botswana, Brazil, and Burma – found it expedient to be represented merely by their resident ambassadors (Berridge, 1994, p. 142). In their absence, it may have been difficult to avoid showing either too much or too little respect. There are also, of course, many other ceremonial occasions when for either practical or political reasons it is simply much more convenient to be represented by a resident ambassador rather than a special envoy. Resident missions are generally of special importance to the prestige of new states and of established ones in declining circumstances.

Promoting friendly relations

In considering the idea that a function of the resident embassy should be to promote friendly relations between sending and receiving states, as noted by the Vienna Convention, it first has to be established that this is a function of diplomacy as such. For the idea has been dismissed as 'cant' by Alan James, and it is easy to see why it is vulnerable to the charge. The first duty of an embassy, or any diplomatic agency for that matter, as he points out, is to promote its country's policy – and this may actually require a diplomat to behave in an unfriendly manner (James, 1980, pp. 937–8). However, it is noticeable that in discussing the representative function, James observes that 'if the ambassador can achieve the respect of the local decision-makers *and get along well with them* [emphasis added] the interests of his state will indeed be well served' (p. 940).

This is the point: a distinction has to be made between the cultivation of friendly relations on the policy level and friendly (or at least civilised and familiar) relations on the personal level, or what in latter-day parlance would be called 'networking'. Another way of putting this is to say that it is an important task of the embassy to promote friendly relations with local elites (non-governmental as well as governmental) *in so far as this is compatible with policy*. The Berrill Report, the fruit of a controversial inquiry into the British diplomatic service which was commissioned by the Labour government in the mid-1970s, called this the 'cultivation of contacts' and commended it (Central Policy Review Staff, 1977, p. 259). This is not surprising since a well 'networked' embassy will obviously find it easier to gain influence and gather information; it will also be better placed to handle a crisis in relations should one subsequently develop. It is for this reason, as well as others, that a good embassy will honour local customs (provided they are not flagrantly at odds with the values of its own country), mark important events in the annual calendar of the country in question, and engage in extensive social contact; in other words, representation is concerned with promoting friendly relations as well as prestige (Heinrichs, 1986, pp. 214–15).

There is, however, another connotation to the objective of cultivating cordial relations, and this is that it is also an important job of the embassy to ensure that gratuitous offence is not given to the host government in the event that some unpleasant message has to be delivered. (This might, perhaps, more accurately be termed the minimising of unfriendly relations.) An ambassador in good standing, an ambassador familiar with the understatement of the profession (Edwards, 1994, p. 81), an ambasssador fluent in the local language, an ambassador properly appraised of conventional procedures, and an ambassador sensitive to the nuances of local prejudice – in short, a professional – is more likely to achieve this than anyone else. In sum, pursuing friendly relations means pursuing these as far as this is possible. Of course, friendly relations can be cultivated by other means but the resident embassy has the greatest opportunities and is likely to have the most appropriate knowledge and skills.

Negotiation

What of the key function of negotiation? As with those already mentioned, it is certainly true that this can be – and is – conducted over the head of the resident ambassador. For example, it appears at first glance from the diaries of Nicholas Henderson, British ambassador to France from 1975 to 1979, that at least by the second half of the 1970s Britain's embassy in Paris had been completely marginalised as far as Franco-British negotiations on bilateral business were concerned. 'I have not been so busy lately,' the ambassador rashly noted in his diary on 29 December 1978 (Henderson, 1994, p. 243). Nevertheless, it is also apparent that the resident ambassador – even, as we shall see, in Paris – usually continues to have more than a walk-on part in negotiations. This is chiefly because there are disadvantages as well as advantages in employing special envoys, such as unwanted publicity, insensitivity to nuances of local sentiment, and the disposition either to break off prematurely or make rash concessions in order to return home on schedule. Even where special envoys take the lead in a negotiation, therefore, it is still common to find the resident ambassador playing an important supporting role, not least in following up negotiations when the envoy has departed. As Trevelyan observes, 'argument breeds argument and negotiation is a continuous process' (1973, p. 72). In other negotiations the ambassador may still take the lead.

To return to the British ambassador in Paris, it is clear that even he played a direct role, albeit a subsidiary one, in at least one highly sensitive matter on the Franco-British agenda: European collaboration in aircraft production. Henderson not only accompanied British Secretary of State for Industry Eric Varley to his talks in Paris with his French opposite number, but kept up the pressure for the British point of view in the intervals between these visits (Henderson, 1994, pp. 214–16, 225–6). It is also interesting that one of the reasons for the need for the ambassador's intervention in this matter was the fact that the British prime minister, James Callaghan, and the French president, Valéry Giscard d'Estaing, were not on 'easy telephoning terms' (p. 214). It is reasonable to suppose that the situation is similar in many other bilateral relationships, not least because of language difficulties.

If embassy staff are still sometimes needed to play at the least a supporting role in important bilateral negotiations where their political masters are now accustomed to take the lead by virtue of geographical and, perhaps, political proximity, it is apparent that the embassy role in important negotiations is usually bigger where the relationship – for whatever reason – is more difficult and also more long drawn out (Central Policy Review Staff, 1977, p. 117). A good example of ambassadorial leadership in an extremely important negotiation is provided by the role of Leonard Woodcock, de facto US ambassador to Communist China, in the talks during 1978–9 which led to the normalisation of relations between Washington and Beijing. 'I have long been in favour', commented US Secretary of State Cyrus Vance on this episode, 'of using ambassadors in place to conduct negotiations whenever possible, rather than relying on pyrotechnics and acrobatics' (Vance, 1983, p. 117).

An even more salutary example, however, comes from Iran in the late 1970s, where it is well known that the British and American ambassadors were in constant touch with the Shah and his advisers on subjects of the greatest delicacy, not the least of which concerned the fate of his regime. Though able to speak directly to the Shah by telephone and fly in special envoys, the American administration was handicapped in its ability to dispense with the negotiating services of its own ambassador – though its distrust of him mounted as the crisis deepened – because of even more serious distractions elsewhere. As virtually admitted by President Carter's National Security Advisor, Zbigniew Brzezinski, the very same man who had earlier tolled the bell for the resident ambassador, the White House was unable to gain direct control of relations with the Shah because of its preoccupation 'on a daily basis with other major issues'. In September 1978 these included the Camp David negotiations for an Egypt–Israel peace settlement (Brzezinski, 1983, pp. 361–2, 396, 526–7). Like it or not, therefore, ambassadors sometimes have to be permitted to play a leading role in important negotiations if only because their political masters cannot be everywhere, or in sustained and informed telephone conversation with everyone, at the same time. Sometimes, too, they are brought back to reinforce the home team. Herman Eilts, US ambassador to Egypt, and Samuel Lewis, US ambassador to Israel, were so respected for their knowledge of their respective countries – see below – that they were brought back to be members of the 11-man US negotiating team at the Camp David summit in September 1978 (Carter, 1982, p. 327).

If embassies are thus still to be found playing either a supporting or leading role in important negotiations, it should hardly be surprising that their role in negotiating on more humdrum matters is very great indeed (Jackson, 1981, pp. 149–51; Henderson, 1994, p. 335). Ministers and senior officials do not want to be bothered with these. Nor should it be surprising to find them heavily involved in lobbying legislators when legislation affecting their countries' interests are being debated, especially where there is a real separation of constitutional powers as in the United States. It is tempting to think of this as a separate function but in principle, of course, it is essentially a form of negotiation.[4] Both Nicholas Henderson and Abba Eban, Israeli ambassador to the United States, report their heavy involvement in this activity during their periods in Washington (Eban, 1977, chs 7–9; Henderson, 1994, pp. 287–8). Furthermore, the very advances in communication which have enabled home ministries to make direct contact with foreign governments similarly make the embassy itself a more responsive instrument in negotiations of all kinds, including that somewhat rudimentary example of the genus: the 'exchange of views'.[5] The Duncan Report, the product of an investigation into the British diplomatic service launched by Harold Wilson's government in the late 1960s, was itself under no illusion that much negotiation would remain to be conducted by overseas missions, even though it felt that the content of those negotiations should be given a much stronger economic flavour (Review Committee on Overseas Representation, 1969, p. 18).

Clarifying intentions

When embassies engage in negotiation they may (they also may not) seek to clarify the intentions of their political masters on the subjects concerned. However, as Alan James points out, governments often need also to communicate with each other on subjects which either directly affect their bilateral relationship but are currently non-negotiable or are altogether beyond the agenda of any current or possible bilateral negotiation (James, 1980, p. 941). One of the most important reasons why they may need to be able to do this is to make sure that the other party knows enough in order to behave conveniently. Depending on the situation, another government may, for example, need to be reassured ('relax – we're only invading your neighbour'), alarmed ('these sanctions are just the first step'), encouraged ('we like what you're doing'), or deterred ('do that and you'll regret it'). If it is an ally, it may need to be warned of an imminent announcement concerning a matter in which it has no vital interest simply in order to make it feel that it has been 'consulted'.

Once more, the resident ambassador is not the only option. Some messages of these kinds can be delivered by other means; some can be delivered better by other means. For example, if special emphasis needs to be given to a message, or if flattery as well as the delivery of information is intended, a special envoy might be sent (Berridge, 1994, ch. 6). It is interesting in this context that, having noted the complaint of US ambassador to Tokyo, Armin Meyer, that he first heard news of the opening to China over Armed Forces Radio while getting a haircut, hindsight did not lead Kissinger to conclude that the 'serious error in manners' represented by keeping the Japanese totally in the dark would have been best avoided by passing news of the imminent announcement to them via the ambassador. 'It would', he concluded instead, 'have surely been more courteous and thoughtful . . . to send one of my associates from the Peking trip to Tokyo to brief Sato a few hours before the official announcement' (Kissinger, 1979, p. 762).

Nevertheless, if there are situations in which a message may be delivered best by other means, there are also situations in which the resident embassy is either at least equally appropriate or distinctly preferable. In the first case, the embassy might be employed in order to avoid erosion of its local reputation, which it needs to preserve for other aspects of its work. In the second, a government may, for example, wish to convey a message of such sensitivity that it does not want it delivered in its entirety in writing or want it to be too vulnerable to electronic recording. A special envoy might well be suitable for such a purpose. However, the matter concerned, while sensitive, may be insufficiently important to justify this; or it may be important enough but fears may exist that a special envoy will excite unwanted interest (which is, of course, one of the reasons why the resident embassy was established in the first place) (Berridge, 1994, ch. 6). In either event, an ambassador can be given instructions to transmit a certain message in writing, and add one or more points orally. The manner of its presentation may also reinforce the message, as may the ambassador's local reputation. If in fact reassurance is the import of a message, a statement by a trusted ambassador will be as good a medium as many and better than most.

Information gathering/political reporting

Gathering information on the local scene and reporting it home has long been recognised as one of the most important functions of the resident embassy. The state of the economy, foreign policy, the morale of the armed forces, scientific research with military implications,[6] the health of the leader, the balance of power within the government, the likely result of any forthcoming election, the strength of the opposition, and so on, have long been the staple fare of ambassadorial despatches. Joseph Grew, US ambassador to Japan from 1932 until 1941, wrote roughly six thousand during the course of his mission (Heinrichs, 1986, p. 222). During recent years political reporting has also taken the form of passing the very latest information to an envoy from home in the car between the airport and the embassy. Immersed in the local scene – scouring the media, mixing with the population in a variety of social and regional settings, routinely contacting government officials and military officers, swapping information with other members of the diplomatic corps, and in some cases regularly encountering government leaders themselves – embassy staff are ideally situated to provide their political masters with informative reports.[7]

Clearly a vital function, this is also one which it is difficult to see ever being adequately performed in any other way. A mission at the UN could obtain some information on, say, conditions in Iceland from the Icelandic mission in New York, but it would be very limited. Special envoys can also obtain information but their slender resources, higher priorities and brief visits make it likely that their reports will be impressionistic. Special envoys sent on specifically 'fact-finding' missions are likely to be treated like tourists in the former Soviet Union. Spies – unless highly positioned agents in place – do not get regular access to senior officials, foreign ministers, and heads of government. Nor do journalists, who in any case do not always ask the questions in which governments are interested (Central Policy Review Staff, 1977, p. 116; James, 1980, p. 939; Edwards, 1994, pp. 54–8), or share the immunity enjoyed by the person and communications with home of the diplomat. A diplomat

who 'strays' into a security zone can at worst be expelled whereas a
journalist may be executed for spying – the recent fate in Iraq of the
British journalist, Farzad Bazoft. And while a journalist's despatch
may be censored, a diplomat's may not. In 'closed societies' the
information provided by a diplomatic mission is especially important (Central Policy Review Staff, 1977, p. 258). Resident missions
are also, of course, extremely convenient bases from which to
operate, or provide support to, spies.

What is particularly impressive is the extent to which governments
need to rely on the reports of their people on the spot for knowledge
of the mind of the local leadership. Such knowledge is particularly
important, of course, if an important negotiation is in prospect – or
in progress. During the American-mediated negotiations between
Israel and Egypt in the 1977–9 period, for example, in which
accurately sensing the mood of the volatile Egyptian president,
Anwar Sadat, was of vital importance to the Carter administration,
great reliance was placed on the reports of the US ambassador in
Cairo, Herman Eilts, who by 28 November 1978 had had more than
250 meetings with the Egyptian leader (Carter, 1982, pp. 320–1;
Quandt, 1986, p. 284). 'Since no American knew Sadat better,'
comments Quandt, 'Eilt's views on what was on Sadat's mind were
read with particular interest' (Quandt, 1986, p. 166). But Carter also
took a keen interest in the analysis of the Israeli view provided by
the US ambassador in Tel Aviv, Samuel Lewis,[8] and generally
appears to have been better disposed towards 'on-the-spot reports'
compared to the Washington-based analyses of the State Department and the National Security Council (Carter, 1982, p. 321).

It is true that in another area of crisis, Iran during the last days of
the Shah, President Carter ultimately lost faith in the reports of his
man 'on-the-spot' in Teheran, William Sullivan. But what is
significant about this case is, first, that Carter continued to rely on
some of Sullivan's reports for some time after the two men found
themselves at odds over policy and, second, that when Carter lost
faith in Sullivan he did not dispense with a resident ambassador but
sent out a second one! This was General Robert Huyser, who was
Deputy Commander of United States forces in Europe (Carter, 1982,
pp. 443–9). The Iranian case, incidentally, also illustrates the point
that intelligence on a foreign government can, of course, be sought
by gentle interrogation of its own ambassadors abroad as well as
through ambassadors posted in its capital. Both Carter (p. 441) and

Brzezinski (Brzezinski, 1983, pp. 359–60) testify to the usefulness in this regard of the Iranian ambassador in Washington, Ardeshir Zahedi, who was known to be close to the Shah.

Policy advice

It follows naturally from the respect still generally accorded to the local knowledge of the competent embassy that its advice on policy is usually welcomed as well, and, even if rejected, at least taken seriously. The tradition of listening to, if not necessarily accepting, the advice of ambassadors has perhaps also been reinforced, at least in the West, by the fact that persons sent to important postings have often been eminent in their own right – and cogent in the expression of their views. For example, it is probably no great exaggeration to say that the Commonwealth Relations Office in London regarded with something little short of awe any major despatch from its High Commissioner in South Africa in the late 1940s, the uncompromisingly pro-consular Sir Evelyn Baring; while President Kennedy listened to the views of J. K. Galbraith, his ambassador to India, not only because of the local knowledge which he acquired but because of his fame as an economist. The advice of an ambassador may be obtained by means of direct communication or by recalling him for consultation. In the United States there has been a tradition of discussing policy at periodic and ad hoc conferences at which chiefs of diplomatic and consular missions from an individual region meet senior State Department officials,[9] though it appears that these have been replaced by the expedient of collecting regional views from Washington (Vance, 1983, p. 126).

The Vienna Convention did not mention policy advice as a separate function, presumably because it regarded this as subsumed under functions such as negotiation and political reporting. (This is reasonable since information, analysis, *and* policy advice are often contained in the same 'reports' or 'despatches'.) However, the Duncan Report picked this point out for special emphasis in 1969,[10] as did the Murphy Commission Report in the United States six years later. 'The ambassador is not only our eyes and ears,' a senior State Department officer, echoing the Murphy Report, informed the Senate Foreign Relations Committee in 1982, 'but a significant part of the brain' (Kennedy, 1982, p. 18).

The ambassador's advice may well include views not only on what the policy of his or her own government should be towards the country of accreditation, but views on broader questions of policy which might bear either directly or indirectly on that country. This was certainly true of the advice with which Gladwyn Jebb, British ambassador in Paris from 1954 to 1960, bombarded London, when he became convinced after the Suez crisis that Britain should throw in with the Europeans. This, of course, was a case of advice spurned. According to Jebb's own account of the 'great debate', the still anti-European Foreign Office was consecutively astonished, alarmed, and indignant at his increasingly strong pro-European sentiment. However, it is probably with justice that he concludes his account of this period by saying that 'All I had perhaps done was to prepare the way for some later change in our policy, and to influence, in some small degree, the thinking of certain key figures in the official machine' (Gladwyn, 1972, p. 298). Another case of advice taken seriously but spurned was, of course, the advice of Sullivan in Teheran that the Shah was doomed and that the United States should make direct contact with Ayatollah Khomeini.

Consular services

Nationals of one state touring, studying in, resident in, or doing business with another have varying interests which may be usefully supported by a resident mission. A tourist charged with a criminal offence will need moral support and legal advice; a visiting businessman may need contacts and guidance in local procedures; and almost all nationals will expect reassurance, advice and an escape route in the event of political upheaval and a serious collapse in public order. As states have become more directly involved in economic life, and as foreign travel has become easier and cheaper, this kind of work – traditionally described as 'consular' – has generally become more important in resident missions or at satellite outposts, though the balance within it between protecting distressed citizens and commercial work has probably changed in favour of the latter. Of course, whether citizens abroad – distressed or otherwise – should be 'nannied' by diplomats is another matter, and the Berrill Report certainly took a severe view of the matter (Central Policy Review Staff, 1977, ch. 9). Nevertheless, as the report admitted, the issue is politically sensitive in a democracy with a welfare state tradition and a free press. Rightly or wrongly, citizens of such states tend to expect this support (Edwards, 1994, ch. 11) and can make life difficult for a foreign minister whose embassies are found wanting in this regard. In short, resident missions with efficient and compassionate consular branches are likely to be vote-winners, or at any rate not vote-losers.

It is, however, the commercial side of consular work[11] which has really gained in prominence in recent decades. This is particularly true of those trading nations such as Britain which since the early 1960s have been increasingly worried by their diminishing share of total world exports. Indeed, the resident missions of some of these nations are now justified principally by the useful contribution which they are believed capable of making to export promotion, especially where military equipment is involved, contracts are large, or the foreign state itself is the customer – and where strong chambers of commerce and industry capable of undertaking this work themselves, as in Germany, are lacking (Review Committee on Overseas Representation, 1969, p. 78; Central Policy Review Staff, 1977, pp. 84–6).

In 1969 the Duncan Report concluded that export promotion 'should absorb more of the [British Diplomatic] Service's resources than any other function' (Review Committee on Overseas Representation, 1969, p. 68), and urged that overseas missions should exert themselves more to seek out fresh opportunities for British exporters on their own initiative rather than spend so much time on responsive work (p. 75).[12] Shortly afterwards, Humphrey Trevelyan confirmed the priority being given to commercial work in Britain's embassies, especially in the developing world (Trevelyan, 1973, pp. 104–5). And shortly after this the Berrill Report reinforced the same thrust. Whether or not the benefits to the balance of payments deriving from diplomatic export promotion are worth the less tangible political costs involved in this distortion of the traditional work of the diplomat is another matter (Donelan, 1969, pp. 612–15). In this regard it is interesting that in the course of his frank account of his belated grasp of what was happening in Iran during the last years of the Shah's regime, the British ambassador in Teheran, Sir Anthony Parsons, should have laid such stress on the fact that 'the Embassy was primarily organised as an agency for the promotion of British exports and for the general commercial, financial and economic interests of Britain. This was true', he continued, 'both of the civilian and the military staff while even the political officers had a brief to be on the lookout for fresh export opportunities' (Parsons, 1984, p. 40). There were, of course, other reasons for this failure in political reporting. These included the imperfect guide to an understanding of Iranian affairs provided by Parsons' previous Arab experience and the restraint imposed on his embassy's information gathering by the need to avoid offending the hyper-suspicious Shah. However, Parsons also seems to be saying that the overwhelmingly commercial outlook of the embassy did not help; and if he is, he is almost certainly right.

As well as protecting the interests of individual citizens abroad, consular services also embrace the processing of categories of potential travellers to the home country who are legally subject to entry control, notably those seeking permanent settlement. In light of the spread of poverty, chaos, and disease in most areas of the world beyond North America, Western Europe, certain parts of the Far East and Australasia, this is no insignificant, technical function. On the contrary, it is of enormous and increasing significance in many bilateral relationships (Herz, 1983, pp. 5–8; Edwards, 1994, ch. 11). Once more, however, there is great variation in the emphasis given to this work between embassies of the same diplomatic service located in different countries. For example, while a significant proportion of the staff of the British High Commission in New Delhi, as well as of its regional offices (notably in Bombay) are allocated to immigration work, it is hardly surprising to find this low on the agenda of British missions in Switzerland (Foreign and Common-wealth Office, 1994). Furthermore, there is also great variation in this regard between the diplomatic services of different countries. In Britain, for example, it is policy to place a great deal of the burden of processing potential immigrants on overseas missions, whereas in others, such as France, most of the processing is done at home. The British view, which is similar to the American one[13] and was underlined by the Berrill Report in 1977, is that, although expensive, this reduces delays at ports of entry, facilitates investigation of the applicant's circumstances, and minimises his or her inconvenience – especially in the event that entry is refused (Central Policy Review Staff, 1977, p. 163). Another probable reason is the avoidance of heart-rending scenes at ports and airports and fear of what the media would do with them.

Propaganda

Foreign propaganda is not diplomacy. It is political advertising designed usually to persuade a government to accept a particular view by persuading to a like one those with influence upon it: its own general public, the media, pressure groups, and foreign allies. Of course, a distinction has to be drawn between propaganda which might be construed as intervention in the 'domestic' affairs of another state and propaganda aimed at influencing its foreign policy. Purveying propaganda of the latter kind is generally considered more acceptable than the former, and is so important in international relations and a hat now worn so frequently by the resident ambassador, that it must be mentioned here. Besides, the embassies of some countries also attempt to influence the foreign policy of the receiving state indirectly; this is the cultivation of political sympathy via the export of a way of life. 'Pedlars of national cultures', notes Trevelyan, 'are found in embassies which have a culture to export' (Trevelyan, 1973, p. 106). In short, in another irony of the history of diplomacy, propaganda – usually seen as the antithesis of diplomacy – turns out in this regard at any rate to be its ally. Why is the resident mission sometimes well placed to conduct propaganda? How does it go about it?

It should, of course, be stated at once that the extent to which the resident mission is well placed to conduct propaganda – even restricted to foreign policy questions – varies considerably, and it varies in the main with the local political culture and the sensitivities of the regime; sometimes, it has to be admitted, it is not well placed to conduct propaganda at all. It would, for example, have been inconceivable for any ambassador in Iran whose government valued its relationship with the local regime – either before or after the fall of the Shah – to make public appeals over the latter's head on questions of any kind unless they were mere echoes of the government's own propaganda. Anthony Parsons, the British ambassador in Teheran, had difficulty enough coping with the Shah's allegations that the Persian language service of 'Radio London' (the BBC) was encouraging his opponents (Parsons, 1984, pp. 72–3). Had Parsons attempted to go public himself – even should this have been practical – he would without doubt have been on the next plane home.

Interestingly enough, it is not only in totalitarian regimes, where the media is under the total control of the government, or in prickly authoritarian ones where it is heavily influenced by the government, that resident embassies may conclude that propaganda is off the agenda. Even where the print media (at least) is free, as in France, there can be problems. As Sir Nicholas Henderson has observed:

> it would be thought odd and might prove counter-productive with the French government for a foreign diplomat in Paris to appear to be advancing his country's cause in public . . . An Ambassador in France is called upon from time to time to make speeches; but he is not expected to use them as a means of exerting influence on the French authorities. (Henderson, 1994, p. 287)

Nevertheless, there remain many countries where the ambassador is able to undertake a propaganda role with relative freedom. In the main, these are the liberal democracies, and the United States is the best and most important example. Again it is convenient to call on the testimony of Henderson, who was moved from Paris to the American capital in 1979: 'In Washington it is quite different . . . It would be regarded there as a sign of lack of conviction in his country's case if an Ambassador did not go out of his way to promote it publicly' (Henderson, 1994, p. 288). And indeed, Henderson put the British point of view directly to the American people on a number of issues of considerable sensitivity in Washington and enormous importance to London. Among these, Northern Ireland (1994, pp. 397–9, 421–5) and the Falklands crisis (p. 450ff) stand out. In the latter case it was essential for the British government, first, to convince the American public that this was a serious crisis and 'not an act from Gilbert and Sullivan'; secondly, 'to expose the unholy alliance between the Soviets and the Argentinians'; and, thirdly, to move the Reagan administration from its initial posture of neutrality between Britain and Argentina to one of allied solidarity with the former. Another former ambassador to Washington, Abba Eban, has also paid unambiguous testimony to the importance of propaganda to the foreign diplomat in the United States: 'my vocation', he notes, 'was to develop an American-Israeli tradition based on a public sympathy that might transcend, and sometimes correct, the direction of official policy' (Eban, 1977, p. 175). But Washington is hardly unique. Foreign ambassadors can be regularly heard on the radio and seen on the television in Britain. And during the Gulf War in early 1991, Iraq's ambassadors in Europe and the

United States – repeatedly appearing on television and radio – were at the forefront of Baghdad's propaganda campaign, which is no doubt one reason why Saddam Hussein did not sever diplomatic relations with the Coalition powers until three weeks after the outbreak of the war (Taylor, 1992, pp. 97–8, 106, 181).

The resident ambassador is well placed, at least in the liberal democracies, to make propaganda for the obvious reason that he or she is attractive to the local media as an interviewee and to a variety of local bodies as a speaker. In the absence of a high ranking visitor from home, the ambassador is the most accessible spokesperson for his or her government; is likely to have mastered the sound-bite and the after-dinner address; is unlikely to make any great fuss about having to appear at an inconvenient time; and will not expect a fee. Like the Iraqi ambassadors, Nicholas Henderson used both television and radio extensively during his tour in Washington, as well as non-broadcast speeches to a variety of influential audiences. The more subtle cultural propaganda is purveyed by means of the embassy's cultural attaché and agencies such as the British Council which have a more or less arm's length relationship to it.

Older-generation ambassadors tend to be sceptical of the 'information' role of embassies, though one suspects that it is a conclusion at which they arrive in part at least via distaste. Trevelyan, for example, in a give-away phrase, refers to it as a 'generally unprofitable form of *exhibitionism*' (emphasis added; Trevelyan, 1973, p. 114), though he adds that at least in the British case foreign public opinion is better influenced by the overseas broadcasts of the BBC, while the foreign media is best briefed in London, where the FO's News Department can provide its correspondents with the latest information direct from the horse's mouth. But, of course, few if any states have as respected an overseas broadcasting service as Britain, and there are situations in which governments will want their message to be unmediated by foreign correspondents, whom they may well not trust. In any case, it is clear that the ambassador can often play an important supplementary role even when other channels of propaganda may be superior in effectiveness. The role of the Iraqi ambassador in France illustrates the former situation and that of Sir Nicholas Henderson in Washington – whose television appearances were widely regarded as extremely effective – the latter. Not surprisingly, as early as 1970 the US State Department affirmed that one of the new functions of the Foreign Service, indeed one of its 'critically important programs', was 'communicating directly with people of other countries through the media of press, radio, and television' (Trask, 1981, p. S33).

The versatility of the embassy

It was noted by way of introduction to this section that the work of resident embassies varies in range and emphasis between different national diplomatic services and, within the same service, between countries of location. In passing, this point has been partially illustrated by reference to the considerable variations between embassies in the emphasis given to core functions such as propaganda and in the range of sub-functions (commercial, immigration, protection) within the consular category which they may or may not fulfil. It is now necessary to elaborate the point that embassies also vary in the range of non-core, subsidiary or optional functions which they fulfil. While not all of these – by any stretch of the imagination – can be defined as 'diplomatic', reference to them as a whole is another way of developing the point that the resident embassy is an extremely versatile institution; and this is a further reason for its reprieve.

The administration of foreign aid plays an important part in the work of many donor country embassies but obviously none at all in that of the missions of the aid-receiving countries; and it also plays none at all in donor country embassies in the developed world. Why have the resident missions in the third world of the aid-granting countries been found particularly useful in the administering of foreign aid? This is partly because they are in the field, partly because the bigger powers commonly have a variety of agencies involved in aid work and the embassy is the natural vehicle for the coordination of their efforts on the ground, and partly because the political relationship between givers and receivers is notoriously delicate. The donors are usually suspected of being politically or commercially motivated, while the receivers are often regarded as cynical and ungrateful (Trevelyan, 1973, p. 106). Apart from policy advice, there are as many as three main tasks in which missions – depending on the practice of individual donor countries – may be involved in this area. The first is direct involvement in aid administration. The second is coordination of the aid activities of all other agencies which may be involved in aid work in the country in question. (The necessity for this was one of the reasons for the introduction of the idea in the US Foreign Service in the early 1950s that the ambassador should be the leader of a 'country team'.) (Blancké, 1969, pp. 137–44). And the third task is to ensure that, as individual projects get under way, the ground rules, for example on the purchase of equipment from the donor country, are followed (Review Committee on Overseas Representation, 1969, p. 91). In so far as an embassy is directly involved in the administration and coordination of aid activity, and no doubt in some cases even if it is not, a major concern will be 'to try and ensure tactfully that it [the aid] is used mainly for its intended purpose' (Trevelyan, 1973, p. 106).

A second non-core function which some resident missions have always pursued – the Vienna Convention notwithstanding – is political intervention, that is, intervention in the domestic affairs of the receiving state. If we ask why the resident mission has survived the communications revolution, part of the answer has got to be that the major powers – during the cold war notably the Soviet Union and the United States – found their embassies to be excellent forward bases from which to conduct operations in unstable but nevertheless important countries. Such operations might be aimed at propping up a friendly regime[14] or undermining a hostile one, and involve anything from the secret channelling of funds, arms, and medical supplies to the friendly faction to organising a military coup against the opposition. Zbigniew Brzezinski, who saw no use for embassies before he joined Jimmy Carter's administration, wanted the US ambassador in Teheran to persuade the Iranian military to seize power. The latter had no objection to this in principle but opposed it simply on the grounds that it would not work.

Thirdly, and in particularly flagrant violation of the Vienna Convention, resident missions have also proved useful to some states in providing cover for the prosecution of their wars, wars against domestic enemies exiled abroad and wars against other states. The embassies of Middle East states throughout the world have been notoriously involved in this sort of activity, the most recent example being the implication of the Iranian embassy in Buenos Aires in the savage bombing of Jewish targets in the Argentinian capital in 1994.

Finally, the work of some embassies in conducting relations between hostile states on the territory of a third might be mentioned. If the United States and Communist China had not both had resident missions in such places as Geneva, Warsaw, and Paris, a channel of communication which played an important role in limiting their conflict and ultimately in facilitating their *rapprochement* would have been unavailable (Berridge, 1994, ch. 5). Similarly, communication between the United States and the Socialist Republic of Vietnam and between the United States and North Korea would have been hindered by the absence of missions in third places – in fact, Bangkok and Beijing respectively. Indeed, this point is an appropriate one on which to conclude this chapter since it underlines the value of the resident mission by illustrating the lengths to which states go to make contact via other resident missions following a breach in relations. These include what elsewhere I have described as 'disguised embassies' (interests sections, liaison offices, consulates, and so on) as well as conventional embassies in a third place (Berridge, 1994, ch. 3; see also James, 1980, p. 943).

SUMMARY

The resident ambassador, concerning whom obituaries were so confidently drafted in the 1970s and early 1980s, is still alive. This is not because he is a geriatric relic kept on a life-support system at the insistence of a powerful constituency. Quite the reverse. As is often pointed out, foreigners are the only constituency of the diplomatic service, which in democracies at any rate tends to be a political liability rather than a political asset. Instead, the ambassador's embassy has survived populist politics and the communications revolution for three broad reasons. It has survived, first, because diplomacy remains transparently essential; secondly, because – with privileges legally reinforced by the Vienna Convention on Diplomatic Relations – it remains an excellent means by which to support if not lead in the execution of key functions; and, thirdly, because it is simply so versatile. It is not surprising that the death of the resident ambassador has been indefinitely postponed.

NOTES

1. While observing, too, that 'jet planes and telephones and the bad habits of Presidents, National Security Assistants and Secretaries of State had now largely restricted ambassadors to ritual and public relations' (Ball,

1982, p. 452), it has to be said that there is no evidence in the memoirs of George Ball that he exercised any great restraint on his own travelling when he was under-secretary of state in the Kennedy and Johnson administrations. The account of the Cyprus crisis of 1964, for example, is largely a description of a 'mission to the centre of conflict' in which resident ambassadors (excepting Raymond Hare in Ankara) get barely a mention (ch. 23).

2. The US embassy was actually occupied twice following the departure of the Shah, in February 1979 as well as in November. On the first occasion the government acted properly to extricate the militants. It was only when the Ayatollah Khomeini publicly endorsed the occupation of 4 November two days afterwards that it was clear that this was an entirely different situation.

3. There is a particularly revealing – and entertaining – account of the naivety of a British government think tank on this point in Henderson, 1994, pp. 126–9. According to Henderson, who was the British ambassador in Paris, the think tank's view was that 'if you represented a tatty country you should accurately reflect it by being tatty also . . . It was suggested that we should give up the Residence and live in a small house in the suburbs.' In its subsequent report, the think tank said of representational activity: 'Little of this contributes to the purposes of the post but it often cannot be escaped without causing undue offence to the local authorities or to diplomatic colleagues' (Central Policy Review Staff, 1977, p. 259). The representative function had also been entirely overlooked by the earlier Duncan Report (Review Committee on Overseas Representation, 1969, pp. 18–19).

4. Evidence that the Berrill Report wrestled with this point, too, is its unconvincing and in any case inelegant distinction between 'negotiation and negotiation-like persuasion work' (Central Policy Review Staff, 1977, p. 50).

5. If an 'exchange of views' is just that, namely a statement made by an ambassador and a reply elicited from a local foreign ministry, then it is merely a summary phrase for the diplomatic functions of clarifying intentions and political reporting. If it is more than that it is a negotiation, however undeveloped. In either event, it does not seem to be the distinct phenomenon suggested by James (1980, p. 941).

6. In ch. 12 of Seymour M. Hersh's *The Sampson Option: Israel, America and the Bomb* (1991) there is an interesting account of the role of the US embassy in Tel Aviv in reporting on the Israeli nuclear weapons programme in the 1960s.

7. There are, of course, exceptions. The position of many embassies in Peking during the Cultural Revolution provides a good example. Virtually besieged by Red Guards, they often had little idea of what was going on (Cradock, 1994, chs 2–7).

8. A previous US ambassador to Israel, Walworth Barbour, who served in the post from 1961 until 1973, had also been prized in Washington for 'his understanding of when and when not to accept every Israeli assertion at face value' (Hersh, 1991, p. 159).

9. In *Envoy to the Middle World: Adventures in Diplomacy* (1983), Ambassador George McGhee – who thought highly of the practice – provides detailed accounts of four such conferences which he chaired in the late 1940s and early 1950s: two on the Middle East in Istanbul, one on sub-Saharan Africa in Lourenço Marques, and one on South Asia in Ceylon.

10. 'Advice on foreign policy. A very important aspect of the conduct of international relations is the reliance which the home government must place upon advice of a general or specific character which its representatives in the field are required to furnish, on their own initiative or in response to enquiry' (Review Committee on Overseas Representation, 1969, p. 18). In the chapter on foreign aid administration, it also listed the first function of missions in this area as: 'evaluation and advice on the amount of aid which should be given to particular countries and the purposes for which it should be given' (p. 91).

11. In diplomatic services such as that of Britain, where commercial work is extremely important, it is now conventional to distinguish it from 'consular work'.

12. 'Responsive work covers all the work undertaken at the request of firms and organisations in Britain, such as the provision of information on local trading conditions, status reports on local firms, advice on possible agents or local partners in subsidiaries, and so on' (Review Committee on Overseas Representation, 1969, p. 75). It also acknowledged, however, the political pressure to give priority to responsive work.

13. 'It is not overstating the case to say that the consular officer is our first line of defense against the entry of dangerous and undesirable elements into our country', P. W. Rodino (Chairman, Committee on the Judiciary, US House of Representatives) in Herz (1983, p. vii).

14. Which might involve encouraging a change in its leadership, which was the role of US ambassador to South Vietnam, Henry Cabot Lodge, in 1963 (Ball, 1982, p. 373).

FURTHER READING

Berridge, G. R. (1994), *Talking to the Enemy: How States without 'Diplomatic Relations' Communicate* (Macmillan: London)

Central Policy Review Staff (1977), *Review of Overseas Representation* ['The Berrill Report'] (HMSO: London)

Cradock, P. (1994), *Experiences of China* (Murray: London)

Donelan, M. (1969), 'The trade of diplomacy', *International Affairs*, vol. 45, no. 4

Eban, A. (1983), *The New Diplomacy: International Affairs in the Modern Age* (Weidenfeld and Nicolson: London)

Edwards, R. D. (1994), *True Brits: Inside the Foreign Office* (BBC Books: London)

Henderson, N. (1994), *Mandarin: The Diaries of an Ambassador, 1969–1982* (Weidenfeld and Nicolson: London)

James, A. M. (1980), 'Diplomacy and international society', *International Relations*, vol. 6, no. 6

Morgenthau, H. J. (1978), *Politics among Nations: The Struggle for Power and Peace*, 5th ed (Knopf: New York)

Parsons, A. (1984), *The Pride and the Fall: Iran 1974–1979* (Cape: London)

Review Committee on Overseas Representation (1969), *Report of the Review Committee on Overseas Representation 1968–1969* ['The Duncan Report'] (HMSO: London)

Sullivan, W. H. (1981), *Mission to Iran* (Norton: New York)

Trevelyan, H. (1973), *Diplomatic Channels* (Macmillan: London)

Watson, A. (1982), *Diplomacy: The Dialogue between States* (Eyre Methuen: London)

3

MULTILATERAL DIPLOMACY

If the role of the resident ambassador has been substantially modified in the course of the twentieth century, this is at least in part because of the explosion in the number of conferences attended by three or more states, an explosion, that is to say, in multilateral diplomacy.[1] These conferences, where communication is conducted principally by means of verbal, face-to-face exchanges rather than in the predominantly written style of bilateral diplomacy (Webster, 1961, p. 152), vary hugely in subject, scope, size, level of attendance, longevity, and extent of bureaucratisation. At one extreme is a relatively insignificant ad hoc conference, say a three-nation conference on air-traffic control, lasting perhaps for a week and attended at the level of officials and experts; at the other a major permanent conference, or 'intergovernmental organisation', such as the United Nations. In 1909 there were already 37 intergovernmental organisations and by 1956 the number had risen to 132. In 1986 a peak was reached when the existence of 369 was recorded (*Yearbook of International Organizations*, 1994, p. 1625).[2] This chapter will consider why this enormous explosion has occurred, and look at the characteristic procedures associated with what in the earlier decades of the twentieth century was called the 'new diplomacy'.

THE ORIGINS OF MULTILATERAL DIPLOMACY

Though it is common to assume that multilateral diplomacy is essentially a twentieth century phenomenon, its origins in fact lie much earlier. It was important in allied diplomacy in ancient India

(Watson, 1982, p. 91) and even in diplomacy beyond alliances in the Greco-Persian world of the fourth century BC (Watson, pp. 85–8). Within the European system of states, multilateral diplomacy began to take on modern form in the early nineteenth century, following the end of the Napoleonic Wars, though somewhat chaotic multilateral conferences devoted to peace settlements (referred to as 'congresses' when of special importance) had, of course, been a feature of the seventeenth century (Satow, 1922, vol. II, pp. 3–4; Webster, 1961, ch. 4; Langhorne, 1981). Since the global states-system of today emerged most directly from the European states-system, the immediate origins of modern multilateral diplomacy are to be found here. Why, then, did it emerge most emphatically in the nineteenth century and blossom in the twentieth?

In order to provide a comprehensive explanation of the development of multilateral diplomacy at this historical juncture, it is insufficient to note the great improvements in transport which made it possible and the advantages which made it attractive; for this leaves out of account accidents of personality and circumstance. With this caveat, it is clear nevertheless that the coincidence of motive and opportunity during these years provides a substantial part of the story, and the emphasis in the following account is placed on the motives which prompted states to embrace multilateral diplomacy with such unprecedented enthusiasm. They include symbolic as well as practical ones because multilateral diplomacy is usually public knowledge.

In the first rank must be placed development of the view that multilateral diplomacy actually provides the best chance for a successful negotiation in certain circumstances. A conference is focused and thus concentrates minds on one issue or series of related issues; it brings together all the parties whose agreement is necessary; it encourages informality (Hankey, 1946, pp. 35–7); its members may even develop a certain *esprit de corps*; it has a president with a vested interest in its success; and – at least if it is an ad hoc conference – it will embody a deadline which will also help to concentrate minds, because it cannot go on for ever (see chapter 8). When issues are complex, when many parties are involved (and more and more have been involved with the great increase in the number of states in the twentieth century), and when speed of decision is of the essence, there is a particularly high premium on proceeding by means of the conference. Sir Maurice Hankey, who played such an important role in the process himself, laid great stress on the impetus given to this device by 'the perils and the overwhelming press of war business' during the great conflict of 1914–18 (Hankey, 1946, p. 14). Whether multilateral diplomacy always has a beneficial effect on negotiation is another matter, and – apart from obvious considerations such as subject matter, relationships between key participants, and skill and influence of the presidency – depends very much on the adequacy with which it is prepared and the procedures which are adopted for its conduct (see below). In the event, there have, of course, been a sufficient number of moderately successful multilateral conferences to sustain the view that this is an effective device. Among recent ones are the Arab–Israeli 'multilaterals' (Peters, 1994) and the Uruguay Round of the General Agreement on Tariffs and Trade (GATT), though the hugely complicated package deal which the latter eventually produced remains unratified at the time of writing (October 1994).

It seems reasonable to suggest, secondly, that multilateral diplomacy was also encouraged because a conference of the great powers – and conferences in the European states-system were essentially conferences of the great powers[3] – was a magnificent device for both identifying and advertising membership of the great power club. Those who managed to secure an invitation to such a conference were, by definition, great powers. This was obviously of enormous value to a state's prestige. For the one which could secure a home venue for the conference, and thus by custom secure the presidency as well, so much the better; this counted in terms of prestige and also in influence over the subjects of immediate concern (Webster, 1961, p. 59 and ch. 9). Because it inevitably raised the question of the authority by which the great powers presumed to dispose of the fate of the world, the great power conference was also an unrivalled opportunity to affirm and justify the special rights of great powers (Webster, 1961, pp. 65–6; Bull, 1977, ch. 9). Finally, such a conference was a subtle device whereby a great power could express respect for, and a bond of solidarity with, its most dangerous rivals. With such a calculus of great power interest behind it, it is hardly surprising that multilateral diplomacy should have developed with such impetus once the idea got off the ground. It reached its twentieth century apogée in the Security Council of the United Nations.

If the great power conferences of the nineteenth century which gave birth to the multilateralism of the twentieth were important because they advertised the great powers, they were also important because they advertised other things, and such conferences remain important today for the priorities or alignments which they proclaim. Indeed, the vastly improved opportunities for propaganda provided by the revolution in mass communications made this an increasingly important consideration. It is easier to demonstrate a sincere commitment to peace, arms control, the environment, and so on, or to lay claim to a leading role in the determination of a regional security question, for example, by 'staging' a conference on the subject than it is by discussing it through normal diplomatic channels. And even if an invitee thinks that a conference on a subject is a complete waste of time from a substantive point of view, it may find it difficult to resist participation: it will be fearful that any decisions taken in its absence may threaten its interests; it may not wish to be thought indifferent to or even hostile to its aims (Webster, 1961, p. 66); and it may desire for any number of reasons to avoid giving offence to the party agitating for the conference. For example, the British were secretly hostile to the conference on West African Defence Facilities which the French were so anxious to promote in the early 1950s but agreed to support it nevertheless. They did this because Paris had been cooperative over an earlier one which they had held themselves in Nairobi, because they were suitably flattered by the French suggestion that Britain as well as France should be an inviting power, and because they saw consolation in the fact that at least the conference would provide 'a welcome opportunity to show Anglo-French solidarity' in colonial Africa at a time when the relationship between the two metropolitan powers was under some strain (Berridge, 1992a, pp. 72–7).

If conference diplomacy has prospered because it has been felt to be a valuable device for advancing negotiations between numerous parties simultaneously, it has also gained support because of the impetus which it can give to bilateral diplomacy. This point has two aspects. First, a multilateral conference can provide opportunities for participants to discuss matters outside the formal agenda and which are only of immediate concern to themselves. This is particularly true of major standing conferences such as the United Nations, and is of special value to states which do not enjoy diplomatic relations (Berridge, 1994). Secondly, a multilateral conference can be held by powerful mediators to kick-start a series of essentially bilateral negotiations which subsequently develop elsewhere. This was the extremely valuable function performed for the Arab–Israeli bilateral talks by the Geneva Conference of December 1973 (Kissinger, 1982, ch. 17) and then by the Madrid Conference in October 1991.

Multilateral diplomacy was also encouraged in the early years of the twentieth century by that strain in liberal thought which emphasises the importance of popular consent in sustaining governmental authority. If governments were to be democratically accountable in the domestic sphere, it followed that they should be similarly accountable in the international one. An important means for achieving this was 'open diplomacy': the conduct of negotiations under the glare of a public scrutiny which (this was axiomatic) was 'creative and pacific' (Keens-Soper, 1985, pp. 76–7). In an extension of the same thinking, the procedures of 'open diplomacy' also permitted some formal influence, however limited, to the smaller states. Of course, conference diplomacy was not necessarily 'open diplomacy'. This was certainly not what Hankey, for example, had in mind when he sang the praises of conference diplomacy in his lecture to the Royal Institute of International Affairs in 1920. Nevertheless, conference diplomacy was a necessary if not a sufficient condition for 'open diplomacy'; hence the one tended to encourage the other. The League of Nations Assembly was the first great example of open diplomacy (Armstrong, 1982, chs 1 and 2), and was followed after the Second World War by the United Nations (Berridge and Jennings, 1985; Luard, 1994).

Finally, multilateral conferences hold out the prospect of making agreements stick. They do this partly by solemnising them through signing ceremonies which display the consensus achieved in the most visible manner conceivable; and partly by their reflexive disposition to provide monitoring or follow-up machinery of one sort or another (Aurisch, 1989, p. 288).

International organisations

The advantages of multilateral diplomacy noted so far do not altogether explain why some conferences have become permanent: standing diplomatic conferences or, as they are more commonly known, 'international' or 'intergovernmental organisations'. No doubt this is partly because, in the case of politically important ones such as the United Nations or the IMF, it suits the major powers to have the world permanently reminded of their status – and because a constant process of constitution, disbandment, and reconstitution would cause those concerning whom a question mark had appeared over their status much anxiety. (Had the UN been replaced by a series of ad hoc great power conferences, Britain and France would probably have lost their seats at the top table many years ago.) It is also fair to note that some multilateral conferences have become permanent under the impact of the enduring functionalist notion that it is out of such structures that regional and perhaps even ultimately global integration will grow. Nevertheless, it seems clear that the multilateral conferences which achieve permanent status do so principally by virtue of an appreciation that the problem with which they are established to grapple is itself a permanent problem, the paradigm case being the problem for the UN of preserving 'international peace and security'.[4]

A permanent multilateral conference normally has full and precisely defined rules of procedure, often contained in a 'charter', and is distinguished by a permanent secretariat and permanently accredited diplomatic missions. It will generally have an executive council which, in important examples such as the UN, will tend to be dominated by the more powerful members and be in virtually permanent session; and it will have meetings of the full membership at less frequent but nevertheless regular intervals. The latter meetings will normally have less formal influence but this may be greater in emergencies, when special meetings can normally be held. An important example is the International Atomic Energy Agency (IAEA), an autonomous organ linked to the UN General Assembly which in January 1992 had 113 states members. This has a 'General Conference' which meets annually, a 35-strong 'Board of Governors' which meets about six times a year, a 'Secretariat' of over 2000, and a plethora of scientific committees, advisory groups, and working groups. In addition to its headquarters in Vienna, it has offices in New York, Geneva, Canada, and Japan. In 1992 it had a regular budget of US$186 million (*Yearbook of International Organizations*, 1994, pp. 783–5).

A multilateral conference which settles down to permanent status has obvious advantages. Among other things, it permits the initial breakthrough to be consolidated; it keeps the problem under constant surveillance; it encourages the accumulation of specialised knowledge; it signals serious commitment; it creates a lobby for the cause in question; it often provides technical assistance to states requiring it; and it does all this without raising the excessive expectations often generated by ad hoc conferences. That rudimentary international organisation, the joint commission, is an expression of exactly the same set of reflexes (Berridge, 1994, ch. 7). There is a price to be paid for this, it is true: permanently constituted conferences tend to freeze the power structure in existence at the time of their creation, together with the culture convenient to it. In this connection it is perhaps significant that the real negotiations seeking to restrain the nuclear ambitions of North Korea have not taken place within the ambit of the IAEA, from which indeed it resigned in June 1994, but in an altogether bilateral context with the United States.

QUESTIONS OF PROCEDURE

Whether multilateral conferences are ad hoc or permanent, they tend to share similar procedural problems – though the solutions with which they come up are by no means identical. Among others, these problems include questions of venue, participation, agenda, style of proceedings, and decision-making.

Venue

This is sometimes a question of symbolic and always one of practical significance in pre-negotiations, and is thus discussed at some length in chapter 6. Nevertheless, it must also be mentioned here since, for obvious reasons, venue is of special importance when the creation of a *permanent* conference, or international organisation, is contemplated; and the more important the organisation the greater the excitement which this issue tends to generate. An outstanding case in point is, of course, the controversy surrounding the site for a permanent home for the United Nations, a question which fell into the lap of the UN's Preparatory Commission in late 1945. Though many different sites were suggested, the argument – inspired in the main by concerns over prestige but rationalised in a different language – basically resolved into one between Europe and America. For Europe it was claimed that the site should be here since this was the major cockpit of international conflict and hence where the UN would have most of its work to do; besides, the old buildings of the League of Nations remained available in Geneva, itself in a neutral country and 'easy to reach from Europe and the Middle East and from the East coast of the Americas' (Gore-Booth, 1974, p. 151). For America 'it was contended that an American headquarters was necessary to retain American interest and avoid a return to isolationism' (Nicholas, 1975, p. 44), while many Latin Americans preferred this solution for practical and political reasons of their own (Gore-Booth, 1974, p. 152). In the end, a decision was made for the United States but the question of precisely where in the United States the UN's permanent home would be located then had to be addressed. New York was finally chosen over the opposition of the Arabs, who 'stood out for San Francisco against the strongly Jewish environment of New York' (Gore-Booth, 1974, p. 152). For sound political reasons, however, the UN's other major agencies were distributed among other important cities, notably Paris, Vienna, Geneva, Washington, and Rome.

Venue may be of special importance for permanent conferences but it is also significant for ad hoc conferences. Today this is principally because only a limited number of cities have the communications systems, hotel space, and reservoirs of qualified interpreters to cope with the huge size of many of these conferences. Venues are also sometimes chosen, however, because it is believed that they will assist the publicity of the conference, which is no doubt why Botswana was chosen as the site for the 1983 meeting of the signatories of the Convention on Endangered Species (Aurisch, 1989, pp. 283–4). Finally, an old and enduring reason why the venue of ad hoc conferences is important is that it is customary for the presidents of such conferences to be the foreign minister or principal delegate of the host country[5] (Thompson, 1965, p. 395; Gore-Booth, 1979, p. 232). Conference presidents have important duties: stating the background and purposes of the conference, and setting its tone in an opening speech; directing administrative arrangements; orchestrating any 'diversions' (which might include showing off local achievements); and, above all, chairing plenary sessions and perhaps drawing up any final report. It is true that the host country will generally have a special interest in the success of the conference and that this may put it under pressure to make concessions of its own to ensure that this is achieved (Putnam, 1984, p. 61). Nevertheless, its possession of the conference presidency is a position of influence, as it was in the Concert of Europe in the nineteenth century. 'The question of president never raised any difficulty,' noted Sir Charles Webster. 'It belonged to the state in whose territory the meeting took place, an advantage', he added, 'of which both Palmerston and Metternich were very conscious' (1961, p. 63).

Participation

The sponsors of conferences dealing with matters of peace and security are traditionally great powers or regional 'great powers'; in other matters, they are those – great powers or not – who have a major interest in the subject, are anxious to get something done about it, are prepared to shoulder the administrative and financial burden (often considerable), and are prepared to risk the possible political complications of staging the conference.

Who should be invited? This is a question which has a parallel in bilateral diplomacy: who should be consulted among the friends and allies of the two parties? However, the question is more sensitive in multilateral diplomacy since the invitation list is usually public knowledge. As a result, prestige – possibly even de facto recognition of a government or a state – is at stake, since an invitation is regarded as acknowledgement of the importance of the invitee to the outcome of the conference, and lack of one the opposite. An invitation also publicly confers legitimacy of interest, which may have far-reaching consequences, especially for a state hitherto somewhat marginal to the question in hand.

Before the twentieth century, the rule of thumb was that invitees should be limited to important states with a direct interest in the subject matter of the conference, while those with an important indirect interest or those whom it was hoped might be encouraged to take a future interest, could be accorded observer status. This has remained the case in the twentieth century with the great majority of ad hoc conferences other than those of the 'open-to-all' type spawned by the UN system. For example, the Geneva Conference on Indo-China in 1954 was limited to the United States, the Soviet Union, France, Britain, Communist China, Vietnam, Cambodia,

Laos, and the Vietminh (Touval, 1989, pp. 160–1); and the Arab–
Israeli multilaterals, inaugurated in January 1992, have been limited
to the main regional parties together with those external parties who
have in effect assumed one or other kind of mediating role (Peters,
1994, p. 6).

However, employment of the criterion of interest in determining
the membership of a conference is often insufficient to remove all
problems. For one thing, the concept of 'interest' itself is notoriously
slippery and the result is that there is ample room for disagreement
on whether or not a state or other agency has a 'legitimate' interest
in a subject. In this connection, it is interesting that while the
twentieth century has witnessed some broadening of the basis of ad
hoc multilateral diplomacy to include small states (total, of course,
in the case of UN conferences), there has been resistance to including
representatives of bodies other than states. This is particularly
noticeable in conferences dealing with the termination of military
hostilities and territorial settlements. For example, the Vietminh
were not admitted to the Indo-Chinese phase of the Geneva
Conference in 1954 until the last minute (Randle, 1969, pp. 159–
60), the Afghan mujahidin were not present at the Geneva talks on
Afghanistan in the 1980s at all, and neither SWAPO, UNITA nor the
ANC were participants in any round of the decisive Angola/Namibia
talks in 1988. In each of these cases there is little doubt that the
excluded, or nearly excluded, parties had an extremely strong
interest in the outcome, and not a little power to influence future
developments.

Apart from the slipperiness of the concept of interest, conference
participation is also problematical since in practice the sponsors are
often influenced by considerations of political rivalry. When this
happens, they sometimes find themselves in a classic dilemma:
wishing on the one hand to refuse an invitation to interested rivals
for fear of adding to their prestige and making the deliberations of
the conference more difficult; and on the other wishing to extend
them an invitation in an attempt to 'carry' them along and forestall
the subsequent sabotage of any agreement reached. This was the
uncomfortable position occupied by US Secretary of State John
Foster Dulles apropos the British agitation to invite the Chinese
Communists to the Geneva Conference on Indo-China in 1954, and
by US President Jimmy Carter in 1977 in relation to the issue of
whether or not to keep the Soviet Union involved in the multilateral

diplomacy over the Arab–Israeli conflict. In view of their quite different reputations, it is ironical that it was Dulles who agreed to open the door to his rival and Carter who decided to keep it closed.

A special case of problematical conference participation which in some measure reflects the dilemma described in the last paragraph is the question of the permanent, veto-wielding membership of the UN Security Council. Fixed at five in the Charter in 1945 and presently consisting of the United States, Russia, Communist China, France, and Britain, there is a growing belief that this membership is no longer appropriate. Supporters of reform urge that the 'Big Five' is a misnomer (perhaps why the preferred nomenclature is now the 'Permanent Five' or 'P5') since Britain and France are no longer great powers, and even Russia is but a pale reflection of the former Soviet Union; besides, the third world is seriously under-represented. The Security Council, it is maintained, would carry more authority if, at a minimum, Germany and Japan (the second largest contributor to the UN's general budget) were to be added to the permanent membership. Among other variations on this theme is the neat but still politically unrealistic suggestion that Britain and France should step down in favour of one seat for the European Union, thereby ensuring their continued de facto representation along with Germany (also, of course, an EU member) and permitting Japan to join without increasing the permanent membership beyond five (Wilenski, 1993, p. 442). Against this it is argued (not least, it is hardly surprising to note, in the Foreign Office and the Quai d'Orsay) that it is silly to tamper with the Security Council when it has at long last started to work – 'if it ain't broke, don't mend it'; that powerful members such as Japan which are outside the formal ranks of the P5 are virtually permanent members in any case since they are re-elected so often to a non-permanent seat; that the P5 rarely in fact move without informally consulting powerful outsiders; that reform which entailed enlargement would make the Security Council 'unwieldy'; and that there is no consensus on how the membership should be altered anyway (Schmidt, 1993). Though it glosses over the issue of prestige, begs the question as to whether the Security Council is working because of or in spite of its present composition (if it is in fact working that well anyway), and stumbles over a contradiction between the claims of broad informal consultation and the feared unwieldiness of formal enlargement, this is a sophisticated rearguard; at least the last point is telling. It is unfortunately true that it generally takes a cataclysmic upheaval to alter the composition of great power councils.

Finally, it is important to note that states or other agencies which are widely acknowledged to have a legitimate interest in a particular subject, and which may be prepared to engage in confidential bilateral discussions, may be reluctant to be observed on the same conference platform. This was a constant problem for the multi-lateral diplomacy in Africa sponsored by the South African government in the 1950s, and – until recently – for all attempts to involve the Israeli government in multilateral talks in which the PLO was a participant.

In many international organisations the problem of participation is in principle solved, as already noted, by admitting all states. These are the so-called 'universal' organisations, which have the added advantage of permitting discreet contact between states lacking diplomatic relations. Of these the United Nations is now probably the paradigm case, though it was certainly not at the start of its life or for many years after, when membership was confined to the founding members and 'all other peace-loving states which accept the obligations' of the Charter and 'are able and willing to carry out these obligations'. This permitted the blackballing of many important governments for long periods (Nicholas, 1975, pp. 86–7), most signally in the case of the People's Republic of China, which was not given China's seat until October 1971. Unpopular countries such as South Africa were also forced out of some international organisations, despite being founder members (Luard, 1994, pp. 164–7).

However, universal or near universal membership brings problems of its own. The most important of these brings us back to the concept of interest. If the determination of conference membership by the criterion of interest may cause trouble because of arguments concerning what constitutes a 'legitimate' interest, throwing the doors wide open tends to cause problems because it permits (and may even encourage) each participant to have a say in the affairs of all of the others – whether they have a direct interest or not. Such problems will be exacerbated if discussion is conducted in public and decision-making proceeds, as it does in the UN General Assembly, by majority-voting on the basis of 'one state, one vote' (see below). In short, universal membership may well be anti-diplomatic, gratuitously worsening relations between states which in an earlier era would either have had little contact at all or would have had contact only on issues where both had a direct interest. It is, for example, unlikely that relations between Britain and Ireland would have suffered as a result of the Falklands crisis in 1982 had they not both been members (the one permanent and the other temporary) of the Security Council of the United Nations.

Agenda

If a state is invited to an ad hoc conference, whether it will attend or not is likely to be significantly influenced by the proposed agenda, on which it might reasonably expect to have been consulted. The agenda can present thorny problems in the lead-up to any negotiation, multilateral or bilateral. It could, for example, contain embarrassing items, a formulation of an otherwise unembarrassing item which nevertheless transparently pre-judges it (such as 'Chinese aggression against Vietnam') (Nicol, 1982, p. 41), or a particular juxtaposition of items which amounts to a thinly disguised deal. As a result, this topic is dealt with at greater length in chapter 6. However, there is an agenda problem peculiar to *permanent* multilateral conferences, and that is that they are provided with a general agenda by their founding charters or statutes, usually under the heading of 'functions' or 'purposes'.[6] This is translated into a working agenda prior to the commencement of each session by the most influential members (Peterson, 1986, ch. 2), and those who do not like it cannot refuse to attend since they have already accepted permanent membership. Even one of the P5 on the UN Security Council cannot veto the inscription of an item on the agenda, or veto its inclusion at a particular point on the agenda, since the customary law of the Council is that these are procedural rather than substantive matters (Nicol, 1982, p. 102; Bailey, 1988, p. 51).

It is true, of course, that devices exist to ensure that the sessional agendas of the permanent multilateral conference are broadly acceptable and that the discomfort which might be inflicted by them on minority states is reduced. Even if vetos are not permitted, special majorities – two-thirds of the members present and voting being typical – tend to be required. And in any case considerable trouble is usually taken in the course of what in the UN are called 'informal consultations' to secure as wide a basis of agreement as possible for the agenda so that a vote is in practice unnecessary. If some states remain nevertheless hostile to the inclusion of a particular item or items on the agenda, they may be mollified in small measure by a vague, general or altogether obscure formulation of it, which is the practice which the UN Security Council has increasingly adopted (Bailey, 1988, p. 49). And in the final analysis they can temporarily absent themselves from meetings or – as South Africa did at the UN General Assembly for several years after November 1956 in protest at this forum's habit of discussing its racial policies – maintain only a token presence.

While in practice, therefore, the difference between ad hoc and permanent conference diplomacy in regard to the question of the agenda is not by any means as great as might at first sight appear, it remains true that states in a minority may have to endure discussion of an embarrassing item on the agenda of a permanent conference, and that to this extent multilateral 'diplomacy' is unlikely to serve the real purposes of diplomacy and may even exacerbate tensions. States in a minority tend to stay for the discussion of items on which they would prefer silence to prevail partly because they want their answer to any charges to be heard, and partly because they have other reasons for wishing to remain a part of the organisation.

Proceedings

It is because of practices under this heading that multilateral diplomacy has, with justice, earned an extremely bad name. When discussion of the agenda items takes place between a large number of delegations in a public setting without any serious attempt to achieve prior agreement in private, as until recent decades was typically the case with both the UN General Assembly and the formal meetings of the UN Security Council, when, that is to say, the style of the proceedings is self-consciously 'parliamentary', the political necessity of playing to the audience outside is inescapable and the give and take of genuine negotiation goes out of the window. Debate is substituted for discussion; propaganda, in other words, is substituted for diplomacy (Keens-Soper, 1985, pp. 78–86). Even 'closed' plenary sessions of conferences are hardly likely to encourage real negotiation when well over a hundred states can easily be represented and the corridors outside are crawling with journalists and lobbyists. At the International Conference on

Population and Development, which was held in Cairo in September 1994, there were 182 participating countries.

Widespread recognition of the drawbacks of over-reliance on public debate in multilateral diplomacy has led to increased employment of sub-committees, private sessions, and informal consultations. Since the 1970s the UN Security Council itself has regularly met informally in private (Berridge, 1991, pp. 3–6) and the P5 have caucused in secret since the mid-1980s (Berridge, 1991, ch. 5). Conferences within the broader UN system have also evolved an elaborate mix of more and less private, plenary, and small group sessions, with the gathering of the conferences themselves preceded by deliberations in a preparatory committee (Aurisch, 1989, pp. 284–5), of which the ILC is in effect an example (see chapter 1). Even in the smaller, more traditional ad hoc multilateral conferences, with no public sessions at all, the real work has almost always been done in small private groups, not least – in a famous irony – at the conference in Paris in 1919, with which the rhetoric of 'open diplomacy' is so closely associated (Nicolson, 1963, p. 43). To take a more recent example, in the Arab–Israeli multilaterals, overseen by a largely ceremonial 'Steering Group', the real business is conducted in five functionally defined and informally conducted 'Working Groups' (on arms control and regional security, environment questions, refugees, regional economic development, and water), and even more in the 'inter-sessional' activities of these groups (Peters, 1994, ch. 3). Where there is a constitutional tradition of public meetings, however, these are generally retained. In any case, while public sessions of conferences which effectively rubber-stamp agreements thrashed out in private might induce cynicism among the cognoscenti, they are as valuable in demonstrating unity as the public exhibition of bitter divisions is damaging.

The number of participants and the technicality of the issues in most multilateral conferences make them extremely complex and, on the face of it, and despite the procedural advances just noted, it might be imagined that this alone would vitiate the advantages of conducting diplomacy by this method which encouraged its initial popularity. This is indeed a problem but it is not normally fatal. This is because in most large conferences the order of battle is simplified by the formation of coalitions, as in the UN Conference on the Law of the Sea which involved more than 150 states but in reality boiled down to the West Europeans, the East Europeans, and the 'Group of 77' (Touval, 1989, p. 164). Furthermore, there is invariably a small number of states which is prepared to make the running, while their need to carry the rest usually inclines them to make their demands with moderation. The opportunities for package deals are also far more numerous than in bilateral diplomacy (Touval, 1989, pp. 165–7).

Decision-making

The method by which decisions are finalised in bilateral talks has never been an issue since it is obvious that when there are only two parties there can be no agreement unless both concur, which is another way of saying that each has a veto. A vote involving two parties where there is disagreement can only result in stalemate. Of course, one might impose its will on the other but in that case it would hardly be a negotiation at all. In short, in bilateral diplomacy the unanimity method is the only method. By contrast, multilateral conferences provide the opportunity to make decisions by voting, and the strength of the democratic idea together with the fear that the unanimity rule might induce paralysis when large numbers of states are involved produced widespread support for majority-voting after 1945. As a result, in the second half of the twentieth century, and despite important exceptions such as the North Atlantic Council[7] and the Organization of Economic Cooperation and Development (OECD) where the unanimity rule is retained (Zamora, 1980, p. 574), it has been at least a formal feature of decision-making in most major international organisations, notably the United Nations.

Where majority-voting is employed there are typically differences in the treatment of procedural and substantive issues, while some international organisations employ weighted voting and others do not, and some require special majorities (Jenks, 1965, pp. 53–5) and others require only simple majorities (over 50 per cent). In the UN Security Council, for example, as Article 27 of the Charter spells out, an affirmative vote of only nine of the fifteen members is required for a decision on a procedural question, while decisions on 'all other matters' require 'an affirmative vote of nine members *including the concurring votes of the permanent members*' (emphasis added) – the great power veto.[8] For its part, the UN General Assembly was authorised to pass resolutions on a simple majority of members 'present and voting', except in the case of 'important questions', which require a two-thirds majority.

In practice, however, majority-voting has not been as significant across the whole spectrum of multilateral diplomacy as might have been imagined. To begin with, ad hoc conferences, especially those involving relatively small numbers of participants and not constituted under the auspices of the UN system, have rarely if ever even claimed to employ majority-voting. Secondly, those which tend to do so, including the permanent ones with large memberships within the system, have generally found it necessary to introduce more or less major modifications to the substance if not the forms of their procedure in the interests of their very survival. This has been observed at least since the mid-1960s (Buzan, 1981, p. 325).

The problem is, of course, that the 'one state, one vote' rhetoric has collided head-on with political reality as a result of the introduction into the states-system, especially since the late 1950s, of a huge number of small, weak states, including 'micro-states' (Berridge, 1992b, pp. 19–23). In these circumstances even the requirement for a two-thirds majority can fail to block the 'wrong' decision (Jenks, 1965, p. 55). As Buzan puts it, then, this has rendered 'majority voting increasingly useless for lawmaking decisions because of the danger of powerful alienated minorities' (1981, p. 326). Having lost its own majority in the UN in the 1960s, the United States emerged as the most powerful of all of these 'alienated minorities' and, as it drastically scaled back its funding of the United Nations in the 1980s in protest at having to provide the lion's share of the money for programmes which it found objectionable, threatened with collapse the organisation itself, as well as specially anathematised satellites such as UNESCO (Berridge, 1991, ch. 4). Moreover, the superficially attractive scheme of weighted voting – giving more votes to the bigger battalions – is politically sensitive because it draws attention to real differences in standing between states when all are supposed to be equal, and raises complex questions concerning the criteria to be employed in computing the differences (Jenks, 1965, pp. 52–3). As a result it has only proved acceptable in specialised economic organisations such as the IMF and the World Bank, and others which subsequently modelled themselves on their procedures (Zamora, 1980, pp. 576–7). In practice, then, what has happened is that multilateral diplomacy has witnessed a growing acceptance of decision-making by 'consensus'

(Buzan, 1981, pp. 325–7; Peters, 1994, pp. 7–8), which is a procedure not exactly light years away from the old method of requiring unanimity, that is to say, negotiated agreement (Jenks, 1965, p. 56).

Is decision-making by the 'consensus system' simply negotiation (the 'unanimity system') by another name? The answer to this question is: substantially but not entirely. Clearly, when states participating in a multilateral conference proceed on the understanding that no decision should be taken unless each of them is prepared to give at least reluctant consent (a situation of consensus), those most in favour of a given proposal must be prepared either to water it down, make concessions to the unenthusiastic in some other area, or alarm them with the prospect of isolation if the necessary concurrence is to be obtained. This is the essence of negotiation (see chapter 6), and to this extent there is no difference between the 'consensus system' and 'unanimity system' (it is also apposite to note here that in conferences where the *unanimity* rule formally prevails, as it did in the Concert of Europe and the League of Nations, minorities are reluctantly dragged along for similar reasons) (Webster, 1961, p. 64; Jenks, 1965, p. 49).

Nevertheless, in practice the more modern system differs from the unanimity system in that it tends to retain on the grand level the formal structure of majority-voting,[9] while ensuring that power realities are reflected in conference discussions by procedural devices on a lower level. The appeal of this somewhat cynical arrangement is obvious: it avoids ruffling the feathers of the weak unduly while in practice usually allowing the powerful to carry the day. It also prevents eccentric vetoes, but still makes them possible where *vital* interests are at stake. The 'consensus system' is the 'unanimity system' adjusted to the prejudices of the twentieth century.

SUMMARY: A 'CRISIS OF MULTILATERALISM'?

Multilateral diplomacy took firm root in the early twentieth century under the impact of world war and democratic ideas. It blossomed after the Second World War with the great expansion in the number of states and the belief of the new states that conference diplomacy within the UN system – based on majority-voting – was their best chance of securing influence. Ultimately they were disappointed, not least in their hopes of achieving by these means a New International Economic Order. The major Western powers became tired of paying for programmes to which they took strong political objection, and gradually – under the name of 'consensus decision-making' – began to make their weight felt.

At the time when the mood really began to change, in the mid-1970s, multilateralism suffered a further blow. This was the failure in 1975 of a conference in Vienna which this time sought to extend to permanent missions to international organisations and delegations to conferences (it was the latter which was especially controversial) the same sort of privileges and immunities in which permanent missions accredited to governments had been confirmed by the earlier conference in Vienna, in 1961. Whereas on the latter occasion the participants enjoyed a strong common interest because all states were both sending and receiving, the 1975 conference effectively foundered[10] because most international organisations are hosted by a small number of wealthy Western states, while the vast majority of states are only sending states. Clearly, the host states were appalled at the extent to which the diplomatic bodies in their capitals would be swollen were this proposal to go through, which would have more than undone the work of the 1961 conference, and in effect they killed it (Fennessy, 1976).

In the 1980s, with the UN system reeling under the impact of American budgetary withholdings and the poorer states increasingly disillusioned with the meagre results obtained by their big voting majorities, a 'crisis of multilateralism' set in (Aurisch, 1989, p. 288). The fashion for creating new international organisations had passed and existing numbers dropped dramatically (note 2 above). Against this, the major powers saw an advantage in returning to the UN in the search for solutions to regional conflicts (Berridge, 1991), and multilateral spectaculars are still staged. As an important mode of diplomacy multilateralism is here to stay. It has weathered its crisis, and it has emerged a little leaner. It has also emerged a little more diplomatic.

NOTES

1. Technically, 'conference diplomacy' and 'multilateral diplomacy' are not synonyms since, of course, conferences may be held between only

two states and thus be a device of bilateral diplomacy. In this connection it is interesting that Hankey's classic lecture on 'conference diplomacy' should have revolved substantially around the Anglo-French dialogue during the First World War, though he naturally goes on to show how the bilateral conference grew into a multilateral one (1946, ch. 1). In general, nevertheless, the two phrases are used interchangeably.

2. Interestingly enough, a decline in the number of intergovernmental organisations set in after this year which was almost unbroken. By 1994 the total was down to 263 (*Yearbook of International Organizations*, 1994, p. 1625).

3. If their vital interests were closely touched, small states might be invited to attend, but they invariably found themselves in the wings rather than centre stage – '*at* but not *in* the conference' (Webster, 1961, p. 60).

4. Of course, the UN is a collective security organisation as well as a standing diplomatic conference.

5. While certainly not merely ceremonial figures, the presidents of plenary sessions of permanent conferences tend to be less influential than the presidents of ad hoc conferences. This is substantially for political rather than procedural reasons. They are commonly chosen from smaller states and also lack the ability to determine the ambience of a conference which is available to a senior politician operating on his or her home territory. UN Security Council presidents in any case rotate every month in the English alphabetical order of the names of the Council's members (Bailey, 1988, p. 96), though this also means, of course, that at least for a third of the time in this case the president comes from the ranks of the Big Five.

6. For example, the Statute of the International Atomic Energy Agency (1956), following a brief statement of 'objectives', lists functions (seven in all) such as encouraging 'the exchange and training of scientists and experts in the field of peaceful uses of atomic energy'.

7. The plenary body of NATO, which is in permanent session at ambassadorial level but also meets twice-yearly at ministerial level.

8. It was subsequently accepted that an abstention did not amount to a veto (Luard, 1994, p. 13).

9. But not always. For example, as early as 1976 a consensus procedure was explicitly formalised in the rules of procedure adopted by the UN Conference on the Law of the Sea (Buzan, 1981, p. 328).

10. As at 31 December 1992 there were only 27 parties to the Convention, an insufficient number for it to come into force. Though the Russian Federation was among this number, it included no other member of the P5 and no major host state at all (*Multilateral Treaties*, 1993).

FURTHER READING

Armstrong, D. (1982), *The Rise of the International Organization: A Short History* (Macmillan: London)

Aurisch, K. L. (1989), 'The art of preparing a multilateral conference', *Negotiation Journal*, vol. 5, no. 3

Bailey, S. D. (1988), *The Procedure of the UN Security Council*, 2nd ed (Clarendon Press: Oxford)

Berridge, G. R. and A. Jennings (eds) (1985), *Diplomacy at the UN* (Macmillan: London)

Berridge, G. R. (1991), *Return to the UN: UN Diplomacy in Regional Conflicts* (Macmillan: London)

Buzan, B. (1981), 'Negotiating by consensus: developments in technique at the United Nations Conference on the Law of the Sea', *American Journal of International Law*, vol. 72, no. 2

Fennessy, J. G. (1976), 'The 1975 Convention on the Representation of States in their Relations with International Organizations of a Universal Character', *American Journal of International Law*, vol. 70, no. 1

Hankey, Lord (1946), *Diplomacy by Conference: Studies in Public Affairs 1920–1946* (Benn: London)

Jenks, C. W. (1965), 'Unanimity, the veto, weighted voting, special and simple majorities and consensus as modes of decision in international organisations', *Cambridge Essays in International Law: Essays in Honour of Lord McNair* (Stevens: London; Oceana: Dobbs Ferry, New York)

Keens-Soper, M. (1985), 'The General Assembly reconsidered', in Berridge, G. R. and A. Jennings (eds), *Diplomacy at the UN* (Macmillan: London)

Kissinger, H. A. (1982), *Years of Upheaval* (Weidenfeld and Nicolson and Michael Joseph: London), ch. 17

Langhorne, R. (1981), 'The development of international conferences, 1648–1830', *Studies in History and Politics*, vol. 11, part 2

Luard, E. (1994), *The United Nations: How It Works and What It Does*, 2nd ed rev. by D. Heater (Macmillan: London)

Peters, J. (1994), *Building Bridges: The Arab–Israeli Multilateral Talks* (RIIA: London)

Peterson, M. J. (1986), *The General Assembly in World Politics* (Allen and Unwin: Boston)

Randle, R. F. (1969), *Geneva 1954: The Settlement of the Indochinese War* (Princeton University Press: Princeton, New Jersey)

Roberts, A. and B. Kingsbury (eds) (1993), *United Nations, Divided World* (Clarendon Press: Oxford)

Thompson, K. W. (1965), 'The new diplomacy and the quest for peace', *International Organization*, vol. 19

Touval, S. (1989), 'Multilateral negotiation: an analytic approach', *Negotiation Journal*, vol. 5, no. 2

Webster, Sir C. (1961), *The Art and Practice of Diplomacy* (Chatto and Windus: London), ch. 4

Zamora, S. (1980), 'Voting in international economic organizations', *American Journal of International Law*, vol. 74

4

SUMMITRY

A great deal of multilateral diplomacy takes place at the summit, at the level, that is to say, of heads of government or heads of state. But this is multilateral diplomacy of a very special kind; besides, bilateral diplomacy also takes place at the summit, as for example in the Franco-German summit which has occurred at regular intervals since 1963, and this is special too. For these reasons, then, it is necessary to treat summitry separately. This chapter will consider the origins of summitry, its advantages and disadvantages, and the bearing on summitry's contribution to diplomacy – as opposed to propaganda – of different patterns of summitry.

THE ORIGINS OF SUMMITRY

Since summitry[1] is often a special case of multilateral diplomacy, it is hardly suprising that the history of its development should have followed similar lines, and for similar reasons. It had ancient origins (Plischke, 1974, p. 2) and at least by the middle ages was, indeed, a normal method of conducting diplomacy. At this time 'countries were little more than the private estates of their absolute rulers' (Ball, 1976, p. 29) and personal encounters were relatively easy to arrange since 'diplomatic relations were largely confined to neighbouring states' (Queller, 1967, p. 225). Interrupted during the modern era by the rise of the modern state and the introduction of the resident ambassador, summit diplomacy once more became a significant technique in the first half of the twentieth century, notably at the Paris Peace Conference in 1919.

Fostered by the pall which had spread over professional diplomacy during and after the First World War, and the belief that the decisions needed could best be taken quickly by men close to the people, unhindered by 'protocol', and above all possessing ultimate authority (Eubank, 1966, pp. 5–8), it expanded in mid-century, when the wartime conferences of the Big Three – Roosevelt, Churchill, and Stalin – were its centrepiece. Stimulated at great power level above all by Churchill (Eubank, 1966, pp. 136–7), it exploded in the post-war period. In half of the time available to President Roosevelt, President Nixon made more foreign trips even than this illustrious and mobile predecessor and, abroad, saw vastly more foreign leaders (*Department of State Bulletin*, 1981).

PROFESSIONAL ANATHEMAS

The return on such a massive scale to this 'mediaeval dynastic practice' (Ball, 1976, p. 30) produced deep unease among professional diplomats and caused many to make it the target of biting criticisms. Since summitry is an insult to their competence and at least a limited threat to their careers, this might be put down to special pleading. Nevertheless, their arguments are persuasive and find loud echoes outside their ranks. Most eloquent among their number is George Ball, who was US under-secretary of state during the Democratic administrations of the 1960s and on whose account this section draws heavily. What is the case against summitry?

The case against summitry turns on certain assumptions about heads of government[2] as a class, among which the following are prominent. First, they constitute the sovereign authority of their regimes, and thus the court of final appeal on all important policy questions. Secondly, they are ignorant of the details of policy. Thirdly, they are vain. Fourthly, they are over-sensitive to the needs of their fellow heads of government, whom they tend to regard as members of the same trade union (Ball, 1982, p. 427). And fifthly, all of their activities are surrounded by massive publicity, by which, indeed, they live; this does not exclude their forays into diplomacy. Many disadvantages for diplomacy flow from these and other characteristics of the typical head of government.

In the first place, heads of government may conclude agreements which are inconsistent with or irrelevant to their national interests, or conclude no agreement at all, out of ignorance of the detail of the issue under discussion, inadequate time (summits have to be brief and much of the time is usually taken up with protocol functions), or a failure to understand nuances in the position of the other side (especially if there is a cultural divide). Diplomatic failure of one sort or another may also occur because heads of government develop either personal likes or dislikes for their interlocutors, because they are fearful that enjoyment of generous hospitality may lead a tough bargaining position to be construed as bad manners (De Magalhães, 1988, p. 55), because they get carried away by the atmosphere – the theatre – of the occasion, or because they fall ill (Eubank, 1966, p. 205). Illusory breakthroughs captured by such slogans as the 'Spirit of Geneva' are a summit speciality (Ball, 1976, p. 303). It is in any case far more difficult for heads of government than for ambassadors or even foreign ministers to contemplate bringing a negotiation to an end without something substantial to show for it. Under the glare of the television cameras, their personal prestige and the prestige of their country is on the line in a way which simply would not be the case even were the negotiations being conducted at foreign minister level. The result is that, even if none of the earlier problems are present, they are always in danger either of making unwise concessions in order to achieve a 'success', or of making a 'tremendous row' (Watt, 1981) and breaking off the negotiations prematurely if it seems that they will be unable to get one. Worse still, since a president is the ultimate plenipotentiary, 'there is no recourse' in the event of a deadlock (Kissinger, 1979, p. 769), and there is no going back – except at the price of great humiliation – on a presidential promise, even if this turns out to have been a mistake:

> If he ignores subtleties of policy or some relevant fact, he may well commit his government to an action he would never favour had he had the chance to study the problem with care, follow the advice of better informed assistants, factor in all relevant information, and prepare a reply in precisely written language that took into account the context of total policy. (Ball, 1976, p. 39)

Dean Acheson made this point more succinctly: 'When a chief of state or head of government makes a fumble, the goal line is open behind him' (Acheson, 1969, p. 480). In short, diplomacy conducted at the summit is not only likely to lead to more mistakes but to irrevocable ones. Finally, and because this is so, relations between the states concerned may actually be exacerbated since there will be an unusually high incentive to argue over the interpretation of any agreement, and the scope for this will be greater since key points may have been vaguely formulated in the absence of aides and even in the absence of any written record (Ball, 1976, pp. 37–9). In any case, agreements or understandings achieved by means of summitry and thereby in some measure personalised tend to be weakened by the fall from office of one or other of the leaders concerned (De Magalhães, 1988, p. 56). In short, summitry 'obscures the concept of relations between governments as a continuing process' (Ball, 1976, p. 40).

Summing the argument up himself, David Watt wrote in 1981 that 'Heads of government, with their massive egos, their ignorance of the essential details and their ingrained belief in the value of back-slapping ambiguity, simply mess everything up.' The examples, of course, are legion, and are quoted sometimes with sadness, sometimes with anger, by the professionals. The mistakes made in the Treaty of Versailles were in part ascribed by Harold Nicolson to the decision of the American president, Woodrow Wilson, to attend in person – an 'historical disaster of the first magnitude' (Nicolson, 1933, p. 71). In order to underline his own hostility to summitry, Acheson chooses the example of President Truman, 'in the privacy of his study', unwittingly altering American policy in a most sensitive area by informing the British prime minister, Clement Attlee, that the United States would not use nuclear weapons without first consulting the British (Acheson, 1969, p. 484). William Sullivan's story is how the Shah of Iran, on a visit to the United States, told President Carter of his belief that the Organization of African Unity was an 'im*p*otent' body, and the president – a Southerner – agreed that it was indeed 'im*poh*tant' (Sullivan, 1981, p. 129). And George Ball, in the course of his own savage polemic, gives us a list of summits which have been a 'source of grief', among them Chamberlain's conference with Hitler at Munich in 1938, from which he returned with the conviction, he said, that he had secured 'peace for our time'; the East–West summits of the 1950s and 1960s which did nothing but raise false expectations; the personal encounters between President Johnson and Harold Wilson in the 1960s which impaired Anglo-American relations because the two men simply did not like each other; the meeting in 1962 at which

Kennedy gave Polaris to Macmillan because he had a soft spot for him, though this fitted ill with American policy on nuclear proliferation and gave De Gaulle an excuse to veto Britain's application to the EEC; the discussions, dogged with misunderstandings, between Nixon and Prime Minister Sato of Japan which blighted American–Japanese relations in the early 1970s; and so on (Ball, 1976, ch. 3). Echoing the professionals, Keith Eubank concluded, after looking closely at seven great power summit conferences between 1919 and 1960,[3] that there was no evidence that the presence of heads of government at these meetings produced better agreements than would have been generated otherwise, while 'often the reverse was true' (Eubank, 1966, p. 196).

But this is not the end of the case against summitry. Leaders who employ the technique find that it mushrooms: despite the cost of these events, they have to attend even more summits for fear of causing offence. Heads of government who overindulge the habit may also find themselves giving insufficient time to domestic affairs, and may as a result even lose their jobs. This was the experience of General Smuts in the fateful South African election of 1948.

CASE FOR THE DEFENCE

Summitry has been so roundly anathematised by historians as well as professional diplomats, that it is at first glance not easy to understand why it remains such an important feature of the international scene. But only at first glance. In fact, of course, summitry is valued chiefly for its enormous symbolic or propaganda potential. For example, during the cold war East–West summits were valued mainly because they enabled both sides to advertise their attachment to peace, while intra-alliance summitry was taken seriously because it advertised alliance solidarity. The end of the cold war was also, of course, advertised by a summit, held in Paris in November 1990, which also bound the countries participating more tightly to their agreements by publicly solemnising them at the highest level. In democracies, summits are of special value to political leaders because they demonstrate to their voters that they are personally 'doing something' about a current problem and are important actors on the world stage. Add to this pot the power of television and sprinkle the surface with exotic locations, and it is clear why summit diplomacy is irresistible – why President Nixon had such a burning ambition virtually to kow tow before Mao Zedong in 1972 (at a time when the United States still did not even recognise his government) and President Bush was so anxious to meet the leaders of the South American drug-producing countries at the so-called 'Cocaine Summit' held in the Colombian seaside resort of Cartagena in February 1990.[4] At the Western Economic summit which was held in Paris in 1989, during the Bicentennial of the French Revolution, 6000 journalists were in attendance on the assembled heads of state and government (Kirton, 1989, p. xxvii).

There is no doubt, however, that while summitry may well be irrelevant and even highly damaging to diplomacy, and may often serve principally foreign and domestic propaganda purposes, it can also be valuable for diplomacy – provided, of course, that it is employed judiciously. It is at this point that it is necessary to do something which is often overlooked when the case against summitry is being made, and that is to distinguish between different types within the same broad species; for while all summits share some of the same purposes and procedures some have different ones.

There are, then, three main kinds of summitry.[5] First, there is what might be called – at the risk of being accused of the subliminal suggestion that summits regularly murder diplomacy – the serial summit conference, a summit, that is, which is part of a regular series. Secondly, there is the ad hoc summit conference, which is generally a one-off meeting though it may turn out to be the first of a series. This usually has a fairly narrowly focused theme, and invariably has a high public profile. Finally, there is the high-level 'exchange of views', which may be part of a series but is more likely to be ad hoc. Rather than being concerned with a set piece negotiation, this kind of summitry has the more modest purposes of clarifying intentions, gaining intelligence, and giving an extra push (perhaps a final push) to a continuing negotiation at lower level; the agenda may be focused but is often a miscellaneous collection; and the summit is more likely to be bilateral than multilateral. While the 'exchange of views' is not necessarily conducted in low-key fashion, it often is, and sometimes it is even secret. What are the diplomatic purposes served by all of these summits, those served more by some than others, and those served by some but by others not at all?

Bearing in mind the functions of bilateral diplomacy discussed in chapter 1, there are five functions which the summit might usefully

advance. These are promoting friendly relations, clarifying intentions, information gathering, consular work (principally export
promotion and interceding on behalf of detained nationals), and
negotiation. Let us consider the degree to which the different types
of summit are suited to carrying out these functions, broad though
these categories are and treacherous though this makes the task of
generalising about them.

Serial summits

Important examples of the serial summit are provided by the
European Council, which normally meets three times a year; the
Franco-German summit, which has met officially at least twice a year
since the signing of the Franco-German Treaty of Friendship and
Cooperation in January 1963;[6] the Western Economic summit,
which meets annually;[7] and the Commonwealth Heads of Government Meetings (CHOGMs), which meet every two years. The
superpower summits had also achieved serial summit status by the
second half of the 1980s, by which time they were taking place once
a year (Whelan, 1990, p. xv).

Of all three types of summit, the serial summit is probably the best
suited to the key function of negotiation, though the extent to which
this is true turns to some extent on its length and frequency. As a
general rule, the greater is each of these the greater will be the
suitability of the summit to serious negotiation during the meeting
itself. The reasons for this are clear. Longer meetings allow subjects
to be treated in greater depth, and – most importantly – allow time
for a return to the table following a deadlock rather than, as with
brief summits, have the onset of deadlock coincide with the
scheduled departure for the airport. The CHOGM, which lasts
between five and seven days, is one of the best in this regard.
Frequent summits at pre-determined intervals are also more
congenial to serious negotiation because they are likely to arouse
fewer public expectations and to have developed clear and
comprehensive rules of procedure. In this regard, the Franco-
German summit, which often meets in practice as many as five or
six times a year, is one of the best. Unfortunately, but not
surprisingly, frequent summits tend to be brief and long ones less
frequent.

Whether serial summits are frequent or separated by a year or more, and whether they last for hours or days, they may contribute to a successful negotiation between the parties concerned for one or more of the following reasons. First, they educate heads of government in international realities: they are forced to do their homework in order to avoid embarrassment at the summit, and the personal encounters there give them a first-hand intimation of the problems experienced by their fellow leaders; 'if no significant domestic pressure for an internationally cooperative line of policy exists, summitry cannot create it, but where such pressure exists, the summit process can amplify its effectiveness' (Putnam, 1984, pp. 73–5, 86). Secondly, and related to this, summits make package deals ('linkage') easier because, sitting astride the apex of policy-making within their own administrations, heads of government are alone able quickly to make trades involving bureaucratically separate issue areas, a capability to which a premium began to attach in the 1970s as matters such as financial markets, raw material, and energy sources soared to the top of the foreign policy agenda (Bulmer and Wessels, 1987, p. 17). Thirdly, summits of this kind set deadlines for the completion of an existing negotiation, or a stage of an existing negotiation, between the parties. (Deadlines in general are discussed in Chapter 8.) Because heads of government may be publicly embarrassed by a failure to announce an agreement at a summit, their junior ministers and officials are put under intense pressure effectively to have concluded much the greater part of the negotiation with their opposite numbers before the summit is held. In short, serial summits sustain diplomatic momentum. Fourthly, if the negotiations have indeed been brought to this stage, the summit – even if brief – may serve to break any remaining deadlocks by virtue of the authority of the assembled negotiators and their greater breadth of vision (point two above). This is the 'final court of appeal' function of the summit.

As for the other functions, it is self-evident that the serial summit – or at least the series of which it is part – is also the best suited to information gathering, including the gathering of information on personalities. Summiteers themselves stress this: in 1992 Chancellor Kohl of Germany noting in support of this point that he had met President Mitterrand of France in excess of 80 times (Bower, 1994, p. 37). The serial summit is probably the best for clarifying intentions as well, not least because these rarely appear more clearly than in the give and take of genuine – and therefore private – negotiations. The serial summit is probably not altogether useless for pressing the case of detained nationals, though its qualifications in this area are not self-evident. Precisely because it is the summit most suited to negotiation, it is also the summit which is perhaps least well suited to the promotion of friendly relations. Serious negotiation invariably generates tensions and these are almost bound to be greater at summits, as their critics have so frequently pointed out, since the protagonists can rarely pretend that their word is anything other than the last word of their governments.[8] Besides, politicians tend to find it harder to resist point-scoring than professional negotiators, which was well illustrated by the acerbic exchanges at the 1988 summit of the South Asian Association for Regional Cooperation (SAARC) in Islamabad between the newly elected Pakistani leader, Benazir Bhutto, and leaders who had been close to her predecessor, Zia ul-Haq, the man who had detained her and hanged her father (*Far Eastern Economic Review*, 1989, p. 10). Summits where serious negotiation occurs often also allow little time for the elaborate courtesies, observance of which is so important to the pursuit of friendly relations by the resident ambassador. On the other hand, serial summits would not exist in the first place if there was not an appreciation of some significant overlap of important interests or strong sense of cultural affinity among the participants, and this will often – as clearly in the case of the Franco-German summit and the CHOGMs – ensure that tensions are not permitted to become destructive. It is worth noting here that the SAARC summit mentioned above was also the setting for a warm encounter between the Indian prime minister, Rajiv Gandhi, and Benazir Bhutto, whose election had been widely welcomed in India.

The paradigm case of the serial summit is the French-inspired European Council, the regular conference of heads of state and government of the European Union which was designed principally to ensure that supranationalism in Europe did not get out of hand. This had its origins in informal summits starting in 1957, formally came into being in Paris in December 1974, and was finally embodied in the treaty regime of the (then) EC in the European Single Act in 1986. Despite a deliberate attempt to maintain flexibility and informality, clear rules of procedure have developed, some of which are to be found in documentary sources (Werts, 1992, p. 77) and some in custom and practice. Among the more important are the requirement that the Council shall meet at least twice a year, though in practice it is normally summoned three times,[9] usually in March/April, June/July and November/December, with ministers and members of the Commission also in attendance. A first draft of the agenda is prepared by the Committee of Permanent Representatives in Brussels but the final draft is submitted by the country holding the presidency; the agenda is only finally agreed, however, at the start of the meeting (Bulmer and Wessels, 1987, pp. 51–3; Werts, 1992, pp. 78–9). The chairman is the head of government of the country holding the presidency. The Council normally lasts for no more than 24 hours, starting at noon and ending at noon on the following day. In order to encourage frank exchanges, and although it can subsequently lead to arguments, no official minutes of the plenary sessions are recorded (Bulmer and Wessels, 1987, pp. 57–8); these sessions are also intimate and restricted (ministers and officials are kept in a separate room), though 'not at all secret' since 'eveybody goes out and tells great numbers of people exactly what they think has happened' (Jenkins, 1989, p. 75). After dinner on the first day, there is a very informal 'fireside chat' on general political questions beyond the formal agenda (Callaghan, 1987, pp. 316–17; Werts, 1992, p. 80), the inner caucus of the Council to which only heads of state and government and the president of the European Commission are admitted (Bulmer and Wessels, 1987, p. 50). Decison-making is, of course, by consensus.

What role has the European Council played? In theory, it was designed to promote frank exchanges of views, and to enable government heads to negotiate agreements on matters of high policy, on questions of policy coordination, and on issues on which the Council of Ministers was deadlocked. In practice, the informal sessions have proved particularly useful, at least during some periods; they appear to have been vital, for example, in facilitating the establishment of the European Monetary System (Bulmer and Wessels, 1987, p. 84). And in general the European Council has proved valuable in signalling to the world European solidarity on some key foreign policy questions. However, to the extent that it has been successful as a negotiating body, this has been increasingly as a final court of appeal, though this is hardly an insignificant role. It must, however, be admitted that as the scene of sometimes extremely tough negotiations in the plenary sessions, it has not been famous for its contribution to the promotion of 'friendly relations'; nor did this begin with the appearance of Mrs Thatcher in its ranks and the bitter and protracted arguments which she stimulated in the 1980s over Britain's budgetary contributions. Even in Paris in 1974, when Britain was represented by Harold Wilson, the exchanges on this subject were 'long, argumentative and tense at times' (Callaghan, 1987, p. 315). But this is simply the price of seriousness.

Ad hoc summits

Examples of this type of meeting are the Sino-American summit and the 'Cocaine Summit' mentioned above. As with the serial summit, the usefulness of this type of summit meeting in negotiation is to some extent a function of its length – the longer the better. The Camp David summit, for example, which took place in September 1978, lasted for a full 13 days. Extremely tough negotiations took place between the American, Israeli, and Egyptian leaders and their senior advisers, and a dramatic breakthrough was eventually made with the announcement of the 'Camp David Accords'. The Camp David summit, in other words, did not merely ratify an agreement made earlier by the 'sherpas'[10] (Quandt, 1986, chs 9 and 10). As ad hoc summits go, however, Camp David was the exception rather than the rule. Most of them last no more than two or three days. Because of this, and because they also tend to generate more publicity than, and lack the clear procedural rules[11] of, the serial summit, ad hoc meetings are unlikely to be so useful for negotiations during the meetings themselves.

Nevertheless, precisely because the ad hoc summit is a more remarkable event, producing more publicity, it is perhaps better suited than the serial summit to generating or regaining diplomatic momentum, rather than simply sustaining it. Moreover, because there is no guarantee of a subsequent meeting to which consideration of an unresolved agenda item can be put back, the ad hoc summit represents a better deadline for an existing negotiation than the serial summit. The ad hoc EC summits of the early 1970s, including the Paris summit in 1974 which launched the European Council, are good examples of summits which (some more than others) had an 'energising' effect on extant negotiations (Bulmer and Wessels, 1987, pp. 27–46). In the same period, in May 1972, the prospect of the Nixon–Brezhnev summit in Moscow put huge pressure on the arms control negotiators of both sides substantially to wrap up the first Strategic Arms Limitation Treaty in time for a signing at the summit.[12] To give a final example, the Camp David summit in September 1978 was expressly conceived by President Carter as a 'dramatic' last throw of the dice to regain the momentum in the Middle East negotiations which had faltered when direct Egypt–Israel talks following Sadat's visit to Jerusalem in November 1977 had failed to make progress (Carter, 1982, p. 305; Brzezinksi, 1983, p. 250).

Since ad hoc summits are characteristically designed principally for symbolic purposes rather than negotiation, it seems reasonable to suggest that, whether they have an emphasis on ceremonial functions or not, they are better suited to the promotion of friendly relations than the serial summit. Indeed, many ad hoc summits are designed deliberately and openly for this purpose: the summit symbolises this and fosters it by providing a format which encourages relaxed encounters between the leaders. A good bilateral example of such a summit is provided by the encounter between President Clinton of the United States and President Hafez al-Assad of Syria in Geneva in January 1994. A multilateral summit with heavy symbolic emphasis and the general aim of fostering increased economic and cultural ties between its participants was the two-day Ibero-American summit held in Mexico in July 1991.

As for clarifying intentions and gathering information, the qualifications of the ad hoc summit are a mixed blessing. On the one hand, the typically low emphasis on negotiation and high emphasis on ceremonial will reduce the opportunities for these purposes to be pursued; on the other, the more relaxed and less adversarial atmosphere may produce a frankness in the exchanges which suits these purposes very well. In the extreme glare of publicity which tends to surround ad hoc summits, and especially if nurturing an old friendship or putting the seal on a new one is the main object of the occasion, it is highly unlikely that it will be an appropriate one for a leader, however strong the domestic pressure, to raise the cases of any detained nationals or nationals under threat of execution; for this will inevitably be seen as intervention in a 'domestic affair'.

An important and interesting special case of the ad hoc summit is the funeral of a major political figure which is attended by high-level delegations from the region concerned or, as is now very common, from all over the world.[13] The 'working funeral', which actually resembles the serial summit to the extent that at least by the 1960s it had established a predictable pattern of procedure, is a special case because it is more or less useless for the diplomatic purpose for which, it has been argued here, the typical ad hoc summit is principally conceived: generating significant diplomatic momentum on a major issue. This is partly because of its theme and partly because of the unavoidable shortness of notice which the countries sending delegations receive. Furthermore, funeral summits carry risks: existing diplomatic schedules are upset; and decisions on attendance and on level of attendance sometimes have to be made in the absence of perfect knowledge about what other states will be doing and of how the delegation will be received.

Nevertheless, funeral summits are of considerable value to the world diplomatic system. This is partly because the shortness of notice available to the 'mourners' has compensating advantages. First, it provides heads of government with an acceptable excuse to break an existing schedule in order to have urgent discussions on a current problem with other leaders in circumstances which will not arouse public expectations. Secondly, a decision to attend is unlikely to prove embarrassing as a result of changed circumstances by the date of the funeral. Thirdly, if attendance at the funeral is likely to cause controversy, there is little time for domestic opposition to be mobilised.

A working funeral is of special diplomatic significance if it is the funeral of an incumbent head of government, since the funeral is almost certain to be the first occasion for foreign friends to confirm that the new leadership remains wedded to their relationship and for foreign rivals to explore the possibility of a change of heart. Warsaw Pact leaders always attended the funerals of leaders of the Soviet Union for the former purpose, while Western leaders attended them for the latter, at least in the 1980s. The funeral summit also provides a perfect cover for discreet consultations between foreign rivals seeking to keep their conflict within peaceful bounds or striving for a way out of an impasse. Funerals of this kind are times of political truce.

Because there is so little time for preparation before or for discussions during the event, funeral summits rarely serve for serious negotiation. Their functions are diplomatic signalling, promoting friendly relations (particularly between the mourners and the bereaved), clarifying intentions, and gathering intelligence.

The high-level 'exchange of views'

Heads of government who visit several countries or more on a foreign tour are usually engaged in this kind of activity, which is extremely common. For example, in September 1994 the British prime minister, John Major, accompanied by officials and business-men, went on a week-long trip of this kind which took in both the Gulf (where he had 'several hours of "very friendly" talks' with King Fahd of Saudi Arabia before proceeding to Abu Dhabi) and South Africa (*Financial Times*, 1994). Newly elected American presidents have a particular weakness for this least ambitious form of summitry, or perhaps are just able to gratify it more readily.

Where new leaders are concerned, the educational argument for this kind of summitry is a strong one, though perhaps more in friendly relationships than adversary ones. In the latter there is hardly likely to be such frankness and, as illustrated by the famous Soviet–American summit encounter in Vienna in 1961, the pitfalls for the inexperienced are in any case more numerous. In the White House discussion in February 1961 on whether or not President Kennedy should seek a 'face-to-face talk' with Soviet leader Nikita Khrushchev, the American ambassador to Moscow, Llewellyn Thompson, urged this strongly on the grounds that 'it was impossible for the new President to get at second hand the full flavour of what he was up against' (Schlesinger, 1965, p. 277). However, while the subsequent encounter in Vienna was clearly educational for both leaders, Kennedy came to the conclusion that Khrushchev's own education had been poor, the latter having wrongly formed the impression that the new American president lacked the necessary resolve to defend Western positions.

With its more modest ambitions and generally relatively low-key proceedings, the 'exchange of views' summit is probably best suited of all summits to promoting friendly relations. It also serves well in the promotion of trade and in taking up serious cases of maltreatment of nationals. It is not self-evident, however, despite its self-styling, that the 'exchange of views' summit is necessarily better at clarifying intentions and gathering information than the serial summit or even the average ad hoc summit. As for serious negotiations, this kind of summit can nudge forward continuing talks and even rescue those deadlocked on a particular point, though it will not generally be up to the serial summit in the last regard or the ad hoc summit in the first.

Secrets of success

It is a cliché of studies of summitry which is some consolation for the professional diplomats and other officials, and no less true for being a cliché, that meticulous preparation is the key to success, whatever kind of summit is involved. Indeed, the conventional wisdom is that the most successful summit is the one which witnesses signature of a treaty or release of a joint communiqué actually negotiated before the summit even commenced (Kissinger, 1979, p. 781; Weihmiller and Doder, 1986, pp. 103–5). This is obviously of greatest importance when the summit is the highly delicate kind which is designed to seal a new friendship between erstwhile enemies, as in the case of the Sino-American summit in February 1972,[14] or is a friendly encounter but is only scheduled to last for hours rather than days, as in the case of the European Council or the Western Economic summits.[15] The preparatory negotiations are normally conducted by ministers or senior officials close to the heads of state or government.

The 'sherpas' who prepare the ascent to the annual Western Economic summits 'typically meet three or four weekends a year, once in the winter to review the aftermath of the previous summit and to conduct an initial *tour d'horizon* for the next, and then roughly monthly from March until the summit itself in June or July' (Putnam, 1984, p. 59; also Kirton, 1989, p. xxxi). First they agree the agenda and then, assisted by contributions from appropriate subsidiary forums such as the OECD, the World Bank, the International Monetary Fund (IMF), and the IAEA, they agree the chief lines of the final communiqué or 'declaration'. At a fairly late stage in the cycle of sherpa meetings,[16] foreign ministry officials join in in order to help prepare the 'political statements' which will be announced separately at the end of the summit in order to preserve the fiction that it is chiefly an economic affair (Kirton, 1989, pp. xxxii–xxxiii). Such, however, is the anxiety to ensure that the summit is a success that it is now usual – as in similar fashion prior to the European Council (Bulmer and Wessels, 1987, pp. 54–5) – for the host head of government to engage in a series of bilateral pre-summit summits not only with the other participants but also with important outsiders (Kirton, 1989, pp. xxv–xxvi). At the Houston summit in 1989, the heads of government actually arrived two days early in order to conduct 'pre-Summit bilaterals' (Kirton, 1991, p. xii).

It is not, however, only the communiqué which ideally should be prepared well in advance of the summit. Prior agreement or agreement at the outset on what might and what might not be said to the media is another important requirement for successful summitry, as, of course, it is for any diplomatic encounter which entails private discussion. There must also be detailed planning of the choreography of the summit, that is, the pattern of meetings and events such as visits, speeches, motorcades, 'walkabouts', joint press conferences, and so on, the mix depending on the character of the summit. Pre-planned choreography is always important but is especially so if symbolism is expected to take precedence over substance, as at the Reagan–Gorbachev summit in Moscow in 1988. In preparation for this occasion, the White House planning group worked for three months to 'write a script that would resemble an American political campaign with strong emphasis on visual impressions' (Whelan, 1990, p. 89). Not surprisingly, the analogy which sprang to Ronald Reagan's own mind was a Cecil B. DeMille epic (Whelan, 1990, p. 89). Among other requirements for successful summitry is avoiding the arousing of excessive expectations. This might involve repeated prior statements that, say, a planned ad hoc summit will merely involve an 'exchange of views', which was the line taken by the Americans in the run-up to the Churchill–Eisenhower–Laniel summit at Bermuda in December 1953 (Young, 1986, p. 901); or that a summit will merely be a 'pre-summit' or 'base camp' as with Reykjavik in 1986.[17]

These 'secrets of success' are, of course, necessary conditions of success; they are not sufficient ones. The best actors can fumble their lines when the curtain goes up, or simply fall ill. Churchill was unwell at the unhappy Bermuda summit, while the French prime minister, Laniel, took to his bed with a high temperature on the second day (Young, 1986, p. 906). Boris Yeltsin, president of the Russian Federation, apparently fast asleep, failed altogether to emerge from his *Tupolev* after it landed at Shannon airport in the Irish Republic in September 1994, though the Irish prime minister, Albert Reynolds, was waiting for him on the tarmac, complete with band, local dignitaries, and red carpet. Unforeseeable external events can also poison the atmosphere of a summit or cause acute embarrassment. The shooting down over the Soviet Union of an American U-2 spy-plane two weeks before the opening of the East–West summit in Paris in May 1960 reduced this event to a fiasco (Weihmiller and Doder, 1986, pp. 38–40). In another example, the occupation of Tiananmen Square in Beijing by pro-Democracy students prior to the Gorbachev–Deng summit in May 1989 turned this into a humiliation for the Chinese Communist leadership. The programme had to be hastily revised and the Soviet leader brought into the Great Hall of the People through the back door (Cradock, 1994, p. 221). In short, thorough preparation can minimise the risks of summitry but not eliminate them.

SUMMARY

Summitry may sometimes be highly damaging to diplomacy and is always risky; and it may serve only foreign or domestic propaganda purposes. Nevertheless, judiciously employed and carefully pre-pared, it can – and does – serve diplomatic purposes as well. This is especially true of the serial summit, an institution to which resort seems to have become reflexive following the establishment of an important international relationship. But the ad hoc summit and the high-level 'exchange of views' are of some importance to diplomacy as well, if only as devices to inject momentum into a stagnant negoti-ation. Moreover, while the pattern of summitry has changed in the past and may change again, there seems little reason to believe that it will go into a general decline as a mode of communication between states as it did with the rise of the resident ambassador at the end of the middle ages. Television and democracy have seen to that.

NOTES

1. The term itself was not used until the 1950s, when it was developed in the press following Churchill's use of the word 'summit' during a speech in Edinburgh in February 1950.
2. Some heads of government are also, of course, heads of state, as in the case of the president of the United States. In these circumstances the following arguments usually apply with even greater force.

3. Paris, 1919; Munich, 1938; Teheran, 1943; Yalta, 1945; Potsdam, 1945; Geneva, 1955; and Paris, 1960.
4. A second was held at San Antonio (Texas) in 1992.
5. The following categories are sometimes sub-divided accordingly as they are bilateral or multilateral in composition.
6. This is actually the tip of the iceberg. Chancellor Adenauer and President de Gaulle met 15 times between 1958 and signature of the Treaty. Moreover, in addition to official meetings, which are those held under the auspices of the Treaty, it is now common to find the French president and the German chancellor meeting 'unofficially' three or even four times a year. The official meetings rotate between Paris in the New Year and Bonn in June or July (Bower, 1994, pp. 28–9 and app. 3).
7. This embraces the G7 countries (France, the United States, Britain, Germany, Japan, Italy, and Canada) plus the European Union and, since 1991, Russia. It was inaugurated at Rambouillet in France in 1975. The venue is rotated as in the parenthesis above.
8. Sometimes they can, though. Where there is a real separation of powers, as in the US system of government, the head of the executive branch could claim that any agreement to which he or she assented was subject to endorsement by the legislative and even judicial branches as well. Furthermore, in a political system with a strong tradition of cabinet government, as in Israel, the Netherlands, or, to a lesser extent perhaps, in Britain, a head of government can make the atmosphere of a negotiation at least a little less tense – as well as improve his or her bargaining position – by suggesting that in effect he or she is little more than an ambassador answerable to the cabinet at home. This was invariably the tactic of Menachem Begin, the Israeli prime minister, during the Camp David negotiations.
9. The original agreement, in 1974, was that it should meet three times a year, which it did over the following decade. It was the Single European Act which changed the rule to 'at least twice a year'. The frequency of meetings thereafter was as follows: 1986 (2); 1987 (2); 1988 (3); 1989 (3); 1990 (4); 1991 (3); 1992 (2) (Werts, 1992, pp. xvii–xviii).
10. The term comes from the locally hired bearers who assist mountaineers in the Himalayas.
11. Except, of course, for the admittedly large number which are generated by the UN system.
12. By contrast, the knowledge that arms control would be on the agenda of another superpower summit before too long was no doubt one reason why the Moscow summit of May/June 1988 failed to generate adequate pressure for the conclusion of an agreement on long range missiles (Whelan, 1990, pp. xi, 84–6).
13. I have written at length on this subject in *Talking to the Enemy*.
14. The famous 'Shanghai Communiqué' released at the end of President

Nixon's visit to Communist China in February 1972 was substantially negotiated by Henry Kissinger on his own visit to China in the previous October. However, it still took Kissinger a further twenty hours of negotiation in the wings of the summit itself to finalise it (Kissinger, 1979, pp. 781–4, 1074–87).

15. Though the original 36-hour encounters of the Western Economic summit had expanded to three days by the late 1980s (Kirton, 1989, p. xxiv).

16. Earlier if, as in 1990, political circumstances warrant it.

17. I am indebted to David H. Dunn for this last point.

FURTHER READING

Ball, G. (1976), *Diplomacy for a Crowded World* (Bodley Head: London), ch. 3

Bulmer, S. and W. Wessels (1987), *The European Council: Decision-making in European Politics* (Macmillan: London)

Carter, J. (1982), *Keeping Faith: Memoirs of a President* (Bantam: New York and London)

Eubank, K. (1966), *The Summit Conferences 1919–1960* (University of Oklahoma Press: Norman, Oklahoma)

Kirton, J. J. (1989), 'The significance of the Seven Power Summit', in Hajnal, P. I. (ed), *The Seven Power Summit: Documents from the Summits of the Industrialized Countries 1975–1989* (Kraus: Millwood, New York)

Kirton, J. J. (1991), 'The significance of the Houston Summit', in Hajnal, P. I. (ed), *The Seven Power Summit: Documents from the Summits of Industrialized Countries. Supplement: Documents from the 1990 Summit* (Kraus: Millwood, New York)

Nicolson, H. (1937), *Peacemaking 1919* (Constable: London)

Plischke, E. (1974), *Summit Diplomacy: Personal Diplomacy of the United States' Presidents* (Greenwood Press: New York)

Putnam, R. (1984), 'The Western Economic Summits: a political interpretation', in Merlini, C. (ed), *Economic Summits and Western Decision-making* (Croom Helm: London; St. Martin's Press: New York)

Putnam, R. and N. Bayne (1988), *Hanging Together: Cooperation and Conflict in the Seven Power Summits*, 2nd ed (Sage: London)

Weihmiller, G. R. and D. Doder (1986), *US–Soviet Summits* (University Press of America: Lanham, New York, and London)

Werts, J. (1992), *The European Council* (North-Holland: Amsterdam)

Whelan, J. G. (1990), *The Moscow Summit 1988* (Westview Press: Boulder)

Young, J. W. (1986), 'Churchill, the Russians and the Western Alliance: the three-power conference at Bermuda, December 1953', *English Historical Review*

5

MEDIATION

Mediation is by definition multilateral and may occur, as at Camp David in September 1978, at the summit. Its extent in international conflicts, and also in civil wars, is vast, though only occasionally does it attract great attention. A recent study cites research showing that 255 of 310 conflicts between 1945 and 1974 enjoyed some form of official mediation alone (Princen, 1992, p. 5). In the mid-1990s it seems even more difficult to find conflicts in which intermediaries are not involved in one way or another. What does mediation involve? What motivates the intermediary? What are his or her ideal attributes? In what circumstances is mediation most likely to be successful? And what are the drawbacks of involving third parties in disputes? These are the questions which this chapter will consider.

THE CONCEPT OF MEDIATION

Mediation is particularly necessary in extremely bitter disputes, especially those in which the parties have been engaged for long periods and are locked into public postures which appear to make compromise impossible without major loss of face. It is also appropriate where the parties have the most profound distrust of each other's intentions, where cultural differences present an additional barrier to communication (Cohen, 1991), and where at least one of the parties refuses to recognise the other. It is important to note, though, that non-recognition does not necessarily make mediation essential, as evidenced by the direct Sino-American contacts in the 1950s and 1960s (Berridge, 1994, ch. 5).

What does mediation involve? It is probably best to think of it as third party diplomatic activity ranging along a continuum from relatively passive to relatively active involvement in a dispute.[1] At the passive end the role of the mediator is limited to making it possible for the parties to communicate with each other. Initially this will involve merely provision of a secure channel of communications but the implications of this are greater than might be imagined. A good mediator is not simply a conveyor but also an interpreter of messages; and equally someone with the ability to show one or both parties how the style, as well as the content, of a message from one party can be made more palatable to the other. Algeria made important contributions in both of these ways to the resolution of the hostages crisis between Iran and the United States at the beginning of the 1980s (Sick, 1985, ch. 15; Christopher, 1985, chs 7 and 8).

But there is even more to being a simple 'channel' of communications than this, for a message passed on by a mediator might be secure, intelligible, and as inoffensive as its substance will allow – but still be regarded as either a pack of lies, a stalling device, or a stratagem which, while truthful as far as it goes, is designed to lure the recipient into a trap. A final vital role which the mediator must play in communication, therefore, is that of providing reassurance. The mediator, in other words, must as far as possible be able to reassure each party that the other means what it says and is sincere in seeking a negotiated settlement. This seems to have been at least one of the roles played in the earliest stage of the Sino-American *rapprochement* in 1969 by the government of General de Gaulle, a figure who still commanded enormous international respect at this time, even though his position was by then seriously weakened at home (Nixon, 1979, pp. 370–4; Hersh, 1983, pp. 351–2).

Via the communications they have exchanged through the 'good offices' of the mediator (on diplomatic procedure as well as political substance), the parties to a conflict may conclude that there is a basis for negotiation between them. In this eventuality, the mediator may be required to facilitate this by arranging for a neutral venue for the talks.[2] This may be on the territory of a mediator, especially if it is a permanent neutral such as Austria. It may also be elsewhere. During the Angola/Namibia negotiations in 1988, which were brokered by the United States, meetings were held in London, Cape Verde, Brazzaville, Geneva, and Cairo, as well as in New York. Talks mediated by the United Nations are commonly held in Geneva or New York but certainly not always.

Having brought the parties together, the subsequent role of the mediator depends on a variety of factors. These include motives (see below), influence, diplomatic skill, and standing with the parties; and whether or not the latter have been brought to a stage where they can bear it to be known that they are talking face-to-face with their enemies. A mediator may lack significant influence with the parties and find that in any case they are by now prepared to talk directly, as in the Sino-American *rapprochement* in the early 1970s in which Pakistan had emerged as the most important mediator. In this case the third party will generally retreat to the wings, while standing ready to assist if necessary.[3] Conversely, the influence of the mediator over the parties may be considerable, especially if the open or tacit support of other important players is available. Furthermore, the parties in dispute may not only find it impossible to meet without the face-saving presence of the mediator but require a constant stiffening of their resolve to continue talking. In such circumstances, it is common for mediators not only to orchestrate the negotiations but to chair them, put forward substantive compromise proposals of their own, and in some cases even make threats and promises to one or both of the parties in order to get a settlement. To reassure them that calamity will not follow non-compliance with any agreement reached, the mediator may also provide tangible guarantees, a vital feature of American mediation in the Arab–Israeli conflict in the 1970s (Touval, 1982, chs 9 and 10). And the mediator may make a final contribution to face-saving on the part of one or both of the antagonists by assisting in construction of an agreement the form of which suggests that any concessions made have been granted to the mediator rather than to the opponent. In the Iran hostages negotiations, for example, the final agreement took the form of a 'Declaration of the Government of the Democratic and Popular Republic of Algeria' (*International Legal Materials*, 1981, p. 224ff; Sick, 1985, p. 332). The paradigm case of mediation at the active end of the continuum, however, remains US mediation in the Arab–Israeli conflict in the 1970s.

In considering the nature of mediation, it is finally important to note that it is not unusual to find more than one mediator active in a particular dispute at the same time, and not just in the early stages. For example, France and Romania played a role in the

Sino-American *rapprochement*, as well as Pakistan. Since the late 1970s the United States has had a 'Special Cyprus Co-ordinator' who is at least as active in the Cyprus negotiations as the UN Secretariat (Berridge, 1992c). The Americans and the Russians, together with EC 'observers', were all present at the Madrid Conference between the Arabs and the Israelis in November 1991. And at the first face-to-face encounter between the chief antagonists in the Mozambique civil war, President Chissano and Afonso Dhlakama of Renamo, which took place in Rome in August 1992, President Mugabe of Zimbabwe, the foreign minister of Botswana, and Lonhro's Tiny Rowland[4] were also present, though the mediation over the previous two years had been conducted 'officially' by the Rome-based religious community of Sant Egidio with the assistance of the Italian Foreign Ministry (*The Independent*, 1991). Why is mediation often a multiple affair?

One reason for this, of course, is that in some conflicts many people want to be involved for reasons of their own which will shortly be explored. But since on the face of it this might appear to be a recipe for nothing but confusion, the issue here is: what if any are the advantages of multiple mediation? From the point of view of the parties, one advantage is that a mediator with rivals is not in a position to command a monopoly price. Another, which is especially important in the early stages, is that it is not immediately apparent which mediator will prove to be the most suited to the particular task in hand. For example, the Americans initially considered Romania for the task of communicating with the Chinese because they thought that a Communist regime which was at the same time noted for its relative independence from Moscow would be especially attractive to Peking. This proved not to be so, probably because the Chinese feared KGB penetration of the Romanian government (Kissinger, 1979, pp. 181, 714).

From the point of view of the mediators, especially if they have a deep national or other interest in a settlement, multiple mediation provides more scope for bringing pressure to bear on the parties and – if success is achieved – increases the cost of any subsequent default by multiplying the ranks of those who will be directly affronted by it. Considerations of this sort clearly influenced the enthusiasm of the current secretary-general of the UN, Boutros Boutros-Ghali, for what he described in his *Agenda for Peace* as 'complementary efforts' to preserve or restore peace (either by mediation or other means) between the UN and regional bodies such as the EU (Boutros-Ghali, 1992, ch. vii). At the negotiation stage, however, one mediator alone normally has formal responsibility for chairmanship; in the Cyprus negotiations, for example, this is the UN secretary-general. However, joint mediations, such as the Owen/Vance mission on Bosnia, are certainly not unknown. Finally, multiple mediation is of advantage to both the parties and the mediators themselves to the extent that it increases the credibility of a message. For example, it is a reasonable supposition that if the Chinese Communists were hearing that the Nixon administration was sincere about wishing to end the Vietnam War and normalise relations with Peking not only from the French but also from the Romanians and the Pakistanis as well, they were more likely to believe it. Paul Gore-Booth, who was permanent under-secretary in the British Foreign Office in the second half of the 1960s, makes the same point about the effects of 'simultaneous advocacy by British and Polish intermediaries' in the Vietnam War in late 1966 (Gore-Booth, p. 357).

In sum, mediation involves at the least the provision of a channel of communications between the parties to a dispute and at the most the active steering of negotiations between them. In addition, it quite often involves more than one participant.

WHAT MOVES THE MEDIATOR?

In a much-quoted though not altogether original line,[5] Touval says that 'mediators, like brokers, are in it for profit' (Touval, 1982, p. 321). There is no doubting this. However, the nature of the profit sought depends on who they are and what kind of dispute they are trying to mediate. First of all, then, who are the mediators?

Some are private but well connected individuals such as the legendary Armand Hammer, the American tycoon whose Russian father, a supporter of the Socialist Labour Party, had emigrated to the United States in the late nineteenth century. Hammer, who died in 1990, made his first money in the world of Soviet–American import/export business in the 1920s, with the personal blessing of Lenin. Subsequently he received much carefully engineered publicity for his personal attempts as a 'citizen-diplomat' to promote East–West detente, though less so – for good reasons – for his efforts on behalf of Soviet Jews at the instigation of Israel. Exploiting to the full his huge experience of the Soviet Union, his vast wealth, and his remorseless energy, Hammer seemed to open doors in Moscow which others found closed. He certainly had political achievements to his credit, though there were many in the US State Department who did not trust him and some at any rate of his efforts on behalf of East–West detente were rendered superfluous by the fact that diplomatic relations between the superpowers were never actually broken off (Hammer, 1987; Weinberg, 1989; Blumay, 1992). Most important mediators in international relations, however, fall into one or the other of the following categories: states, regional associations of states (such as the EU, OAU or ASEAN), churches (notably the Roman Catholic Church in South America and the Church of England in southern Africa), and international organisations such as the UN, the International Committee of the Red Cross, and so on.

The major powers, who held a virtual monopoly over the activity until the twentieth century (Princen, 1992, p. 6), have generally involved themselves in mediation for three main reasons. First and generally foremost, they have traditionally offered themselves in this role in order to defuse crises which threaten global stability, including global economic stability. Against the background of the massive increase in the price of oil associated with the Yom Kippur War in October 1973 and an increasingly strained detente with the Soviet Union, these were certainly major considerations prompting successive US administrations in the 1970s to make a settlement of the Arab–Israeli conflict a high priority.

Secondly, the major powers have from time to time thought it prudent to mediate in conflicts within alliances or looser associations of states in which they play leading roles in order to maintain internal solidarity and pre-empt offers of assistance from outside. In some cases this inclination has been reinforced by a lingering sense of imperial responsibility and 'ethnic' lobbying at home. These have been key factors leading the United States and Britain to interest themselves in the Cyprus dispute, which, of course, involves two of the most important members of NATO's southern flank – Turkey and Greece. Britain also has legal guarantor obligations towards the Republic of Cyprus, while the island itself contains important NATO military installations and the Republic is a member of the British Commonwealth. Considerations of in-group solidarity and leadership have also no doubt been behind Britain's long-standing attempts to mediate in the dispute over Kashmir between leading Commonwealth members India and Pakistan, an offer renewed as recently as June 1992 (*The Independent*, 1992a).

Finally, it is clear that the major powers have also seen mediation in general as a means of enhancing their reputations for diplomatic weight and extending their networks of dependent clients; in other words, they have seen it not only as a means of preserving existing influence but of projecting it into areas where previously it had not been great. This prompted Soviet mediation in the India–Pakistan conflict, at Tashkent in January 1966, at a time when both of these South Asian powers were disgruntled with the West, and, as Humphrey Trevelyan observes, 'must have made Lord Curzon turn in his grave' (1971, p. 200). It was also behind the American role in the Angola/Cuba–South African negotiations which were finally brought to a success at the end of 1988 (Berridge, 1989).

The major powers, however, are not the only kind of states which involve themselves in mediation efforts. Medium powers, or regional 'great powers', periodically play this role and for reasons related to those which lead to its adoption by the major powers. In the cases of Austria and Switzerland, however, middle powers which have assumed postures of permanent neutrality, the reasons are somewhat different, though Austria at any rate has certainly sought influence through mediation. These states are anxious to contribute to the peaceful settlement of disputes in order to sustain the stability in which they flourish; this was particularly true of Austria, given its position in Central Europe, during the Cold War. But another important motive for both is the need to deflect the free-rider criticism of neutrality. It is no accident that both Vienna and Geneva have been the venues of so much sensitive diplomacy, that Geneva should host the European headquarters of the UN, or that in 1979 – at a very considerable cost to the Austrian taxpayer – a new 'International Centre' for the use of UN agencies should have been opened in Vienna (Stadler, 1981, p. 14). It is also no accident that both Switzerland and Austria are frequently employed by states in conflict as 'protecting powers'.[6]

It should be noted, however, that while both permanent neutrals have been prominent at the passive end of the mediation continuum, Austria, which prides itself on its 'active neutrality', has also played a more positive role from time to time. This was particularly true under the leadership of the Jewish but nevertheless anti-Zionist Socialist, Dr Bruno Kreisky, who took a particular interest in the Arab–Israeli conflict in the mid-1970s, and was the first Western statesman to recognise the PLO; he allowed it to open an 'information office' in Vienna. In 1977 he hosted a famous encounter in the city between South African prime minister, John Vorster and US vice-president, Walter Mondale, and later visited Teheran on behalf of the Socialist International in an unsuccessful attempt to break the impasse in the hostages crisis (Stadler, 1981, pp. 16–17). Austrian minister of foreign affairs from 1959 until 1966 and federal chancellor from 1970 until 1983, Kreisky, according to Kissinger, was 'shrewd and perceptive . . . [and] . . . had parlayed his country's formal neutrality into a position of influence beyond its strength, often by interpreting the motives of competing countries to each other' (Kissinger, 1979, p. 1204). However, with the election to the federal presidency in 1986 of Dr Kurt Waldheim, the former secretary-general of the UN whose war record had shortly before received much unfavourable press scrutiny, Austria's ability to act as a mediator was seriously impaired. Waldheim, for example, was personally barred from visiting the United States.

It is important to note that small states, too, sometimes mediate in international conflicts, including those involving far larger states than themselves. An excellent case in point which has already been mentioned is the mediation of Algeria in the hostages crisis between the United States and Iran at the beginning of the 1980s. Clearly, Algeria was interested both in the huge prestige which successful mediation in this most serious crisis would bring in its train and the increased influence in Teheran and Washington which it would produce as well.

International organisations (universal and regional) and churches mediate in international disputes chiefly out of duty, though political calculations of the sort that move states to this activity also play a part. The UN, for example, is virtually bound to mediate in conflicts between member states when called upon to do so, while for the Vatican it is a spiritual as well as political requirement. It is worth noting in passing, however, that for much the greater part of the post-war period Communism and religious divisions have together severely restricted the mediating capacity of the Vatican diplomatic service. In breach of diplomatic relations with the entire Communist world (including Communist China) until the end of the 1980s, and having refused to recognise the State of Israel, the Vatican has been as much in need of mediation itself as it has been available as an appropriate intermediary. In practice, its activities under this heading have been confined to the Catholic world, as, for example, in its mediation of the Beagle Channel dispute between Argentina and Chile, diplomacy which began in 1979 and culminated successfully six years later (Lindsley, 1987; Princen, 1992, ch. 8).

THE IDEAL MEDIATOR

While it is obvious that the attributes of the ideal mediator (additional to routine diplomatic skills) will vary according to circumstances, three observations in this regard of general relevance might be suggested without serious risk of banality. First, the ideal mediator should have influence relative to the parties; secondly, possess the ability to devote sustained attention to their dispute; and, thirdly, be perceived as impartial on the specific issues dividing them although not necessarily be thought to hold them in equal affection on a broader level. However, in the particular case of mediation by the United Nations, a fourth 'ideal' attribute, leadership of the effort by a 'distinguished statesman', which has recently been given some emphasis by the UN secretary-general, Boutros Boutros-Ghali, should be treated with more reserve.

While influence relative to the parties is less important if the mediation is confined to the passive end of the mediation continuum, it is clearly vital at the active end. This point has been very ably developed by Saadia Touval in his study of mediation in the Arab–Israeli conflict (*The Peace Brokers*, 1982), and hardly needs labouring here. Suffice it to say that power, typically in the form of economic and military aid, is of the greatest use to the mediator in cajoling antagonists to a settlement. (Jimmy Carter said that he was wary of 'buying peace' in the Camp David negotiations – but he did.[7]) Furthermore, it is also vital in providing any necessary guarantees against the consequences of non-compliance. It is for these reasons that the ideal mediator is often a great power, like the United States in the Middle East, or – better still – a great power acting with the support of a regional grouping and another great power. This was the ultimately happy position of the United States in south-western Africa in the mid-1980s, when it came to enjoy the support of the Front-Line States and the Soviet Union, among others (Berridge, 1989; Crocker, 1992, pp. 472–3). It is interesting in this context, however, that the UN Secretariat is now giving active consideration to ways of mobilising the resources of all of the UN's notoriously uncoordinated agencies and programmes in order to provide 'positive leverage' behind the UN's own mediation efforts (Boutros-Ghali, 1992, para. 40).

Next, it is important that the mediator should be able to give continuous attention to a conflict, possibly over many years. The conflicts which require mediation are the most intractable, and intractable conflicts do not dissolve, or resolve themselves, over-night. Continuous involvement produces familiarity with the problem and key personalities, enables relationships of personal trust to develop which reinforce calculations of interest, fosters a routine which reduces the likelihood of false expectations being generated, and makes possible procedural breakthroughs and even breakthroughs of principle which in turn make seizing a propitious moment for settlement that much easier. This is where international organisations, and the UN in particular, tend to have the edge over states, especially in the mediation of disputes where great power interest is at most moderate. The reason for this is that even in stable political regimes like that of the United States, which have foreign ministries capable of pursuing consistent policies over long periods, electoral cycles as well as a constantly changing international context tend to make mediation an episodic rather than continuous affair (Quandt, 1986, ch. 1). This has been a marked feature of American mediation in the Middle East, though it is fair to note that Chester Crocker, the US assistant secretary of state for African affairs who successfully negotiated the Angola/Namibia Accords of December 1988, was able to devote the full period of both Reagan administrations to the task. Not surprisingly, Crocker himself emphasises the value of continuity in his memoir of this negotiation (Crocker, 1992, pp. 468–70).

As for impartiality, the mediator needs this in order to be trusted by both parties: trusted to exchange messages between them without distortion, trusted to give well-founded reassurances about their mutual sincerity, trusted with their confidences, and trusted to propose and support – if this is desired – compromises which are of equal benefit to both. Impartiality is thus a necessary if certainly not a sufficient attribute of the ideal mediator.

However, a little more needs to be said on this point because the influential work of Touval on mediation has tended to denigrate the importance of impartiality. He suggests, indeed, that not only is it not a necessary attribute of the ideal mediator but that its absence is actually a positive advantage. This is because the mediator's influence in the negotiations will be increased by the possibility of alignment with one side rather than the other. With this possibility open – ruled out by impartiality – the favoured party may make concessions to the mediator out of fear of losing the mediator's favour, while the other may make them in an attempt either to win it or at least to reduce the intermediary's support for the opposition. Extravagant one-sidedness on the part of the mediator will be restrained by an interest in a settlement acceptable to both, by an interest in future dealings with each party, and possibly by an interest in being retained as a mediator in different conflicts or sought as a mediator in future ones. Historical cases of successful mediation conducted by biased intermediaries are cited by Touval, and by Zartman and Touval in support of this view.

Touval is right to point to the greater bargaining possibilities of a situation in which the mediator is not fixed in a posture of rigid neutrality; and also right to point out that a generally partisan mediator may in any case have to be accepted because mediation is unavoidable and the alternative mediators are worse,[8] though the less favoured party pays a price in prestige in accepting this situation. However, Touval's position – which in the end turns out to be nowhere near as radical as it first appears – requires heavy qualification.

In the first place, it does not bring out with anything like sufficient force and clarity the vital distinction between the mediator's general attitude ('sympathies and sentiments', or 'underlying sympathy' (Touval, 1982, pp. 277, 325 resp.)) towards the parties involved in a dispute and the attitude of the mediator towards the particular issues over which they are at odds. In fact, what emerges is that when he is talking about impartiality, or its absence, he has in mind the former and not the latter. And, quite obviously, what really matters to the parties to a dispute, and what Touval himself appreciates, is the potential mediator's attitude to the dispute in question. Thus it is likely that a party generally less favoured relative to the opposition will find a mediator acceptable provided the latter is more even-handed on the specific issues currently dividing them. Furthermore, this may be deduced by the less favoured party from a correct interpretation of a biased intermediary's own interest in a settlement, as the Egyptians did in regard to Kissinger's mediation in the Middle East in the aftermath of the Yom Kippur War (Touval, 1982, p. 277). In short, Touval does not challenge the importance of impartiality on the issues in dispute.

In the second place, Touval's thinking glosses over the question of the sources and intensity of the mediator's general bias and thus implies that the biased mediator has virtually unlimited freedom to shift its weight from one side to the other as the course of the negotiation demands; in fact, this may not be possible. In the Camp David negotiations, for example, Jimmy Carter, who was personally extremely even-handed on the issues dividing the parties, could not persuade the Israelis to make the concessions on Gaza and the West Bank which he thought were necessary for a comprehensive settlement of the Arab–Israeli conflict. And the reason was that they knew – and he knew – that, as a result of the strength of the Jewish lobby in Washington and the imperatives of the American electoral cycle, he could not credibly threaten them where it would really hurt (on arms sales and economic aid) in order to achieve this objective. Despite the clear evidence which Carter gave of his personal sympathy for the Egyptian leader, Anwar Sadat, and the strong commitment to human rights which made him responsive to the plight of the Palestinians, on the West Bank, therefore, the Israelis remained relatively relaxed. In short, the generally favoured party (Israel) did not have to make significant concessions in order to retain the mediator's favour because the objective roots on which it rested meant that that favour could only be diluted so far. As for the generally unfavoured party, it is true that Sadat made important concessions in order to gain Carter's personal friendship but only at the cost of ostracism in the Arab world and, ultimately, of his life.

In the third place, general bias of the sort which Touval has in mind may have the bargaining advantages of which he speaks but obviously this is only pertinent if the mediation actually involves the third party in substantial bargaining. It is by no means clear that the mediation of Algeria in the hostages crisis, for example, which tended towards the passive end of the continuum, would have been assisted by any pronounced general bias towards either the Iranians or the Americans; or that such bias would have in any way assisted the UN secretary-general in any of the mediation efforts in which he was engaged, sometimes successfully, in the late 1980s – rather the reverse (Berridge, 1991). Moreover, if by contrast a generally 'biased' intermediary is driving the negotiations, generalised sympathy for one side rather than the other has disadvantages as well as the advantage stressed by Touval. First, the unfavoured party may not be certain that the interpretation of the mediator's own motives on which the necessary trust must be based is correct, and is likely to have less confidence in this interpretation by virtue of the difficulties placed in the way of intelligence gathering by the very fact of being historically 'unfavoured'! Secondly, the guarantees offered by the mediator on which Touval rightly places such emphasis are likely to be considered with much greater scepticism by the unfavoured party. Guarantees, after all, may be expensive to deliver, may have to be delivered in circumstances in which the mediator's calculation of interest has significantly changed, and are thus ideally underpinned by those very 'sympathies and sentiments' which are by definition unavailable to the unfavoured party. Perhaps Touval overlooks this because his generalisation has a narrow historical base: the Arab–Israel conflict, in which it has always been the party more favoured by the Americans, that is to say, Israel, which has been the more anxious for security guarantees. In short, it is by no means self-evident that general bias has any advantages at the passive end of the mediation continuum, and has distinct disadvantages at the other.

Distinguished statesmen and UN mediation

The argument for employing 'distinguished statesmen' in mediating roles has been developed by Boutros-Ghali in the context of his observations on UN mediation in *An Agenda for Peace* (1992, para, 37). According to the secretary-general, the advantages of employing such persons in UN mediation efforts, of which there is 'a long history', are threefold. In the first place, they have personal prestige; in the second, they have experience; and in the third, they do not compose a shallow labour pool into which the overstretched UN might dip – on the contrary, says Boutros-Ghali, 'there is a wide willingness to serve in this capacity'. What are we to make of these arguments?

Personal prestige certainly counts for something in mediation, if only because it is attention-grabbing and likely to dissuade the parties from taking the propaganda risks of an immediate rebuff of the individual concerned. Thus the despatch of a distinguished statesman to mediate a conflict would be likely to give the negotiation some initial momentum, while the injection of such a personality into a stalled mediation effort would be likely at the least to give it fresh impetus. Experience is also obviously of the greatest value, and plenty of national statesmen have had experience of mediation. Boutros-Ghali might have added, too, that superannuated statesmen of major powers – the obvious example from recent times being Cyrus Vance – also bring to the UN their knowledge of the levers of real power and the personal contacts which will help them to keep nudging, if not positively pulling, them in support of a UN effort. Statesmen still on the national payroll who are 'loaned' to the UN by a major power – as in the case of Ellsworth Bunker and the West New Guinea dispute between Indonesia and the Netherlands in 1962 – are even more useful, of course. However, in these circumstances it is a moot point whether the major power's diplomat is being borrowed for a UN-driven negotiation or if instead it is the face-saving trappings of 'UN auspices' which are being borrowed for a negotiation essentially driven by the major power. It is interesting in this connection to compare the accounts of the Bunker mediation, in which Robert Kennedy also played an important and high-profile role, provided in American and UN sources; the UN is all but overlooked in the former (Schlesinger, 1965, pp. 463–6; Thant, 1977, pp. 48–9).

On the other hand, it is not self-evident that all 'distinguished statesmen', and certainly not those who have reached the pinnacles of national authority, have the kind of experience which makes them a great asset to UN mediation efforts. To begin with, even to the extent that their reputations are built in some measure on achievements in *diplomacy*, as, say, was Richard Nixon's via his policy towards China, they generally are the result of the labours of those below them, as was noted in the previous chapter. The vision, energy, and political courage may be that of the statesman – and these are not disadvantages in UN mediation – but the laborious negotiations with their unavoidable attention to detail are generally not.[9] Secondly, the great majority of these statesmen will at best have had only limited experience of the UN's own bureaucracy and style of diplomacy.[10] Among other drawbacks to bringing in outsiders may thus be a greater difficulty in exerting pressure on the parties to a dispute by subtle coordination of the rewards and threats available through the whole UN network.

As for personal prestige, two points come to mind. First, it is difficult to disentangle the prestige of statesmen from the prestige of their states, or at least of the governments in which they played leading roles. On their own, without the trappings of national power and bureaucratic support, such figures can, despite their formidable personal qualities, suddenly look lonely and even pathetic: Edward Heath in Baghdad on the eve of the Gulf War; and Cyrus Vance in South Africa in July 1992, in the aftermath of the Boipatong massacre. Secondly, the prestige of many statesmen is in any case acquired by means which rule them out as potential mediators in many conflicts – they are too partisan. It is unlikely, for example, that Mrs Thatcher or Jimmy Carter would be acceptable mediators in any conflict involving Iran; or that Anwar Sadat, had he lived, would have been acceptable as a mediator in many inter-Arab disputes.

In practice, then, it is not surprising that distinguished statesmen seem to serve the UN only rarely, despite their apparent willingness to come forward as mediators. It is perhaps also significant that, with notable exceptions such as Vance and Thorvald Stoltenberg, the Norwegian foreign minister who replaced him in Bosnia in mid-1993, the distinguished statesmen employed by the UN as mediators have tended to be citizens of neutral states such as Sweden (Bernadotte and Jarring in the Middle East, Olof Palme in the Iran–Iraq war). Apart from the fact that these statesmen had little success, it was more likely their neutrality than their personal distinction which made them seem suitable. In the Iran–Iraq war both the UN and Waldheim personally were unacceptable in Teheran (Berridge, 1991, p. 50).

The UN's diplomatic advances in the 1980s – from Afghanistan to the Gulf – were all achieved either by Secretariat professionals or by the secretary-general himself, all of whom seemed better placed than 'distinguished statesmen' such as Olof Palme to provide that dogged continuity to mediation efforts which is one of the UN's few strengths. In light of this and in light of the foregoing considerations, it might have been better had *An Agenda for Peace* emphasised the need to recruit and train more mediators rather than give the impression that this is unnecessary in view of the availability of so many distinguished statesmen. At best, Boutros-Ghali has made a virtue out of a financial necessity; at worst he is guilty of contempt for his own staff and extraordinary complacency. The last possibility seems to be supported by his attitude towards Giandomenico Picco, the senior Secretariat official who played such an important role in negotiating the release of the Western hostages in Lebanon; Picco resigned after being asked to look after Afghanistan, 'the UN equivalent of being sent to Siberia' (*The Independent*, 1992b).

IN WHAT CIRCUMSTANCES IS MEDIATION LIKELY TO SUCCEED?

Provided there is to hand an ideal mediator appropriate to a particular dispute, with strong motives for promoting a resolution, mediation is most likely to succeed in the circumstances in which any negotiation is most likely to succeed: when the antagonists have both arrived at the conclusion that they are better off with a settlement than without one (Haass, 1988), or at the least better off resuming direct contact than continuing in a state of frozen hostility. In the latter case, well exemplified by Sino-American relations at the beginning of the 1970s, mediation is assisted by its limited goal.

Where the conflict in which mediation is involved is relatively narrowly focused and has involved fighting, a 'hurting stalemate' might be fostered by the mediator, especially if it is a great power. This was certainly part of Kissinger's approach to the Arab–Israeli conflict after the Yom Kippur War (Touval, 1982, pp. 228–38) and equally part of Crocker's strategy in south-western Africa (Berridge, 1989). In such cases, the mediator also needs to judge properly whether it is best to seek a 'comprehensive' solution to the dispute, or approach it in a 'step-by-step' manner. Since conflicts would not require mediation if they were not singularly intractable, it is often best to adopt the latter approach. This emphasises the need to build both trust and momentum by confining the initial negotiations to subjects of only limited political implications, such as the disengagement of military forces (Golan, 1976; Zartman and Berman, 1982, pp. 33–4). Besides this, the mediator needs to employ a judicious combination of deadlines and press manipulation in order to sustain diplomatic momentum. A fair share of luck is also needed, since a local incident can sour the atmosphere at a critical juncture while the eruption of a major international crisis can at best distract attention from the dispute in question and at worst seriously alter the calculation of interests on which one or more of the parties – including the mediator – had previously agreed to proceed.

Finally, it is worth noting that, while there are advantages to multiple mediation, this can generate crossed lines, divided responsibility, and general confusion, especially when the mediation is at the active end of the continuum. This is not least because the motives of the different parties involved in the mediation attempt will almost certainly not be identical. It is clear that this happened in the Bosnian crisis in 1992, in which the UN secretary-general, the Security Council, and the European Community were all involved. It may be, too, that the extremely visible role of the American 'Special Cyprus Co-ordinator' in the Cyprus negotiations, for which the UN secretary-general has always been formally responsible, has hindered rather than helped a solution to the conflict on this Eastern Mediterranean island. Here it might have been better had the United States either lent its full weight discreetly to the UN through normal diplomatic channels, or assumed full responsibility for the mediation. In the event, Washington was assumed to be the fulcrum of the negotiations and the position of New York was thus to some extent undercut; but partly because the prestige of the United States was not committed to the success of the negotiations its incentive to drive them forward was commensurately reduced (Berridge, 1992c). In short, active mediation is most likely to succeed when responsibility and power are clearly united. Supplementary mediators, whose resources should certainly be harnessed during the mediation, are best brought into the open when success seems in sight, as in the Mozambique civil war in August 1992. This commits them to the settlement and underlines – for the benefit of the antagonists – the weight of support behind it.

THE DRAWBACKS OF MEDIATION AND THE LURE OF DIRECT TALKS

If an important reason for seeking mediation is to secure guarantees of any settlement from the mediator, as has generally been the case in the Arab–Israeli conflict, then the parties to a dispute will seek it even if in different circumstances they would have been prepared to make direct contact with each other. However, when the antagonists are major powers and when, as a result, it is extremely unlikely that any external guarantee of a settlement between them will be available, they have an incentive to dispense with the mediator or mediators as soon as possible. This is because, to return to the major theme of Touval's work, 'mediators, like brokers, are in it for profit' – and some of this may be anticipated in the form of direct payment from the antagonists themselves, albeit generally in kind rather than in cash. It is well known, for example, that the American 'tilt' to Pakistan in its conflict with India in the early 1970s was in part precipitated by Nixon's indebtedness to the Pakistani leader, Yahya Khan, for acting as intermediary in the early approaches to Peking. Rewarding intermediaries in this manner, or simply enabling them to increase their prestige by acting in this role, may also be distasteful for another reason: since the intermediary also has to have good contacts with one's enemy, dislike for the former may be only marginally less evident than hostility to the latter. This sort of consideration encouraged Dulles to keep at arm's length the repeated offers to mediate between the United States and Communist China which were made by neutralist India in the mid-1950s.

But minimising the rewards of intermediaries is not, of course, the only reason for dispensing with their services at the earliest moment decently possible. Using intermediaries inevitably causes delays, increases the number of foreigners who share one's secrets, carries the risk that messages may be garbled in transmission, and usually brings into the negotiations an additional source of complaint about one's own 'reasonable' demands as well as a source of support in the diplomatic campaign against the wholly 'unreasonable' position of one's enemy – and how this will all work out is rarely predictable. Not surprisingly, Hersh records, apropos the budding Sino-American *rapprochement*, that as early as mid-1970 both Nixon and Kissinger were anxious 'to get rid of all the middlemen' (Kissinger, 1979, pp. 722–3; and Hersh, 1983, p. 364).

SUMMARY

Mediation is third party diplomatic activity ranging along a continuum from relatively passive to relatively active involvement in a dispute. The attributes of the ideal mediator, who is generally motivated by a desire for influence and prestige, vary according to circumstances and his or her position on the mediation continuum. Passive mediation requires little power relative to the parties, active mediation a great deal. Impartiality on the issue dividing them is usually indispensable. Mediation is often needed and often accepted; but it is often refused as well, and, if accepted, sometimes discarded. The lure of direct talks, even at a high political price, is always strong.

NOTES

1. There is a tradition that the term 'good offices' should be applied to activity at the relatively passive end of this continuum, that activity midway along it should be described as 'conciliation', and that the term 'mediation' should be reserved exclusively for the active end of the range (Touval, 1982, p. 4). However, in the real world of diplomacy careful use of this terminology has long since been abandoned. For example, the extremely active role of the UN secretary-general in the Cyprus dispute is officially described as his 'mission of good offices'. As a result, it seems best to refer simply to more, or less, active mediation.

2. This is by no means essential. In the final Iran hostages negotiation, the Americans shuttled between Washington and Algiers, the Algerians shuttled between Algiers, Teheran and Washington, and the Iranians remained in Teheran.

3. After Kissinger's secret visit to Peking in July 1971 Chou En-lai suggested to him that they should continue to use the Pakistani channel occasionally since there was a saying in China that 'one shouldn't break the bridge after crossing it' (Kissinger, 1979, p. 745).

4. The London and Rhodesia Mining and Land Company, of which Tiny Rowland was managing director from 1961 until 1994, has extensive interests in central and southern Africa, including ownership of the Beira–Mutare oil pipeline, which traverses Mozambique from the Indian Ocean to Zimbabwe. On Rowland's political as well as commercial activities, see Richard Hall, *My Life with Tiny: A Biography of Tiny Rowland* (1987), and 'Private diplomats: Tiny in Africa' (1992, p. 69).

5. For example, in a memorandum of 29 April 1955, Robert Murphy, US Deputy Under-Secretary of State, having noted that 'volunteer intermediaries [between the US and China] are not wanting', added that 'this might be profitable brokerage for them . . .' (Murphy, 1986, p. 532).

6. Strictly speaking – but only strictly speaking – this is not a mediating role since a protecting power acts for one party only (Berridge, 1994, pp. 32–5).
7. With $3 billion in concessional loans in order to enable the Israelis to build new airfields in the Negev to compensate for the ones they would have to surrender in the Sinai (Quandt, 1986, p. 241). As for Egypt, by 1980–1 (the year following signature of the Egypt–Israel Peace Treaty) Egypt was the top recipient of US official development assistance (Berridge, 1992b, table 7.2).
8. Princen also makes this point (1992, p. 62).
9. There are exceptions to this, of course; for example, Jimmy Carter at Camp David.
10. There are also exceptions to this, such as Lester Pearson, former prime minister of Canada and president of the UN General Assembly, who was considered by U Thant as a suitable UN mediator for Northern Ireland (Thant, 1977, p. 55).

FURTHER READING

Berridge, G. R. (1989), 'Diplomacy and the Angola/Namibia Accords, December 1988', *International Affairs*, vol. 65, no. 3

Berridge, G. R. (1991), *Return to the UN: UN Diplomacy in Regional Conflicts* (Macmillan: London)

Berridge, G. R. (1992), 'The Cyprus negotiations: divided responsibility and other problems', *Leicester Discussion Papers in Politics*, no. P92/7

Berridge, G. R. (1994), *Talking to the Enemy: How States without 'Diplomatic Relations' Communicate* (Macmillan: London)

Boutros-Ghali, B. (1992), *An Agenda for Peace: Preventive Diplomacy, Peacemaking and Peacekeeping* (United Nations: New York)

Christopher, W. and others (1985), *American Hostages in Iran: The Conduct of a Crisis* (Yale University Press: New Haven and London)

Crocker, C. A. (1992), *High Noon in Southern Africa: Making Peace in a Rough Neighbourhood* (Norton: New York and London)

Lindsley, L. (1987), 'The Beagle Channel settlement: Vatican mediation resolves a century-old dispute', *Journal of Church and State*, vol. 29, no. 3

Princen, T. (1992), *Intermediaries in International Conflict* (Princeton University Press: Princeton, New Jersey)

Quandt, W. B. (1986), *Camp David: Peacemaking and Politics* (Brookings: Washington, D. C.)

Touval, S. (1982), *The Peace Brokers: Mediators in the Arab–Israeli Conflict, 1948–1979* (Princeton University Press: Princeton, New Jersey)

Zartman, I. W. and S. Touval (1985), 'International mediation: conflict resolution and power politics', *Journal of Social Issues*, vol. 41, no. 2

II

THE ART OF
NEGOTIATION

6

PRE-NEGOTIATIONS

Negotiation in international politics is a technique of regulated argument which normally occurs between delegations of officials representing states, international organisations or other agencies. It takes place with a view to achieving one or other of the following objectives: identification of common interests and agreement on joint or parallel action in their pursuit; recognition of conflicting interests and agreement on compromise; or, more often than not, some combination of both. Negotiation, as will already be clear, is only one of the functions of diplomacy and in some situations not the diplomat's most urgent or even practical task. However, it is in general the most important function of diplomacy, and it is now common to think of it as proceeding to its conclusion in distinct stages.

Students of negotiation, notably Zartman and Berman, divide negotiations into three such stages: the pre-negotiations stage, the formula stage, and the details stage. This chapter and the following one will hinge on these distinctions. They will analyse the characteristics of each stage, including their characteristic difficulties. However, two cautions must at once be registered. First, the concept of sequential stages of negotiation is an analytical construct: in reality, the stages usually overlap and sometimes, as well, the difficulties of a particular stage are so acute that 'back-tracking' (return to an earlier stage) is unavoidable. Secondly, the notion of three-stage negotiations has developed principally out of analysis of talks on issues where the stakes were high, typically between previously or still warring parties. In negotiations between friendly powers on matters of relatively low importance the pre-negotiations stage will present few problems and may barely be noticeable at all. Since negotiations between recently or still belligerent states, however, are clearly the most important, it is this kind which will be principally in mind in this chapter.[1]

At first glance, the term 'pre-negotiations' is a terrible misnomer, in fact, a contradiction in terms. It seems, that is to say, clearly illogical to describe the first stage of negotiations as '*pre-negotiations*'. Indeed, a great deal of negotiation is conducted in this stage; furthermore, some of this negotiation, albeit disguised, concerns substantive issues. Nevertheless, it is common to find states continuing to place great emphasis on instruments of conflict during this period as well, so perhaps it is not so misleading after all. 'Pre-negotiation', then, is the whole range of activity (possibly war as well as negotiation) conducted prior to the first stage of formal substantive, or 'around-the-table', negotiation (Saunders, 1985). It is directed at achieving agreement on three matters. The first of these is agreement on the possibility that negotiation may prove advantageous to all parties concerned. The second is agreement on an agenda for talks. And the third is agreement on the manner in which the talks should be conducted – questions of procedure.

AGREEING THE NEED TO NEGOTIATE

It is an unusual situation in which the parties to a conflict, whether principally military, economic, or waged by means of propaganda, are equally convinced that a stalemate exists or, in other words, that each has a veto over the outcome preferred by the other. It is also an unusual situation in which, even if there is widespread acceptance of a stalemate, all are equally agreed that negotiation is the only way forward. One party may believe that time is on its side, for example because of some anticipated technical development which it hopes will alter the balance of military power, or because of a possible change of leadership on the part of a major power which will alter the diplomatic context in its favour. And even if there is widespread agreement that the time is ripe for a negotiated settlement, it is also an unusual situation in which all are equally prepared to acknowledge this – suing for peace, after all, is a sign of weakness.

It should not be surprising, therefore, that establishing the need for negotiations is often a complicated and delicate matter, 'in many cases . . . more complicated, time-consuming, and difficult than reaching agreement once negotiations have begun' (Saunders, 1985, p. 249). For one thing, because establishing the need for negotiations rests fundamentally on gaining acceptance of the fact that a stalemate exists, any party to whom suspicions of weakness attach may feel that it actually has to raise the temperature of the conflict while simultaneously putting out feelers for negotiations. Third parties may be calling instead for 'gestures of goodwill' but stepping up the pressure will safeguard the balance and protect an antagonist's flank from domestic hard-liners. If on the other hand powerful third parties are positioning themselves to act as mediators, they may be able, for example by regulating the flow of arms to the rivals, to engineer a stalemate themselves.

In bitter conflicts where the stakes are high, for example in the Middle East and until recently in South Africa, acceptance of a stalemate nearly always takes a long time. When the issues concern core values and perhaps even survival itself, it is obvious that there will be enormous reluctance to accept that another party has the ability to block achievement of one's aspirations or permanently threaten an otherwise satisfactory status quo. Acceptance of a stalemate in such circumstances requires repeated demonstration of power and resolve by both parties. In the Arab–Israeli conflict it took four wars (five including the War of Attrition from 1967 until 1970) before Egypt made peace with Israel, in 1979, and then it required the assistance of sustained top-level American mediation and the application of heavy pressure to both sides. It was a further 14 years before the PLO and Israel reached out for the olive branch. Acceptance of a stalemate may also require each party to lobby the allies of the other, for if these powers concede that there is a stalemate this is more likely to be accepted by the parties themselves.

If in the end existence of a stalemate is accepted by the parties, they next have to acknowledge the possibility that a negotiated settlement (though not of course *any* negotiated settlement) may be better for all concerned than continuing with things as they are. This is perhaps the true beginning of 'pre-negotiations'. Through direct or indirect contacts between rivals and through propaganda directed at allies and domestic constituencies, this generally means conveying the following messages: first, that the parties have important common interests as well as interests which divide them;[2] secondly, that disaster will be inescapable if negotiations are not grasped; and thirdly, that there is a possible solution. Such a solution may involve the suggestion that negotiation of the dispute in question be 'linked' to another in which the parties are also on opposite sides, thus increasing the scope for trade-offs.

Indeed, encouraging the belief that negotiations are at any rate worth a try means floating a 'formula' or 'framework' for a settlement. This will have to give something to both sides, and at the least suggest that enlisting intelligence, imagination and empathy, that is to say, diplomacy, may be able to produce a solution. It will, however, also have to be fairly vague because a vague formula avoids giving hostages to fortune in a world in which circumstances are constantly changing; such a formula is also meat and drink to that ubiquitous individual, the wishful thinker, and at this early stage, when nothing which will help to launch the negotiations can be spurned, the wishful thinker is the negotiator's ally.

When parties to a conflict start to explore the possibility of a negotiated settlement they do not, of course, do this in a political vacuum. A variety of circumstances, at home and abroad, will affect the likelihood that negotiations will be launched successfully. To begin with, it is obviously necessary for the leadership on both sides to be domestically secure. This will enable them to ride out any charge that they are proposing to 'sell out' to the enemy, whereas such a charge might bring down a weak leader or fear of one make diplomacy seem to risky in the first place. In democracies, this consideration argues for rapid movement after elections, when a new government has the opportunity to take unpopular action in the reasonable expectation that the voters will either have forgotten or secured compensating blessings by the time they are next able to express a view. It was a calculation of this sort which prompted American president, Jimmy Carter, to move as fast as possible on the Arab–Israeli front after his inauguration in January 1977, because he knew that the kind of settlement which he had in mind would cause some anguish to the powerful Jewish lobby in the United States (Quandt, 1986, ch. 2). In autocracies domestic hard-line opponents have to be dealt with in some other way before negotiations, at any rate substantive negotiations, can be launched. Lin Piao, the pro-Soviet minister of defence in Communist China who opposed any *rapprochement* between Peking and Washington, died in a mysterious air crash in early 1972.

If the leaderships of the parties contemplating negotiations should be domestically secure, it is a commonplace – but worth repeating for all that – that it is a further advantage for them to have a record of especially pronounced hostility to the other side. With such a record they are invulnerable to the charge that their disposition to negotiate is prompted by secret sympathies for the enemy or an inadequate grasp of their own national or ideological priorities; and they are the best placed to hold their own conservatives in line. Such was the case in the early 1970s with US president, Richard Nixon – who had won a reputation for fierce anti-Communism two decades earlier – as he approached the *rapprochement* with Communist China, the abandonment of South Vietnam, detente with the Soviet Union, and the return of Okinawa to Japan (Safire, 1975, pp. 366–7). Another leader whose 'superhawk' reputation stood him in good stead when it came to making peace with his enemy was the Israeli prime minister, Menachem Begin. Begin, who headed the Likud Coalition which triumphed in the elections in mid-1977, was a former leader of the Jewish underground movement, the Irgun, and currently leader of its political successor, the Herut Party. Herut had a reputation for extremism and Begin's name itself was traditionally linked to the policy of absolute refusal to surrender territory to the Arabs – 'not one inch' (Weizman, 1981, pp. 36–7). This reputation, among other things, helped him to carry the Knesset through the protracted and difficult negotiations from 1977 through to early 1979. These negotiations produced the return of the Sinai to Egypt and an agreement on the West Bank which to some at any rate looked like the thin end of the wedge of a future Palestinian state on land Herut believed was forever Israel.

Finally, it is perhaps worth noting that pre-negotiations are most likely to make progress if incidents which cause public alarm are avoided. Of course, this is true of all stages of negotiations, as the Hebron massacre in March 1993, which occurred while Israel and the PLO were trying to settle the details of their 'framework agreement' of the previous September, so tragically demonstrated. However, it is particularly true of the pre-negotiations stage because this is the most fragile. In this stage, relatively little prestige will have been tied to a successful outcome and retreat from negotiations will not, therefore, generally carry a high price (Stein, 1989, pp. 482–3). A high premium attaches, therefore, to the avoidance of incidents such as exchanges of fire along a ceasefire line, hostile popular demonstrations, or virulent press attacks. And the reasons for this are obvious: they put pressure on leaders to increase their demands; they also give them a pretext, if they want one, to avoid or break off initial contacts with the other side.

AGREEING THE AGENDA

If the need for negotiations is recognised and conditions are propitious, it becomes possible to discuss an agenda for talks. This means not only agreeing on what will be discussed but on the order in which the agreed items will be taken. This often creates more difficulties than might be imagined. Why?

There are three main reasons why agenda content might be controversial. The first is that implicit in a proposed agenda might well be a proposed deal. As a result, accept the agenda and, in principle, one accepts the deal. This is why the United States resisted the suggestion of Saddam Hussein that the Palestinian question as well as Iraqi occupation of Kuwait should be on the agenda of talks to avert fighting in late 1990 and early 1991. Had this proposal been accepted, Washington would have conceded that it was reasonable to give Baghdad something for the Palestinians *in return for* withdrawal from Kuwait. But it had no intention of doing this, since it would have rewarded Saddam's aggression with a major propaganda victory and compromised utterly the American policy of persuading Israel to maintain a low profile in the crisis. Sometimes, nevertheless, proposed agendas containing implicit deals are accepted, especially if the deal has been floated earlier as a possible 'formula' or 'framework for agreement' and eventually been accepted as at least a basis for negotiation. Such was the case with the American proposal, first made in the early 1980s, that the issues of South African withdrawal from Namibia and Cuban (plus ANC) withdrawal from Angola should be 'linked', that is, discussed by the parties simultaneously, the assumption being that the withdrawal of the one would be the price of withdrawal by the other. (Linkage is discussed further in the section below dealing with the formula stage.)

The second reason why serious difficulties can be caused by agenda content is that agendas are sometimes used as weapons of propaganda. This is possible because while it is a proper inheritance of the French system that the cut and thrust of negotiations should remain secret, it is normally accepted that the subjects of discussion, that is, the agenda, should – at least in broad outline – be public knowledge. This being so, the parties to potential negotiations can suggest agenda items which they know will never produce concessions from their rivals merely in order to advertise their own priorities. If for some reason the victims of this treatment feel bound to permit their inclusion on the agenda, they will not only have handed a propaganda victory to the opposition but perhaps created all manner of trouble for themselves with friends and allies. It was for reasons such as these that the South African foreign minister, Eric Louw, wanted items like the arming of blacks and Asian immigration into East Africa on the agenda of a white man's conference in 1955 (Berridge, 1992a, pp. 133–7) and that Chou En-lai insisted that Taiwan should be on the agenda of the Nixon visit to China in February 1972. Louw was only thwarted with difficulty, while Chou was not thwarted at all – the stakes for the Americans were too high to be jeopardised by a refusal to concede on this issue.

The third common source of argument over the content of the agenda concerns its generality or vagueness. It is certainly true, as already indicated, that this might with advantage be a feature of any formula floated in the early days of pre-negotiations. However, when the agenda itself is being constructed a party which knows that it will never get the other to agree to inscription of a specific item may strive to secure a vague agenda in order to be able to bring up the issue in which it is interested once the real talks get under way (Webster, 1961, p. 62).

As for the order of the agenda, this can create difficulties because the parties to any negotiation generally approach them in the expectation that they will have to give concessions on some items and receive them on others. As a result, it is natural for them to demand that the latter should be taken first. There are two reasons for this. First, the side which has to wait until later for the items on which it needs concessions may be induced to be generous on the early items in order to increase the likelihood of reciprocal treatment when its turn comes round. Secondly, the side which gets early concessions avoids an impression of weakness and so avoids encouraging the opposition and – if there are leaks – trouble at home. A good example of the importance of the order of the agenda was provided in negotiations between the South African government and the shipping companies in the Europe–South Africa trade in late 1965 and early 1966. On this occasion, the government, which expected to have to make concessions to the companies on the issue of an increase in freight rates, managed to hold back discussion of this item until the very last of 33 formal meetings. In the meanwhile, it won concession after concession from the shipping lines on other items, such as the shipment of arms in national flag vessels (Berridge, 1987, pp. 102–8).

Of course, the signficance of the order in which agenda items are taken is reduced if it is possible to make the grant of early concessions conditional on receipt of later ones; and this sometimes happens. On the other hand, conditionality cannot entirely erase the image of weakness created by the early granting of disproportionate concessions by one side. Indeed, the party which agrees to permit early consideration of items on which it expects to have to give most concessions has already conceded a point – or missed a trick. Furthermore, since the principal beneficiary of negotiations on the first items will generally maintain that it has made some concessions on these points as well, it may not always be easy to secure payment later – and if conditionality is evoked too forcefully this may lead to a charge of bad faith. In general, then, the order or sequence in which agenda items are taken is unlikely to be a matter of indifference.

AGREEING PROCEDURE

With the agenda agreed[3] the final task of the pre-negotiations stage is agreement on procedure. Here there are four main questions to resolve: format, venue, level and composition of delegations, and timing.

As to the format of the negotiations, will they be direct (face-to-face) or indirect? Direct talks between enemies have many practical advantages, and have been mentioned earlier (see pages 113–14 above). If, because of problems of 'face' or legal recognition, the talks nevertheless need an intermediary, who will this be? Will the mediator be required to play an active or relatively passive role in the negotiations? (On mediation, see chapter 5.) Whatever the role of the mediator, can the negotiations be made somewhat easier by taking the form of 'proximity talks', as in the case of the UN-mediated talks between the Afghan Communist government and the Pakistanis which were held in Geneva in the mid-1980s (Berridge, 1991, p. 64)? In such talks an intermediary is employed but the delegations of the principal parties are prepared to base themselves in close proximity to each other, typically in the same hotel or conference centre. This obviously makes the mediator's job easier.

If more than two parties are to be involved in the talks, as is often the case, will they be conducted by a series of parallel bilateral discussions, a multilateral conference, or some combination of both? Bilateral discussions have in their favour maximum flexibility, speed, and secrecy. On the other hand, they are likely to inspire suspicion among allies that one or other among their number is seeking a separate deal with the enemy; they also lack the propaganda value of a big conference. If a combination of bilateral discussion and multilateral conference is preferred, what powers shall the multi-lateral 'plenary' conference have relative to decisions made in its bilateral 'sub-committees'? Do the latter merely report to the former as a matter of courtesy, or do they give it a veto? If a key player fears it may be in a minority in the plenary it is highly unlikely that it will agree to the latter course. Apart from established conventions, choice of format is thus influenced by the degree of urgency attending a negotiation, the state of relations among allies, and the determin-ation of the most powerful or most resolute among the parties as to which format will suit its own interests best. Not surprisingly, the question of format was a serious and complicated problem in the case of Carter's Middle East diplomacy in the late 1970s.

Carter's initial assumption was that the Arab–Israeli talks which he was so anxious to promote would only succeed if the 'Geneva Conference' format was employed in some way. This format had its immediate origins in the aftermath of the Yom Kippur War, when the UN Security Council called in Resolution 338 for immediate talks between the Arabs and the Israelis 'aimed at establishing a just and durable peace in the Middle East'. A conference was duly held in Geneva in late December 1973. It had six signal features. First, it was held under UN auspices.[4] Secondly, it was effectively co-chaired by the superpowers, the United States and the Soviet Union. Thirdly, all immediately interested parties were invited, which meant the Israelis sitting down with the Arabs. Fourthly, it consisted chiefly of 'a battery of public speeches' rather than serious secret negotiation (Kissinger, 1982, ch. 17). Fifthly, neither superpower would be present in negotiations at the sub-committee level (Quandt, 1986, p. 143). Lastly, the plenary conference was to have no right of veto over decisions taken in any subsequent bilateral negotiations.[5]

With the drastic decline in Soviet influence in Egypt which had preceded the Yom Kippur War, the United States was firmly in the driving seat as far as negotiations to resolve the Arab–Israeli conflict were concerned. And Washington's view was that, while secret bilateral diplomacy was the only format which would be likely to achieve any breakthrough, Geneva was an essential pre-condition. Among other things, this would 'symbolize trends toward making peace' and thus put pressure on the radicals, minimise the chances of the Soviet Union disrupting the process out of pique at being excluded and, above all, legitimise direct Arab–Israeli contact. In each of these regards the Geneva Conference had some degree of success. However, by the time that Carter inherited the mantle of Middle East brokerage in 1977 circumstances had changed.

Carter's reasons for initially supporting a reconvening of Geneva, albeit after significant progress had been made in bilateral talks (Quandt, 1986, pp. 61, 76), were essentially the same as those of Kissinger: protecting the flank of the moderate Arab states on the Palestinian question (there would be 'Palestinian' representation of some kind at Geneva as well as representation of all Arab states); advertising the peace process; and limiting the potential of the Soviet Union for trouble-making (pp. 118–21, 137–43). However, Egypt had moved much further away from the Soviet Union by 1977 and was worried about the influence which the Geneva format might give it over a settlement. This format, especially if it involved a unified Arab delegation, would also reduce its flexibility in negotiations with Israel. These considerations were now the more important for Egypt since the relatively easy steps of military disengagement had by now been achieved, and what was left were the big questions: sovereignty over Sinai and the future of the West Bank, in that order. Geneva might help Egypt but, as it was shaping up, it was more likely to prove a trap. In the event, the delay in reconvening Geneva, caused in part by the enormous difficulty of agreeing on how the Palestinians should be represented, gave Sadat the pretext for sabotaging this route by making his spectacular journey to Jerusalem in November 1977. After this, the Geneva format was a dead letter, despite the fact that much of the top-level and time-consuming diplomacy of 1977 had been concerned with preparing for it.

Choice of the format of a negotiation sometimes goes a long way towards dictating where they shall take place, their venue. For example, had the Arab–Israeli talks of the Carter years in fact followed the 'Geneva Conference format', it is likely that they would have taken place in Geneva. Indeed, the American proposal was that, as in 1973, the UN secretary-general should once more issue the invitations, and there is no suggestion in the public record of the discussions at the time that an alternative venue was ever seriously considered. It was likely, then, that the talks would have taken place in Geneva – but not inevitable. When the next international conference on the Middle East, co-chaired by the superpowers and in most essentials resembling the 1973 Geneva Conference,[6] actually took place, in the aftermath of the Gulf War in November 1991, it did not take place in Geneva but in Madrid. This was not because the Swiss city had been destroyed by fire or was suffering acute dislocation of its airport as a result of a strike by air-traffic controllers. Why is venue often an important matter in pre-negotiations and why does it, as a result, often cause considerable difficulties?

The venue of negotiations between rivals is important because of its symbolic and practical impications. If, for example, one state is able to persuade its rival to send a delegation to its own shores, this will not only be of great practical convenience to the former but suggest very strongly that it is the more powerful: the travellers will have suffered a serious loss of face. It is hardly surprising, therefore, in light of the speed and efficiency with which images and other kinds of information can be flashed across the world, that this happens only rarely, and that alternative solutions are the subject of discussion in the pre-negotiations stage. In fact, there are three common strategies for getting over this problem: neutral ground, meeting 'halfway', and alternating (rotating, if there are more than two parties) home venues.

Some venues are chosen for negotiations because either by convention or law they are neutral ground. This, of course, explains the popularity of venues in Switzerland and Austria, both permanently neutral states in international law. Vienna, the capital of Austria, has the added advantage of unique historical association with the development of modern diplomacy, from the Congress of 1815 to the Conference on Diplomatic Relations in 1961. To take another example, The Hague was chosen as the site of the Iran–United States Claims Tribunal in 1981 because although the Netherlands is a NATO member, The Hague is home to the International Court of Justice and also the Permanent Court of

Arbitration, which, indeed, provided the Tribunal with its first quarters in the city (Berridge, 1994, p. 124).

Another traditional device for saving face is to choose a venue for negotiations which is roughly equidistant between the capitals of the rival states. Since compromise is of the essence of diplomacy, it is appropriate as well as face-saving if the parties agree to meet somewhere which is geographically 'halfway' between their own countries. This, of course, was yet another ingredient of the appeal of Vienna during the Cold War, since it is roughly equidistant between Moscow and the capitals of the European members of NATO. And it was the whole of the appeal of Wake Island in the Pacific Ocean as the venue for the highly sensitive and subsequently controversial talks in October 1950 between President Truman and his troublesome general, Douglas MacArthur – virtually the American 'emperor' of Japan, who had not visited the United States since 1938 and whom Truman had never met.[7] What is particularly interesting about the convention of 'meeting halfway', however, is that its appeal is so great that a state may even be content to forgo neutral ground and meet a rival on the territory of the latter's ally – provided it is 'halfway' between them. For example, when the Soviet leader Mikhail Gorbachev proposed in 1986 a US–Soviet summit preparatory to the one already arranged in Washington, he suggested that he and President Reagan should meet 'somewhere halfway', and mentioned as possibilities either London or Reykjavik, though both Britain and Iceland are NATO members (Adelman, 1989, p. 25). In the event, they settled on Reykjavik. In the case of neighbouring rivals it is, of course, traditional to choose a venue on the frontier. A classic example of this in recent times was the conference in August 1974 between white supremacist Rhodesia and its Zambian-supported black nationalist opponents. This was held in a South African railway carriage positioned on the Victoria Falls bridge spanning the border between Zambia and Rhodesia.

Finally, states can avoid any loss of prestige over the issue of venue by agreeing – should there be a need for lengthy negotiations – to alternate between their respective capitals. Since someone has to be the first to travel, however, taking it in turns is a solution which is generally acceptable only after some diplomatic breakthrough and general improvement in relations. There has to be, in other words, reasonable confidence that a sequence will be established, that each will share the benefits of negotiating at home. For example, after the initial superpower summits in the 1950s and early 1960s, which were held on neutral ground (Geneva and Vienna), a rough pattern of alternation was established in the early 1970s. At about the same time, the Americans and the Chinese Communists agreed to meet alternately in their embassies in Warsaw (Berridge, 1994, p. 88). Following the settlement of the Angola/Namibia conflicts in 1988, the venue of the regular meetings of the joint commission created to consolidate the agreement rotated between the capitals of the full members (Berridge, 1994, box 7.1, p. 121). And this is the procedure adopted for summit meetings of the member states of the EU, the European Council, as noted in chapter 4.

Venue, however, is not only of symbolic importance because of its implications for prestige; it may also be of symbolic significance because of the ability of a particular venue to assist one or other of the parties in making some propaganda point. For example, Israel has generally wanted talks with the Arabs to take place in the Middle East itself rather than outside, as was the case with some of the negotiations with Egypt after 1977 and some with the PLO after 1993. One of the reasons for this preference was that it would emphasise the point that Israel is a legitimate member state of the region rather than a temporary foreign implant. For the same kind of reason, among others, South Africa was much more enthusiastic about holding the 1988 talks on Angola and Namibia in Africa rather than in Europe or North America.[8] And to return to the Middle East, it seems likely that one of the reasons why Madrid rather than Geneva was chosen for the 1991 conference on the Middle East was the need to find a venue which did not have UN associations. This was because it was necessary to underline for the benefit of Israel – which did not like the UN's identification with the version of the 'international conference' proposal associated with Saddam Hussein and the PLO at the time of the Gulf War – that it would be in no sense a UN-driven conference.[9] Madrid was also ideal because while Spain retained strong historic ties with the Arab world, its relations with Israel had improved markedly in recent years.

Practical considerations, as hinted earlier, are also of first class importance in influencing preferences for the venue of negotiations. It is generally for these reasons, as well as reasons of prestige, that states prefer their rivals to come to them. In true Middle Kingdom tradition, 'the Chinese', as Binnendijk points out, 'unquestionably prefer to negotiate on their own territory as it facilitates their internal communications and decision-making procedures and maximises their control over the ambiance of a negotiation' (1987, p. 9). If states nevertheless have to send delegations abroad to negotiate, it is thus generally an advantage if they do not have to send them too far. Proximity usually makes communication with home easier and also makes it easier to respond quickly to any sudden developments by flying in more senior personnel or recalling negotiators for consultation. If the venue has to be more remote, it is an advantage if it is in a country where they have a sizeable embassy. This will provide them with local back-up and reliable communication facilities with home. The force of this point was brought home to the American delegation which accompanied President Reagan to the summit with Gorbachev in the Icelandic capital of Reykjavik in October 1986. The secure 'bubble'[10] in the US embassy was the smallest ever built and could seat only eight people. At one point this maximum had already been reached when the President himself turned up. Being closest to the door, US Arms Control Director Kenneth Adelman at once surrendered his chair to his chief. 'I then plopped down on the only square foot of unoccupied floor space,' he reports, 'leaning solidly against the President's legs and with nearly everyone's shoes touching my legs' (Adelman, 1989, p. 46).

Some venues also have air services, conference facilities, hotels, entertainment, and security which are vastly superior to those available to others. Some also have better climates! The Mozambique capital of Lourenço Marques was quite rightly rejected as the venue for a major conference on southern African transport in the early 1950s partly on the grounds that the weather in the chosen month, February, was intolerably hot and humid.

A third procedural point requiring agreement is the nature of the delegations, which embraces level, composition, and size. The last aspect is not normally controversial, unless a state proposes to send a delegation which is so small that it implies lack of seriousness of purpose or so large[11] that difficult problems of accommodation and security are raised. Level and composition of delegations is, however, another matter altogether.

Whether or not talks should be held at ministerial or merely official level has always been an issue in pre-negotiations, since the higher the level the more priority might reasonably be assumed to be implied and the more rapid progress reasonably expected. (This now generally subsumes the question of whether or not the delegation has 'full powers'.) For example, in the 1950s, the South African government, ever anxious to persuade the British government to signal high priority to defence talks on Africa, was constantly urging London to conduct negotiations at senior ministerial level. By contrast, Britain, which did not share the enthusiasm of Pretoria for this subject and was anxious to avoid over-identification with its racial policies, was generally adamant that they should be 'written down' to the level of officials. In some regimes, of course, the line between 'officials' and 'ministers' never had any meaning, and even in those where it did it now seems more blurred. Nevertheless, it remains fairly obvious who is important and who is not, and the greater ease of foreign travel has made it more difficult for states to resist the notion that their most senior people – including those at the 'summit' – cannot take part in a negotiation abroad on grounds of practical impossibility. This may even hold true if they are very ill, which was certainly the case with the American President, F. D. Roosevelt, when he travelled to Yalta in February 1945. One answer to this problem is mixed delegations, which seem increasingly common, including delegations in which ministers participate for short periods. This is often the case with negotiations which it is formally agreed should be held at 'foreign minister' level. Of course, if there is a huge disparity in status between the states in question, the issue of level of delegations is less likely to be troublesome: micro-states know that, as a general rule, matters to which they are happy to have their presidents attend cannot command the personal attention of the leader of a superpower.

The level of a delegation obviously has an intimate bearing on its composition. Nevertheless, level might be agreed but problems of composition remain. This is especially the case where a multilateral negotiation is proposed but there is hostility to participation by certain parties *at any level*. This is typically because of the non-recognition of one potential participant by another, for example the non-recognition of Communist China by the United States at the time of the Geneva Conference on South-East Asia in 1954. To take another example, the refusal of Israel to have anything whatever to do with the PLO, together with the insistence of the Arab states and increasingly the United States as well that talks on the future of the West Bank and Gaza would be meaningless without the participation of this 'terrorist organisation', led to a horrendous wrangle in 1977. As in the case of the issue of the agenda, this dispute illustrated that 'pre-negotiations' can in fact disguise the most vital points of substance. For had the Israelis conceded separate Palestinian representation (whether by the PLO or in some other manner), they would have conceded a separate Palestinian identity – and thus, on grounds of national self-determination, the right of the Palestinians to their own state. It was much better from the Israeli point of view, therefore, that, if the so-called 'Palestinians' were to be represented at all, it should be as part of a Jordanian delegation, since it was a widely held view in Israel that the Palestinians were 'really' Jordanians.[12]

The final procedural question is timing. When should the talks start, and should they have a deadline? The possibility that favourable circumstances are unlikely to last for ever argues for a prompt start – but pressing for this may suggest weakness. Other commitments have to be considered as well. As for deadlines, these are so important to the question of diplomatic momentum that it is better to leave their discussion until chapter 8.

SUMMARY

It should never be forgotten that states sometimes engage in pre-negotiations, and even substantive negotiations for that matter, merely in order to buy time or obtain the propaganda advantages which may attach to being seen seeking a 'peaceful solution'. Prevaricating or, as the British government used to call it, 'playing it long', has a long history in diplomacy. In pre-negotiations, then, and bearing this in mind, states first have to agree that it may be in their mutual interests to negotiate at all. Having agreed that negotiating may be better than not negotiating, they then have to agree an agenda and all of the multifarious questions that come up under the heading of procedure. This being so, it may be thought surprising that states ever get round to substantive negotiations at all. That they do is testimony not only to the remorseless logic of circumstance but to the fact that diplomacy is a professionalised activity.

NOTES

1. The chapter will also have bilateral rather than multilateral negotiations in mind, though multilateral talks – while presenting some different problems and possibilities – proceed through the same stages (Touval, 1989).
2. In the pre-negotiations phase of the Soviet–American arms control negotiations which followed the Cuban missiles crisis this meant, of course, emphasising the mutual interest in avoiding nuclear war.
3. Failure to iron out every last detail of the agenda does not – surprisingly enough – necessarily prevent progress into the negotiation proper (Stein, 1989, p. 490).
4. The venue was the UN's European headquarters, and the UN secretary-general issued the invitations and presided in the conference's opening phase.
5. This conference was itself, of course, in direct line of descent from earlier multilateral conferences on regional questions chaired by major powers from opposite sides of the Cold War, and for that matter also held in Geneva. These included the Geneva Conference on South-East Asia (1954), which was co-chaired by Britain and the Soviet Union, and reconvened in 1961–2 in order to discuss Laos.
6. It was co-chaired by the United States and the Soviet Union and consisted of all interested parties, including the PLO (though this was included in a 'joint delegation' with Jordan). However, the UN, at Israeli insistence, was only present in an observer capacity.
7. On this intriguing episode, see Miller, *Plain Speaking: An Oral Biography of Harry S. Truman* (1976, pp. 314–20); Acheson (1987, pp. 456–7); and Lowe (1986, p. 194). Although in *Plain Speaking* Truman claims that Wake Island was a 'halfway point', Merle Miller points out that the president had to fly 4700 miles from San Francisco while the general only had to fly 1900 miles from Tokyo.
8. In the event, Brazzaville and Cairo were the settings for some rounds of the negotiations.
9. Madrid was also conveniently placed for the PLO, which was headquartered in Tunis, while the Spanish government was currently enjoying a *rapprochement* with Israel following the establishment of diplomatic relations in 1986 and the constitutional recognition of Judaism in 1990. Interestingly enough, Spain was one of three foreign venues which came up in a conversation between Brzezinski and Carter in July 1978 as possibilities for the Middle East summit which was, in the event, held at Camp David in the subsequent September. The other two were Portugal and Morocco (Brzezinski, 1983, p. 250).
10. All US embassies contain a 'bubble': 'a square, transparent plastic room

specially coated to assure that it cannot be bugged' (Adelman, 1989, p. 45).

11. American delegations led by the president, for example, typically number between six and eight hundred people (Kissinger, 1979, p. 75), though these are obviously not all diplomats.

12. On the various options for getting over this problem which were considered by the Americans, see Quandt, 1986, pp. 74–5.

FURTHER READING

Cohen, R. (1991), *Negotiating Across Cultures: Communication Obstacles in International Diplomacy* (US Institute of Peace Press: Washington, D. C.)

Gross-Stein, J. (ed) (1989), *Getting to the Table: The Process of International Pre-negotiation* (Johns Hopkins University Press: Baltimore)

Quandt, W. B. (1986), *Camp David: Peacemaking and Politics* (Brookings: Washington, D. C.) chs 3–7

Saunders, H. (1985), 'We need a larger theory of negotiation: the importance of pre-negotiating phases', *Negotiation Journal*, vol. 1

Zartman, I. W. and M. Berman (1982), *The Practical Negotiator* (Yale University Press: New Haven and London), ch. 3

7

'AROUND-THE-TABLE' NEGOTIATIONS

If pre-negotiations are successfully concluded, the next task for the negotiators is to move into 'around-the-table' mode.[1] This is generally more formal and there is usually more public awareness of what, in broad terms, is going on. First comes the task of trying to agree on the basic principles of a settlement. If this is achieved, the details then have to be added.

THE FORMULA STAGE

For the broad principles of a settlement there are many deliberately anodyne synonyms, among the more common of which are 'guidelines' and 'framework for agreement'. The UN, which has a legendary reputation for fecundity in this department, currently seems to favour the term 'set of ideas'. Zartman and Berman (1982) prefer 'formula' and, since it is short and clear, so do I. Among classic examples of formulas agreed in negotiations in recent years and at the time of writing (October 1994) still a 'basis for negotiations', are those on Cyprus and the Arab–Israeli conflict. The 'high-level agreements' on Cyprus of 1977 and 1979 provided for a deal in which the Greek Cypriots would admit a federation[2] in return for surrender by the Turks of some of the territory seized in the invasion of 1974. As for the Middle East, in UN Security Council Resolution 242 of November 1967, passed following the Six-Day War, it was agreed that Israeli forces would withdraw 'from territories [not, famously, from *the* territories] occupied in the recent conflict', in return for Arab recognition of the

137

state of Israel and an ènd to the state of belligerency with it: the 'land for peace' formula.

The chief characteristics of a good formula are fairly obvious: comprehensiveness, balance, and flexibility. Clearly, the best one will offer solutions to all points of dispute between the parties. However, this is often not practical politics and a formula is not vitiated if this is impossible (Zartman and Berman, 1982, pp. 109–14). Some issues may be registered but postponed for later consideration, as with Taiwan in the Shanghai Communiqué in February 1972; others may be fudged, as with the question of a state for the Palestinian Arabs in the Camp David Accords of September 1978; and others may be omitted altogether, as with multiple independently targetable re-entry vehicles (MIRVs) in SALT I in May 1972. Whichever strategy is employed will depend on the priorities of the moment and the nature of the external pressure on the parties. It was, for example, unnecessary for the United States and the Soviet Union to fudge, or pretend to have made progress, on MIRVs in SALT I since neither party was under overwhelming pressure on this particular score. By contrast, Egyptian leadership of the Arab world turned on whether or not there appeared to be something for the Palestinians in the Camp David Accords; in the event, of course, it was not enough. Secondly, something has to be given to both sides in an exchange which is generally thought to be roughly balanced. And, although the formula must not be as vague as the kind floated in the pre-negotiations stage, it must still contain sufficient flexibility to permit each side to believe that it might be improved in the details stage of the negotiations. So much is fairly obvious. What is sometimes less obvious is the best way to obtain this formula.

The nettle of general principle may be grasped immediately by the negotiators in the formula stage; this is sometimes described as the 'deductive approach' (Zartman and Berman, 1982, p. 89) and requires no further comment. It is the logical way to proceed. Alternatively, the nettle may be approached with caution, by stealth, perhaps from its flank, and always slowly. Sometimes described as the 'inductive approach', this is more commonly known as 'step-by-step' diplomacy. One of the most advertised cases of the latter approach in recent years was the Middle East diplomacy of Henry Kissinger in the years following the Yom Kippur War of October 1973 (Golan) though it has also been essentially the approach of the 'functionalists' to European integration since the end of the Second World War. This approach does require further comment.

The step-by-step approach is usually considered appropriate to the negotiation of a dispute characterised by great complexity and mistrust. In such circumstances it normally makes sense to begin the negotiations on an agenda limited in scope and restricted to items which are relatively uncontroversial. This makes the negotiation more manageable (especially important if the diplomatic resources of the parties are also limited), permits mistrust to be gradually broken down, builds faith in the efficacy of diplomacy by making early successes more likely, and familiarises the parties with the procedures involved in dealing with each other ('learning to walk before trying to run'). The idea, of course, is that, as confidence builds, the more difficult questions can gradually be addressed with more prospect of success; they may even turn out to have been implicitly broken down already (Zartman and Berman, 1982, p. 90). If the initial negotiation is predicated on the hope that more recalcitrant parties will be drawn in later, the step-by-step approach also has the advantage of establishing precedents. Thus it was Kissinger's hope, in the event justified, that having negotiated a limited disengagement agreement between Israel and Egypt, the Syrians would be emboldened to take a similar step themselves.

The step-by-step approach, however, is not without its problems. It can mislead by suggesting a relative lack of concern over the bigger questions; it carries the risk of 'paying the whole wallet' for just one item (Zartman and Berman, 1982, p. 178); above all, it takes time. Because it takes time, the favourable circumstances which made launching the negotiations possible may change for the worse, the moment may be lost. Of course, there may have been no alternative to employing the step-by-step approach but this is the risk which it always carries.

If and when a formula for a settlement is agreed, it is commonly announced to the world, sometimes in a huge blaze of publicity. Such was the case with the 'Camp David Accords'. However, if the formula is based on 'linkage', that is, the trading of concessions in unrelated, or only remotely connected, issue areas, the negotiations may at this point run into difficulties. (This may have happened earlier if the deal was suspected from the nature of the agreed agenda.) The reason for this is that while linkage, or negotiating on a 'broad front', is more likely to break an impasse by increasing the scope for imaginative solutions, it is deeply offensive to those who believe that issues should be treated on their merits, especially if their interests are harmed in the process without any quid pro quo on their own issue. As Hoffmann points out, 'on each issue, a separate constituency develops, which objects to being treated as a pawn in a global log-rolling game' (1978, p. 61). This is why Kissinger's problems with members of the anti-defence spending lobby were magnified when it became clear early in the first Nixon administration that he was contemplating trading US concessions in arms control negotiations for Soviet help in places such as Damascus and Hanoi – the issue of nuclear weapons, they believed, should be dealt with on its merits. It is also why many members of the OAU were enraged when it became clear that the Americans and the South Africans were insisting on Cuba's departure from Angola as the price for South Africa's withdrawal from Namibia – Cuban troops were in Angola at the invitation of the recognised government, whereas the occupation of Namibia was illegal and South Africa was obliged to get out anyway. Nevertheless, in a formula based on linkage, there are winners as well as losers; this helps.

THE DETAILS STAGE

If a formula is agreed by the parties to a negotiation, whether by immediate, head-on talks following pre-negotiations or by the more oblique step-by-step approach, and whether based on linkage or not, the final stage involves fleshing it out – agreeing the details. This is by no means as simple as it sounds. Indeed, in so far as it is possible to generalise about negotiations, the details stage is a strong candidate for the dubious honour of being called the most difficult stage of all.

One aspect of the formula agreed on Cyprus in the late 1970s was that the island should have a new constitution. This would be a bi-communal, bi-zonal federation. The composition of the central government and its agencies, in other words, would have to reflect the division of the population between Turkish Cypriots and Greek Cypriots (roughly 2 to 8), while the island itself (effectively partitioned following the Turkish invasion of 1974) would become a federal state based on two geographical zones, a Turkish zone in the north and a Greek one in the south. So far so good. But this left a myriad of sensitive details to be agreed, as might be imagined. Not the least among these was where *exactly* the line would be drawn on the ground between the two zones. To take another example, when it was agreed in mid-1988 that South Africa would withdraw its forces from Namibia and permit the country to become independent in return for the withdrawal of Cuban troops from Angola, this left a large number of vital issues of detail to resolve on which the interests of the parties were clearly divergent. In the case of the Cuban troops alone, these included the following. When would the departure commence? When would it terminate? Would the withdrawal be front-loaded, end-loaded, or consist of a uniform stream (the same number of troops leaving in each month)? From which areas of Angola would the first troops be withdrawn? And so on. Why is the details stage often so difficult and why, as a result, do talks often founder here?

The first reason, of course, is that the details stage, by definition, is complicated. It may not be more complicated than pre-negotiations (though it usually is); but it is invariably more complicated than the formula stage. In addition to providing a difficulty in itself, complexity also means as a rule that bigger teams of negotiators are required in the details stage; and this brings in its train much greater scope for disagreement *within* the negotiating teams. It is, for example, a commonplace of American commentary on the detailed arms control negotiations between the United States and the Soviet Union in the 1970s that the really tough negotiations took place not in Vienna or Helsinki but between the various agencies of the American government itself in Washington.

Secondly, it is in the details stage that careful thought has to be given to the definition of terms, or to establishing a common language. This is obviously necessary to avoid misunderstanding but can be extremely problematical because some definitions serve the interests of some parties better than others. Definitions proved to be a nightmare in the US–Soviet arms control negotiations, where wrangles over some terms – chiefly concerning categories of weapon – lasted for years. It was, for example, not until 1986 – 16 years after SALT I began in 1970 – that Soviet negotiators abandoned their view that 'strategic' weapons were those capable of reaching the territory of a potential adversary irrespective of their location (Adelman, 1989. p. 52). On such a definition, US 'forward-based systems' such as those in Western Europe would be included in any regime to limit 'strategic weapons' while Soviet missiles targeted at Western Europe but unable to reach the United States would not.

Thirdly, because the details stage of negotiation is complicated and time-consuming, and usually requires the participation of specialists (Vance, 1983, p. 232), the negotiating teams are normally composed of individuals of lower authority than those involved – or at any rate leading – in the negotiations during the formula stage. This may well cause delays as they will need to refer back for guidance to their political masters or mistresses. The stickiness of the details stage caused by this situation may well be compounded further since, having returned home, their principals will be under less pressure from the other side and more from their own constituencies. This may lead to a reversion to a tougher attitude and cause hard-line instructions to be issued to the negotiators saddled with fleshing out the formula. This is precisely what happened after the Camp David formulas had been agreed in the rarified atmosphere of the American presidential retreat in September 1978: 'Isolating the leaders from the press and their own public opinion', as Quandt notes, 'had no doubt been a prime ingredient in reaching the two framework agreements. Now, however, each leader would have to return to the real world in which domestic constituencies would have their say. As each of the Camp David participants felt compelled to justify what he had done at the summit,' Quandt continues, 'the gap separating them began to widen again' (1986, p. 259; also pp. 262, 270, 271, 275). Indeed, it was only after the resumption of top-level participation in the talks, not least by President Carter himself, that at least an Egypt–Israel peace treaty was finally produced five months after the 'framework' had been agreed.

A fourth reason why the details stage is often particularly difficult is that it may well present an opportunity to one or both sides to load the balance of advantage in the agreed formula in their favour, and – enmeshed in the details – in a manner not necessarily easy to detect (Zartman and Berman, 1982, pp. 149–52). In other words, and especially if trust between the parties is minimal, the atmosphere in the details stage is likely to suffer simply because of the fear that each side may be trying to redraft the formula by massaging the details.

Finally, what often makes the details stage the toughest of all is the simple fact that it is *the last stage*: the moment of truth. What is agreed here has to be acted on, so if the negotiators get it wrong they will really suffer. When the details stage is concluded, it may mean soldiers surrendering positions in defence of which they have lost brothers, settlers giving up land in which they have sunk roots, exporters losing prized markets, or workers losing their livelihoods. There should thus be no vagueness and no inconsistencies – and the deal should be defensible at home. Magnanimity is thus generally at a discount in the details stage of negotiations.

Detailed agreements are negotiated either by one or the other of two ways, or – more usually – by some combination of both. The first method is to compromise on individual issues, for example by splitting the difference between the opening demands of the parties on the timetable for a troop withdrawal. This is what happened in regard to the Cuban troops in Angola during the American-brokered negotiations in 1988. The South Africans, of course, wanted them out as soon as possible and had in mind a timetable of months; by contrast, the Marxist government of Angola, anxious to retain the protection afforded by Castro's 'internationalist military contingent' for as long as possible, was thinking of a timetable for its withdrawal in terms of three or four years. In the end, they compromised on a year and a half.[3]

The second method for making concessions is to give the other side more or less what it wants on one issue in return for satisfaction on a separate one.[4] Described by Zartman and Berman as 'exchanging points', this works best when each party is able to acquire from the other something worth more to it than what it has had to surrender in return. This was elaborated by the sociologist George Homans in a work published in 1961, and is thus sometimes known as 'Homans's theorem' (Zartman and Berman, 1982, pp. 13–14, 66, 175–6). A simple example of such an exchange would be agreement on a high cash price for a long-lost Renoir between a rich art collector and a poor man with no interest in art who had found the painting in his attic: general jubilation. (A compromise on the Renoir would have been no good to either party since this would have meant cutting it in half.)

A variant on Homans's theorem is a deal in which one party trades something which it values highly but which it knows it is going to have to surrender anyway, irrespective of whether or not it gets a quid pro quo from the other side. In principle, both parties can do this as well. The trick here, of course, is to make sure that the other side does not share the same information. This is where liberal democracies are at a severe disadvantage compared to authoritarian regimes, which was a constant lament of Henry Kissinger in the 1970s. Thus in seeking to trade a US freeze in the deployment of Anti-Ballistic Missiles (ABMs) in return for Soviet limitations on offensive nuclear forces, Kissinger was seriously hampered by the obvious determination of Congress to kill off the ABM programme anyway (Kissinger, 1979, pp. 194–210, 534–51). Nor did it help him in his negotiations with the North Vietnamese in Paris that, under even more fierce Congressional pressure, his major trump card – US military power in South Vietnam – was slipping remorselessly from his grasp with every fresh public announcement of further troop withdrawals. When the other side knows that it is going to get what it wants anyway, it has little incentive to pay for it in concessions of its own. It merely has to wait.

Whichever strategy for making and seeking concessions, or whichever combination of them, is adopted will depend on circumstances and the established style of the negotiators. In the last regard, there are significant variations between different national cultures. Where the negotiators come from different cultural traditions, this can naturally cause problems (Cohen, 1991). There remains, however, the issue of the general attitude to strike in negotiations, whether, that is, the negotiators should be accommodating or tough. Each has obvious advantages and disadvantages, and since the circumstances of different negotiations vary so enormously generalisation in this area is a risky business. Nevertheless, at the price of inviting the charge of banality, the following might be hazarded. First, extremes of flexibility and rigidity are both inconsistent with the logic of negotiation. Secondly, since this involves concessions by both sides (by definition), it is usually believed to be best to make them in one fell swoop in order to avoid the impression given by making small concessions incrementally that there are always more for the asking (Zartman and Berman, 1982, p. 171).[5] Thirdly, if concessions are, nevertheless, extracted incrementally, the impression of weakness may be reduced by exploitation of various tactical expedients. Among these are making the concessions contingent on a final 'package deal', periodically suspending the talks in order to remind the other party that too much pressure might lead to collapse, and raising the question of the formula again. Fourthly, a tough attitude in negotiations is most appropriate to parties which are confident that they can walk away without major damage to their position, which helps to explain the attitude of the Begin government during the Camp David negotiations; or to those such as regimes based on religious fanaticism or police terror which are able to impose major costs on their own people and allies in the event of diplomatic failure.

SUMMARY

Negotiation is thus generally a lengthy and laborious process, proceeding through 'pre-negotiations' and a formula stage to the details phase. In each stage there is risk of breakdown, though this is probably most acute in the first and last – in the first not least because the 'exit costs' (Stein, 1989, p. 482) are low, while in the last because this is the negotiators' moment of truth. The momentum of the negotiations may thus falter even if both parties in a bilateral negotiation, or a majority of parties in a multilateral negotiation, are serious about making them a success. How diplomatic momentum might be sustained is thus a serious question, and it is to this that we must next turn.

NOTES

1. I owe this phrase to Saunders (1985).
2. This would give the Turks sovereignty over some of their affairs; the independence constitution of the island was a unitary one.
3. The timetable was spelled out in detail in an Annex to the agreements; see Berridge, 1991, pp. 159–60, where this is reproduced.
4. This is in principle the same as 'linkage', discussed earlier. The difference is that here the issues, while separate, are of the same species.
5. Kissinger somewhere describes the incremental approach as 'salami tactics'.

FURTHER READING

Berridge, G. R. (1989), 'Diplomacy and the Angola/Namibia Accords, December 1988', *International Affairs*, vol. 65, no. 3

Binnendijk, H. (ed) (1987), *National Negotiating Styles* (Center for the Study of Foreign Affairs, Foreign Service Institute, US Department of State: Washington, D. C.)

Cohen, R. (1991), *Negotiating across Cultures* (US Institute of Peace Press: Washington, D. C.)

Faure, G. O. and J. Z. Rubin (eds) (1993), *Culture and Negotiation: The Resolution of Water Disputes* (Sage: Newbury Park, California, London and New Delhi)

Golan, M. (1976), *The Secret Conversations of Henry Kissinger: Step-by-Step Diplomacy in the Middle East* (Quadrangle: New York)

Quandt, W. B. (1986), *Camp David: Peacemaking and Politics* (Brookings: Washington, D. C.), chs 8–12

Touval, S. (1989), 'Multilateral negotiation: an analytic approach', *Negotiation Journal*, vol. 5 no. 2

Vance, C. (1983), *Hard Choices: Critical Years in America's Foreign Policy* (Simon and Schuster: New York)

Webster, Sir C. (1961), *The Art and Practice of Diplomacy* (Chatto and Windus: London)

Zartman, I. W. and M. Berman (1982), *The Practical Negotiator* (Yale University Press: New Haven and London), chs 4–6

8

DIPLOMATIC MOMENTUM

The momentum of a negotiation may falter even if the parties are serious about proceeding. This was a recurring problem with the Uruguay Round of GATT negotiations, which started in September 1986 and was not finally completed until April 1994. Why might momentum falter? Why is it serious? And what might be done to prevent it? The first two questions are not especially problematical and have in any case already been touched on. As a result, the greater part of this chapter will be concerned with the practical stratagems which fall under the heading of the third, other than inducements such as side payments and guarantees offered by a mediator, dealt with in chapter 5.

Three reasons why momentum might be lost, especially in the details stage of negotiations, have already been mentioned. First, there is the characteristic withdrawal of senior ministers or officials following conclusion of the formula stage, which may well lead to a slackening in pace because of the greater need to refer home for instructions when difficulties occur. Secondly, there is the deliberate delay caused by a party feeling on the defensive in order to impress the other side with the difficulty which it is having in granting certain concessions. Thirdly, there is the effect of the sheer complexity of much contemporary international negotiation, especially multilateral negotiation.

Talks may also be slowed down or even temporarily interrupted, however, by a host of others factors. Key personnel may be drawn away from any stage of negotiations by the need to attend to even more urgent matters, including time-consuming commitments in annual national and international calendars such as party congresses, the opening of new parliamentary sessions, regular summit meetings, the start of the new session of the UN General Assembly in September, and so on. They may be delayed by disputes within delegations, which was notoriously the case with the EC delegation in the GATT negotiations. They may be delayed by the serious possibility of a change in government of one or more of the parties, especially if it is feared that any agreement negotiated will be disavowed or in practice circumvented by the new government, or alternatively if it is anticipated that the new government will agree to better terms. Final-term American presidents in their third and fourth years have notorious difficulty in being taken seriously as negotiators. (Of course, if one party expects worse terms from a new government the talks may gain rather than lose momentum; see below.) The talks may be delayed by the genuine illness of a key player. They may also be interrupted, as the Israel–PLO negotiations on the withdrawal of Israeli forces from Gaza and Jericho were interrupted for over a month, by an incident such as the Hebron mosque massacre on 25 February 1994, which makes it unseemly for one or other party to be seen pursuing negotiations for the time being.[1] And they may even be interrupted by national holidays, which is one good reason why states generally include a compendium of national holidays in their regularly up-dated *Diplomatic Lists*.

If there is a lull in the talks for any reason, the great danger is that it will drag on and become permanent. There are four main reasons why this may be a real danger. First, an absence of progress may demoralise the negotiators and, just as important, demoralise their supporters. Secondly, such a development will provide the enemies of negotiations with a fresh opportunity for sabotage and provide them with further ammunition as well: 'we told you so!' Thirdly, since the parties are still likely to be on their best behaviour towards each other (everything is relative), one or other may be led to draw the false conclusion that perhaps the status quo is not so bad after all, and that the price of a deal is too high. Finally, and perhaps most fatally of all, a lull in negotiations permits the attention of key personnel to be drawn to other items on the crowded international agenda. This at one time seemed to be the likely fate of the Uruguay Round in early 1991, when the Gulf War literally blew up at just the point when a pre-Christmas crisis left the talks drifting aimlessly and urgently in need of top-level attention. In such circumstances, what can be done to sustain momentum, and to regain it if lost?

One way to maintain high momentum is, of course, for one side to give in to the other on every item on the agenda; but this would be a capitulation rather than a negotiation. Nevertheless, an important method of sustaining momentum in a genuine negotiation is to employ the step-by-step approach discussed earlier. This minimises the risk of stalemate by proceeding in piecemeal fashion, usually from the less to the more difficult issues; and by building up a list of tangible achievements over a relatively long period demonstrates the value of diplomacy. A good recent example of such an achievement used to this end was the Cairo accords on security, signed between the PLO and Israel in early February 1994, which broke months of deadlock in the details stage of this negotiation but left other issues for later. If ratification of the initial achievements is contingent on a package deal, the step-by-step approach also gives the negotiators – who will not normally wish to see their achievements thrown away and have to admit that their time has been wasted – a vested interest in driving the talks towards a final conclusion. The step-by-step approach, however, is rarely able to maintain momentum unaided, not least because it has a downside, too. Its unavoidable slowness, together with the impression which it generally gives of ducking 'the main issues', can generate exasperation. It is, then, perhaps the step-by-step approach which is the strategy of negotiation most in need of special assistance in the maintaining of momentum. How can this be provided?

DEADLINES

A traditional device regularly employed by negotiators in order to keep up the momentum of their talks is to employ deadlines, that is, calendar dates by which either some partial, interim, or final agreement must be reached. Effective deadlines, however, must meet two clear conditions.

In the first place, real penalties must flow from failure to reach agreement by the specified date. If a deadline is missed, this means either a clear risk that the opportunity for a settlement will slip away; or, while a settlement itself may not be seriously jeopardised, an equally clear risk that one or more of the parties concerned will have to pay a higher price for it.

Deadlines which are determined by best estimates of the time required for the negotiation but are in other regards arbitrary, do not usually carry penalties of this kind. Such *notional deadlines*, it is true, may have some small, positive impact on the momentum of talks, especially if they are publicly announced; after all, failure to meet them will be a minor blow to the professional reputations of the negotiators. On the other hand, they can usually gain more than compensating marks from their supporters by maintaining – which may well be true – that they would have been failing in their duty to settle by the agreed date since the terms achieved remained unsatisfactory; missing the deadline was evidence of a 'tough' stand rather than incompetence, sloth or lack of seriousness of purpose. The best deadlines are thus those which are either deliberately pegged by the negotiators (or their masters) to some date which has significance more or less independent of the negotiations, or which are forced on the negotiators by circumstance. In the first case, the symbolic deadline, professional competence will be at issue (as with the notional deadline) but so will the negotiators' respect for the event commemorated. In the second, the practical deadline, reputation for professional competence may be less at stake but another kind of penalty could be far more serious.

Symbolic deadlines are much favoured by negotiators anxious to bring negotiations to a conclusion. Such deadlines are often dates which would have symbolic significance for the subject of the negotiations whether the negotiations were taking place or not. Good examples in peace negotiations are the anniversaries of the outbreak of a war, a cease-fire resolution, or – especially suitable – some spectacular, grisly and altogether gratuitous massacre. The birthday or anniversary of the death of a great leader may, however, serve equally well, as may the date of the founding of some major international organisation. And, such is the fascination with multiples of 10, that the most prized anniversaries are half-centenaries, centenaries and bi-centenaries; even mere tenth anniversaries are eagerly commandeered. Dates in the calendars of the great religions are also useful, in the Christian tradition especially, of course, Christmas itself.

The importance of symbolic deadlines is not difficult to understand. Dates of symbolic significance have long been exploited for propaganda purposes by lobbyists for whom they are important and, partly for this reason and partly because they are ideal 'pegs' on which to 'hang' articles and broadcasts, they have long been the stock in trade of the mass media. In the modern world, therefore, it is highly unlikely that any date of symbolic importance for some group or other will go unnoticed. In early 1994 the story of the Bosnian conflict was on more than one occasion pushed from the headline news in Britain by coverage of wrangles over the best way to commemorate the 50th anniversary of the Normandy landings of 6 June 1944, which presaged the defeat of Hitler in the Second World War.

The pressure exerted by a symbolic deadline, therefore, is this: with unusual media attention focused on the negotiations in the weeks immediately preceding it, the negotiators can expect unusually high marks for meeting the deadline and unusually low ones for letting it slip by. For this is an important date, and concluding by this time will show proper respect for the event which it commemorates, while letting it slip away will imply – whatever the protests to the contrary – at best indifference to and at worst contempt for its significance. The penalty is a propaganda penalty. A good example of such a date was the suggestion of 29 September 1988 by the superpowers as the deadline by which they expected the Angola/Namibia negotiations to be completed. The appeal of this was that it was the tenth anniversary of the passing of UN Security Council Resolution 435 on the arrangements for the independence of South African-controlled Namibia. Not taking this deadline seriously, therefore, would imply not taking seriously the question of Namibian independence – a 'motherhood' issue (Berridge, 1989, pp. 475–6).

The usefulness of a symbolic date as a deadline will obviously vary with the importance attached to the event which it commemorates, and will be significantly reduced if it is forced by mediators on parties whose own estimation of the event varies. This was the case with the proposed deadline used as an illustration in the previous paragraph, because South Africa itself – a key player in these negotiations – could hardly have been expected to have been unduly worried by the prospect of appearing indifferent to the celebration of the passage of what was a transparently anti-South African resolution. In the event, at South Africa's suggestion, the deadline for the Angola/Namibia negotiations was brought forward to 1 September (Berridge, 1989, p. 476). Nevertheless, the regularity with which symbolic deadlines are employed in negotiations is testimony to the value attached to them.

There is little doubt, however, that, as the name for them which comes most readily to mind suggests, *practical deadlines* are usually the most valuable when it comes to sustaining momentum in negotiations. These are deadlines imposed by events which are either completely beyond the control of the negotiating party or only cancelled at considerable cost. In the last category fall deadlines imposed by summit meetings, which have already been discussed in chapter 3. In the former fall deadlines imposed by such events as scheduled elections, the opening of other conferences where the subject at issue may be high on the agenda, the expiry of the negotiating authority of a key party, the expiry of a cease-fire agreement, the expiry of the mandate of a peacekeeping force, and previously announced dates for the commencement and completion of military withdrawals where the details remain to be negotiated.

In *Camp David: Peacemaking and Politics*, William Quandt gives a brilliant exposition of the practical deadlines imposed by the US electoral cycle on American diplomacy, particularly on important negotiations such as those on the Middle East in which the president plays a personal role (1986, ch. 2). Only in the first year of the president's maximum of two four-year terms is he relatively free of the pressure of electoral deadlines, and in this first year the emphasis is in any case usually on pre-negotiations. In the second year he begins to look for diplomatic breakthroughs in advance of the mid-term elections for Congress in November. In the third year it is not long before he is worrying about the effects of his diplomacy on the notoriously protracted presidential nominating process. And in the fourth year, unless it is his second term, he is obviously worrying about the general election in November itself.

It is not altogether accidental that it was just two months before the mid-term elections in 1978 that President Carter devoted 13 days to summit diplomacy on the Middle East at Camp David, and that his 'clear priority after Camp David was to conclude the [detailed] treaty negotiations as quickly as possible, literally within days' (Quandt, 1986, p. 260). It is, however, interesting that his sense of urgency was also heightened by an even tighter practical deadline: the ninth Arab League summit which was scheduled to meet in Baghdad in late October. For it was feared that Jordan, whose participation in 'autonomy' talks in regard to the West Bank was believed to be vital, and Saudi Arabia, whose support for Sadat was also regarded as critical, would both come under intense pressure at the summit from the radical Arab states[2] to denounce the Camp David Accords and cause Sadat to lose his nerve (Carter, 1982, pp. 404–9; Vance, 1983, p. 229; Quandt, 1986, p. 260). By the beginning of 1979, at which point the details stage of the Egypt–Israel negotiations had still not been completed, Carter was of course in his third year. It is also worth adding here that the presidential election in November 1988 put pressure on Chester Crocker to make tangible progress in the Angola/Namibia negotiations since, although Ronald Reagan was retiring, the Republican candidate, George Bush, was obviously anxious to use as many foreign policy achievements as possible in his own election campaign.

Of course, if a party with which the United States is negotiating in a presidential election year expects to get a worse deal from the rival presidential candidate, and if there is a real possibility that the latter might win, the prospect of this election can also put considerable pressure for a settlement on America's negotiating partner. This was the calculus which was at work on the South Africans in the Angola/Namibia negotiations in 1988, for they knew that they were unlikely ever to get a better deal from the Americans than under Ronald Reagan, and certainly not from the liberal Democrat, Michael Dukakis, who was running against George Bush. It was also at work on the Iranians in the Iran hostage negotiations eight years earlier, which, partly in order to complete their humiliation of Jimmy Carter and partly out of fear of the attitude of the new administration, they finally settled on the very day of Ronald Reagan's inauguration, 20 January 1981.

Another good example of a practical deadline in a negotiation sorely in need of every aid to the maintenance of its momentum was the Brussels ministerial meeting in GATT's Uruguay Round in the first week of December 1990. Urgency was injected into these talks because the negotiating mandate of the American delegation granted by Congress was due to run out on 1 March 1991, and there was a real fear that – because of hostility in the United States to the direction of the negotiations – the mandate would not be renewed. Since any package negotiated would thus have to be submitted to Congress by this date, Carla Hills, the US trade representative, insisted that she would need the time between December and the end of February in order to prepare the necessary legislation; hence the effective deadline on the negotiations was the December ministerial meeting.

Finally, the practical deadlines imposed on the details stage of the Israel–PLO negotiations by the dates agreed in the Declaration of Principles of September 1993 for the withdrawal of Israeli forces from Gaza and Jericho might be mentioned. On this occasion it was announced that the withdrawal would commence on 13 December 1993 and be completed by 13 April 1994. These dates were of particular importance to the PLO leader, Yasser Arafat, who was under intense pressure to deliver tangible progress from his own supporters as well as from more radical Palestinian elements. Furthermore, while the Israeli prime minister, Yitzak Rabin, subsequently declared that 'there are no sacred dates' (*The Independent*, 1994) it is clear that failure to take them seriously would lead to intense international criticism, not least from the United States, and might destroy the man who remained Israel's most promising negotiating partner – Yasser Arafat. The Palestinian self-rule agreement was finally signed on 4 May under the equally intense pressure generated in the previous week by the public announcement on 28 April of a 'pre-signing summit' between Arafat and Rabin in Cairo, to which more than 2500 guests and 40 foreign ministers were invited – another practical deadline.

If the first condition of an effective deadline is that real penalties must be expected to flow from failure to meet it (whether in the event they do or not is not the point), the second is that they must not be too tight. They must, in other words, and with the proviso that this will not apply to some practical deadlines, which are in any case often beyond the control of the negotiators, allow sufficient time for the negotiations to be concluded. In short, effective deadlines must be realistic as well as real.

It often happens, of course, that 'effective' deadlines, whether symbolic or practical, are missed: they slip by with the negotiations still incomplete. The Angola/Namibia negotiations were not concluded by 1 September 1988, the Egypt–Israel Peace Treaty was still unsigned at the time of the American mid-term elections and the Arab League summit in early November 1978,[3] and the Uruguay Round plodded on for over three years following December 1990. Nevertheless, it is reasonable to conclude that, in light of the urgency which these deadlines visibly injected into the negotiations, they would have taken even longer in their absence and may not have been concluded at all.

METAPHORS OF MOVEMENT

A particularly interesting and perhaps sometimes almost subconsciously employed device for sustaining momentum in negotiations is the metaphor of movement. Closely allied to deadlines but nevertheless distinct from them, metaphors of movement help to prevent loss of momentum by influencing the view of the negotiators and their supporters of the process in which they are engaged: make them believe that they are on something which is *by definition* mobile and they will be more likely to want to keep it moving, even if the metaphor is treacherous and this may be risky to their interests.

A logical corollary of the deadline is the metaphor of the race – a collaborative race of the parties against their common enemy, time, rather than a competitive race of the parties against each other. (It now becomes clear, incidentally, that a 'deadline' in negotiations is itself a significant metaphor, a metaphor of collaboration.) If the negotiation is like a 'race' there will be no prizes for 'not finishing' or 'dropping out early'. If obstacles which are met in the negotiation are 'hurdles' it is the duty of everyone, including those for whom an early shower might in reality be the best option, to 'clear' them. Negotiators of countries on the verge of war, as in the case of the United States and Iraq in early 1991, are now generally expected to go 'the extra mile for peace'.

Another common metaphor of movement used in negotiations is that of the automobile, even if, described as such, this is usually implicit. If the negotiation is being 'driven forward' like a car it will be capable of high speeds and versatility in manoeuvring around obstacles in the road. If it comes to a stop this is because it has 'stalled', a condition caused either by technical failure or embarrassing incompetence which it is necessary to rectify as soon as possible. The 'road map', employed by the Americans in their negotiations with the Vietnamese in the early 1990s, is a recent variant on this invented by the metaphor machine of the US State Department.

Perhaps even more common than either the car or race metaphor, however, is the metaphor of the train. If the negotiation is like 'a train', it will be dangerous for anyone to get off before it pulls into 'the station'. It will also be dangerous for everyone if it does not stay 'on the track', if, that is to say, it is 'de-railed', in any case a very rare occurrence. And general exasperation will ensue if it gets 'shunted into a siding'. The train metaphor is particularly useful because it can cope with lulls. Trains, after all, stop in stations – but only briefly. Trains also run to timetables, so the metaphor reinforces the use of deadlines. And they *always* arrive at their terminus eventually. The popularity of the train metaphor is not difficult to understand. In the Angola/Namibia negotiations the Americans used it repeatedly (Berridge, 1989, p. 477). Complicated negotiations are also commonly described as 'dual track' or 'multi-track'. The potency of such metaphors, especially if picked up, embellished and repeated by the mass media may be difficult to resist.

PUBLICITY

It is a cliché of studies of diplomacy that publicity is the enemy of negotiation, and this is substantially true, as noted on more than one occasion in earlier chapters of this book. However, employed judiciously, publicity about a negotiation can also help to drive it forward. It can do this in at least three ways: first, by flying kites to see how the other side will react; secondly, by mobilising popular support for a negotiated solution; and thirdly, by 'talking up the talks'. Propaganda and diplomacy are thus not necessarily antithetical; it all depends on the nature of the propaganda. This is one of the reasons why the press office is such an important department of heads of government and their foreign ministries (Dickie, 1992, p. 248).

Floating formulas or flying kites, both publicly and privately, is obviously of special importance in pre-negotiations, as already noted, but it is not confined to this stage. For example, during the 14 weeks of substantive negotiations held on Rhodesia at Lancaster House in London in 1979, the head of the News Department at the Foreign Office, Sir Nicholas Fenn, often aired suggestions for the press to report (Dickie, 1992, p. 249). Flying kites openly can expedite negotiations by preparing the public for an eventual settlement. It can perhaps do this even more by permitting negotiators to gain greater insight into the ambitions and anxieties of their interlocutors by noting their reactions when the kites sail up. An idea *publicly accepted*, or at least not dismissed outright, will be regarded as a serious basis for negotiation because this will be an indication that the party concerned believes that it could sell this at home. According to John Dickie's well-informed account of the Lancaster House talks, 'it was of great interest to Sir Anthony Duff, as head of the British negotiating team, to gauge the public and private reactions of the other delegations to what appeared as a result [of the News Department's briefings] in the Press' (1992, p. 249).

Since even authoritarian regimes ignore their own popular opinion at their peril, as the Shah of Iran discovered, and are in any case almost always anxious to influence foreign opinion, mobilising the public in support of an important negotiation will be a priority for any government committed to the talks, especially if they appear to be flagging. This, of course, was why the Egyptian leader, Anwar Sadat, took the literally dramatic step of journeying to Jerusalem itself in November 1977 to address the Israeli people over the heads of their government; and why the Carter administration also decided shortly afterwards to 'mount a public campaign' directed at both American and Israeli opinion to bring pressure to bear on the government of Menachem Begin (Quandt, 1986, p. 162).

Another important way of sustaining momentum in negotiations is to give the impression to the public that they are nearer to success than is in reality the case. 'Talking up the talks' cannot be done repeatedly or in circumstances when it is manifestly obvious that success is nowhere in sight. This will result in a loss of public credibility. It may also rebound by angering the delegation of the more recalcitrant party, which may find itself – unfairly – in hot water with its own supporters. Nevertheless, used sparingly and when clear progress in one or other stage of the negotiations has been made, talking up the talks can prove very useful indeed. This strategy was employed by the British foreign secretary, Lord Carrington, at the Lancaster House talks on Rhodesia (Dickie, 1992, p. 250), by the UN mediator in the Afghanistan talks in the 1980s (Harrison, 1988, p. 35), and also by Chester Crocker in the Angola/Namibia negotiations. Crocker's tactic, as in the case of the other two negotiators, was to sound optimistic at press briefings once it was clear that there was a genuine chance of a breakthrough. Clearly, his calculation was that if he could entrench the public belief that success in these talks was just around the corner, then any party which deserted them or behaved in an obstructive manner would be the target of attack from the many influential quarters which, in the current atmosphere of superpower *rapprochement* and war-weariness in southern Africa, favoured a settlement. A report written a few days after the final breakthrough at Geneva, in November 1988, summed up this particular ploy very neatly, as well as highlighting the use of the train metaphor in these negotiations:

Once a little momentum was achieved, Mr Crocker would drive the talks train faster and faster, briefing journalists on how well negotiations were going and how close to agreement they were. If the participants tried to stop the train or get off they would be seen as wreckers. It failed a few times, but each time Mr Crocker put the train back on the tracks and started again. 'If anyone had got off the train when they arrived in Geneva they would have sprained a wrist,' one US official said after agreement was reached on Tuesday night. 'If anyone tries to get off now they will break both legs.' (*The Independent*, 1988)

RAISING THE LEVEL OF THE TALKS

If it is clear that a negotiation has lost its momentum by virtue of the inadequate authority of the teams employed rather than by interruption, the obvious solution is to raise the level of the talks, that is, to insert or reinsert more senior personnel – if they can be spared. This actually has more than one advantage. First, and most obviously, it injects into the negotiations people who are more likely to have the authority to make the difficult decisions entailed in granting concessions. Secondly, it brings these decision-makers once more face to face with the realities of the negotiation and dilutes to some extent the influence on them of their home constituencies. Thirdly, it may also provide an opportunity to bring *different* people into the process, with fresh ideas. And fourthly, providing it is done publicly, it will be symbolically significant: raising the level of the talks, in other words, will indicate that the parties to the negotiation continue to attach high priority to progress. This will generally raise public expectations of success and thus increase the pressure for a settlement.

There are at least four different ways of raising the level of negotiations. The most obvious but not necessarily the most common is to do this in set-piece fashion. For example, following confirmation at the Leeds Castle conference in July 1978 that no further progress in the Egypt–Israel negotiations could be made at foreign minister level, Jimmy Carter decided to propose a summit at

Camp David (Quandt, 1986, pp. 165, 199). The same tactic was employed, as already noted, in the Israel–PLO negotiations in May 1994. Another method, however, which is perhaps more common, is to inject senior personnel into a negotiation in a more ad hoc manner, as for example when – 'to speed up the talks' – Jimmy Carter briefly joined the foreign minister level negotiations which were held at Blair House in Washington in October 1978 in order to flesh out the details of the Camp David Accords agreed the previous month (Quandt, 1986, p. 272). A third method is to create a second channel at a higher level and often in a different place, while leaving the lower level channel untouched. This has the advantage of achieving a division of labour on the agenda while retaining the lower level channel as an all-purpose fall back in the event of difficulties. For example, US–North Korea talks began to take place at ministerial level in New York following admission of Pyongyang to the UN in September 1991 but counsellor level talks continued in Beijing.

Finally, it is important to stress a variation on the latter strategy: the creation of a higher level channel which on important issues short-circuits the lower level channel and concerning the activities of which the latter is kept in complete ignorance. This, of course, is what Henry Kissinger called a 'backchannel' (Kissinger, 1979, pp. 138–40, 722–3). Illustrated notably by his Washington discussions with Soviet ambassador to the United States, Anatoly Dobrynin, on arms control, a subject under formal negotiation alternately in Helsinki and Vienna (1979, pp. 805–23), the advantages of backchannels are secrecy, speed, and the avoidance of internal bureaucratic battles. They are also a tactic notoriously favoured by Yasser Arafat.[4] The disadvantages of backchannels are the possibility of overlooking key points, their deleterious effects on morale, and the related difficulty of getting those who have been excluded from the decision-making to support the implementation of any agreement which they have helped to generate.

SUMMARY

The momentum of negotiations may falter for any number of reasons, even though the parties remain committed to progress. This is serious because a slowdown can turn into a lull, and a lull can become a dead end. In order to prevent this, negotiators character-istically resort to notional and symbolic deadlines, and lean on such practical ones as are to hand. They also employ metaphors of movement and publicity, and they raise the level of the talks as a last resort. If an agreement is eventually reached, with or without the assistance of these devices (and it will be the rare one which needs none of them), it will still need to be packaged. It is to this final question which we now turn.

NOTES

1. On 19 March, the Middle East Editor of *The Independent* noted that 'it is unlikely that the PLO will return to talks until after the traditional 40-day period of mourning and the celebration of the Muslim feast of Eid al-Adha next month.'
2. Algeria, Libya, South Yemen, Syria and the PLO had already held a summit of their anti-Sadat 'Steadfastness and Confrontation Front' in Damascus on 23 September (Lukacs, 1992, pp. 469–70).
3. Though Quandt (1986) reports that this summit was scheduled for 'late October', it actually took place between 2 and 5 November.
4. 'Only three others are said to have been fully aware of the secret Norway negotiations with Israel. When Dr Haidar Abdel Shafi, the widely respected leader of the Palestinian team during 10 rounds of talks with Israel, arrived in Tunis last August for further instructions, it was to be told a deal had already been struck behind his back' (*Financial Times*, 26/27 Feb. 1994).

FURTHER READING

Berridge, G. R. (1989), 'Diplomacy and the Angola/Namibia Accords, December 1988', *International Affairs*, vol. 65, no. 3

Carter, J. (1982), *Keeping Faith: Memoirs of a President* (Bantam: New York)

Harrison, S. (1988), 'Inside the Afghan talks', *Foreign Policy*

Quandt, W. B. (1986), *Camp David: Peacemaking and Politics* (Brookings: Washington, D. C.)

9

PACKAGING AGREEMENTS

Diplomatic agreements vary in form to an almost bewildering degree. They vary most obviously in title or style: 'Treaties', 'Final Acts', 'Protocols', 'Exchanges of Notes' – even 'Agreements', for example. However, they also vary significantly in textual structure, language, and whether or not they are accompanied by 'side letters'. They also vary, though since Woodrow Wilson's campaign for open diplomacy at the time of the First World War there has become entrenched a presumption that they should not, in whether they are publicised or kept secret. The purpose of this chapter is to explain this variation and to indicate what form an agreement might take depending on its subject matter and the political needs of its authors.

There are four main reasons, aside from accident and changing linguistic preferences, which help to explain the multiplicity of forms taken by international agreements. The first is that some create international legal obligations while others do not. The second is that some forms of agreement are better at signalling the importance of the subject matter, while others are better at disguising its significance. The third is that some are simply more convenient to use than others; they are easier to draw up and avoid the need for ratification by a popular assembly. And the fourth is that some are better than others at saving the 'face' of parties who have been obliged to make potentially embarrassing concessions in order to achieve a settlement.

The form taken by any particular agreement will depend on what premium is attached to each of these considerations by the parties to the negotiation, the degree of harmony between them on these questions, and – in the absence of harmony – the degree to which concessions on form can be traded for concessions on substance.

The parties to a negotiation may agree that the subject of their agreement is not appropriate to regulation by international law. This may be because it is obvious that it is more appropriately governed by municipal law, as are a great many commercial accords; or because the agreement merely amounts to a statement of commonly held principles or objectives, such as the Atlantic Charter of 1941 or the Helsinki Final Act of 1975, which was the product of the 35-nation Conference on Security and Cooperation in Europe (Gore-Booth, 1979, pp. 238–9; Shaw, 1991, p. 562). If, however, they concur that their agreement should create obligations which are enforceable in *international* law, then they must put it in the form of a treaty.

A treaty (the term derives from the French verb *traiter*, to negotiate) was defined by the Vienna Convention on the Law of Treaties, 1969, which came into force in 1980, as 'an international agreement concluded between States in written form and governed by international law, whether embodied in a single instrument or in two or more related instruments and whatever its particular designation'. It is important to add to this that in order to be 'governed by international law', an agreement must (under Article 102 of the UN Charter) 'as soon as possible be registered with the Secretariat and published by it', since unregistered agreements cannot be invoked before 'any organ of the United Nations', which includes the International Court of Justice (Ware, 1990, p. 1). In short, parties who want their agreement to create international legal obligations must write it out and give a copy to the UN; in so doing, they have created a 'treaty'.

In view of the widespread cynicism about the effectiveness of international law, why might the parties to a negotiation want to create an agreement entailing international legal obligations? They do this because they know that such obligations are, in fact, honoured far more often than not, even by states with unsavoury reputations (Henkin, 1979, p. 47). Among other reasons, this is mainly because the obligations derive from consent, because natural inhibitions to law-breaking exist in the relations between states which do not obtain in the relations between individuals, and because a reputation for failing to keep agreements will make it extremely difficult to promote policy by means of negotiation in the future (Bull, 1977, ch. 6; Berridge, 1992b, pp. 157–62).

SIGNALLING IMPORTANCE AT A PREMIUM

Creating a treaty is one thing; calling a treaty a 'treaty' is another. In fact, treaties are more often than not called something quite different. A few of these alternative titles were mentioned at the beginning of this chapter; others include 'act', 'charter', 'concordat', 'convention', 'covenant', 'declaration', 'exchange of correspondence', 'general agreement', *'modus vivendi'*, 'pact', 'understanding', and even 'agreed minutes'.[1] Some treaties are nevertheless still called 'treaties' and there is a consensus that this style is adopted when there is a desire to underline the importance of an agreement.[2] This is because of the term's historical association with the international deliberations of princes or their plenipotentiaries, and because the genuine treaty is composed in an imposing manner, complete with seals as well as signatures.[3] Agreements on matters of special international significance which have, accordingly, been styled 'treaties' include the North Atlantic Treaty of 4 April 1949 which created the Western Cold War alliance, the Treaties of Rome of 25 March 1957 which created the European Communities, and the various Treaties of Accession of new members to the EC (Gore-Booth, 1979, pp. 239–40). Agreements ending wars are, of course, commonly called 'peace treaties', as in the case of the Treaty of Peace between the Arab Republic of Egypt and the State of Israel of 26 March 1979. And agreements providing all-important guarantees of a territorial or constitutional settlement are invariably called 'treaties of guarantee'. In this case a good example is the Cyprus Guarantee Treaty of 16 August 1960. These, however, are not so common today as they once were.[4]

If an agreement is believed by its authors to be of great political importance but is not of such a character as to warrant creation of legal obligations of any kind, obviously its importance cannot be signalled nor its binding character reinforced by calling it a 'treaty';

it is not a treaty. However, precisely because the parties have rejected the possibility of clothing their agreement in international law but remain 'politically' bound by it as well as deeply attached to the agreement's propaganda value, it is doubly important to dress it in fine attire of a different kind. Hence the use of imposing titles such as Atlantic 'Charter' and Helsinki 'Final Act', as mentioned in the previous section.[5]

CONVENIENCE AT A PREMIUM

Since states today negotiate on so many matters, an international agreement does not have to be of a merely routine character for convenience to be an important consideration in dictating its shape (Aurisch, 1989, p. 281). Convenience argues for informal agreements: treaties not styled as 'treaties', or agreements which, because they remain unpublished, are treaties in neither form nor substance. What inconveniences are avoided by packaging an agreement informally?

First of all, the complexities of formal treaty drafting and its attendant procedures, such as the production of documents certifying that the plenipotentiaries have 'full powers', are avoided. This is probably of special benefit to smaller and newer foreign ministries but is also likely to be regarded as an advantage by the over-burdened ministries of the bigger powers as well. Not surprisingly, therefore, Exchanges of Notes or Letters, which consist simply of a letter from one of the parties spelling out the terms of the agreement and a reply from the other indicating acceptance, are now the most common form of treaty. They require none of the elaborate construction of the treaty-by-name; nor do they require the presentation of full powers (Gore-Booth, 1979, pp. 247–8).

The second inconvenience which may be avoided by informal packaging, though it will not necessarily be avoided, is ratification of the agreement. Ratification, which means confirmation on the part of the negotiators' political masters that they will honour an agreement negotiated and signed on their behalf, became normal practice when poor communications made it difficult if not impossible for there to be any certainty that negotiators had not exceeded their powers – or that their masters had not changed their minds altogether since despatching them on their diplomatic errand.

The revolution in communications has, of course, virtually removed this problem, but ratification is still widely valued and provision for it is a feature of almost all written constitutions and, indeed, of the unwritten constitution of the United Kingdom (Ware, 1990, p. 1; Shaw, 1991, pp. 568–9).

Sometimes, of course, for a reason not far removed from the original theory of ratification, it is in the interests of the immediate political masters of the negotiators, the governments themselves, to insist on a form of agreement which requires ratification. This may be because they have certain anxieties about the agreement – perhaps because it had to be negotiated rather hurriedly – and themselves want time for second thoughts. They may also insist on such an agreement because, although they may feel no need for further reflection themselves, they know that it is of such significance that it will be politically insupportable at home (and thus unimpressive to the other party or parties to the negotiation) in the absence of some expression of popular approval, typically by a special majority in an elected assembly. The ultimate, though rare, form of ratification is a referendum, as when the Labour government in Britain held a referendum in 1974 on the issue of whether or not the United Kingdom should remain a signatory of the Treaties of Rome.

There are, nevertheless, clearly many occasions when neither of these considerations apply. In these circumstances governments are naturally anxious to avoid at best the delay in the coming into force of an agreement caused by the need for its ratification by a popular assembly and at worst the demand for its renegotiation which this might entail – the notorious fate of the Treaty of Versailles, signed in June 1919 but in the following November and again in March 1920 refused the two-thirds majority by the US Senate needed for American ratification. This failure was a doubly searing experience for the United States because the strain of campaigning for ratification, coming as it did on top of the mental and physical exertions of the peace negotiations themselves, had caused the American president, Woodrow Wilson, to have a severe stroke from which he very nearly died (Dimbleby and Reynolds, 1988, pp. 70–3). Six decades later, President Jimmy Carter had a similar problem with the second Strategic Arms Limitation Treaty.

An executive which itself feels no need for ratification is, then, unlikely to invite certain delay and possible trouble by casting its agreements in a form which requires ratification by a popular assembly. Since the American view is that treaties, by definition, require ratification (Shaw, 1991, p. 569),[6] it is thus obvious that the United States executive branch itself will avoid this form of agreement in these circumstances, and will probably have little difficulty in persuading its negotiating partners to concur. In fact, as is well known, it is in order to avoid the possible embarrassments of the ratification process in the Senate (in practice, in the Foreign Relations Committee of the Senate), that there has been massive resort to the 'executive agreement' in place of 'treaties-by-name' by successive American administrations since Wilson's time. Technically, these are international agreements entered into by the president either after Congress has by law given him a *general* authorisation in the field concerned (Bradshaw and Pring, 1973, pp. 407–8); or, in the case of 'pure' executive agreements, by virtue of certain unfettered plenary powers, for example as Commander-in-Chief, devolved on him by the constitution (Franck and Weisband, 1979, pp. 144, 149). In practice they are simply any international agreement entered into by the US executive branch which is not called a treaty and therefore does not require the 'advice and consent of the Senate' (pp. 141–2). Since the Second World War, US presidents have entered into roughly seven times more executive agreements than treaties; of the 1271 international agreements entered into by the second Reagan administration, only 47 were treaties (Ragsdale, 1993, pp. 76–7).

Another way of sidestepping the Senate is for the United States executive branch and its foreign negotiating partner each to issue a 'unilateral non-binding declaration', which in practice nevertheless is expected to be politically effective. The classic example here is provided by the separate but virtually simultaneous declarations of the United States and the Soviet Union immediately prior to the date of expiration of the Interim Agreement on Strategic Offensive Arms on 3 October 1977. Each indicated in its separate statement that, provided the other showed similar restraint, it would continue to honour the provisions of the technically dead Agreement (Glennon, 1983, pp. 267–9).

One of the titles common to a large proportion of the thousands of executive agreements to which the United States government is a party, as well as to a large proportion of the international agreements entered into by other states, is, as already mentioned, the Exchange of Notes or Letters. This does not normally require ratification, and so comes into force immediately upon signature. As a result, it is popular for this reason as well as because it avoids the formal complexities of the treaty-by-name. Informal agreements with other titles may, however, also be so framed in order to avoid pressure for ratification.

The final inconvenience which may be avoided by packaging agreements informally is the inconvenience of unwanted publicity, that is, publicity which may stir up political opponents at home or present intelligence gifts to unfriendly foreign states. To avoid the former, agreements on sensitive matters may be published (and thus become binding) but in such informal style as to be unlikely to attract attention. Two examples here might be cited. The first is the so-called Simonstown Agreements between Britain and the Union of South Africa which were concluded in 1955. The British wanted to play these down because they entailed surrender to Nationalist control of imperial facilities (the Simonstown naval base) and at the same time close military cooperation with racist South Africa. The agreements took the form of an 'Exchange of Letters' (Berridge, 1992a, ch. 5). The second good example is the Anglo-Argentine agreement on the Falkland Islands of 1971. The Argentines were not anxious to advertise this because they had gained nothing on sovereignty, while the British were not anxious to advertise it either because the practical schemes dealing with access and technical cooperation to which they had agreed could nevertheless have been interpreted as the thin end of the wedge of surrendering sovereignty. The agreement took the form of a 'Joint Statement' initialled by delegation heads on 1 July rather than signed, thus indicating only that negotiations were closed (Wood and Serres, 1970, p. 221); and secondly, an Exchange of Notes on 5 August between the British chargé d'affaires in Buenos Aires and the Argentine minister of foreign affairs, which referred to and qualified this Joint Statement (Grenville and Wasserstein, 1987, pp. 11, 433–6).

To avoid presenting intelligence gifts to unfriendly foreign states, the parties to a successful negotiation may not only conclude an informal agreement but withhold publication. Of course, this means that it is not a treaty, that it is, in other words, legally non-binding. But there are circumstances in which this is relatively unimportant, for example in the case of certain kinds of defence agreements between close allies, bound to each other by urgent common interest and perhaps by ties of sentiment as well. As Ware has noted, a good example of such an agreement is the UK–US Memorandum of Understanding on British participation in the Strategic Defense Initiative, which was signed in 1985 but, in Britain, revealed in its details only later, and in confidence, to the Defence Select Committee of the House of Commons (1990, p. 3).

SAVING FACE AT A PREMIUM

Questions of legal obligation, signalling or concealing importance, and administrative and political convenience are thus clearly important influences on the form taken by an agreement. It is obvious, nevertheless, that what especially excites interest in the form taken by an agreement in politically sensitive negotiations – where publicity for any agreement achieved is unavoidable and even desirable – is the issue of 'face': the necessity to save the 'face' of parties who have been obliged to make potentially embarrassing concessions in order to achieve a settlement. This is a particularly important consideration in 'shame cultures' such as those of the Arab Middle East (Cohen, 1991, p. 132).

Where face is a vital issue, the form – meaning chiefly the composition and structure, as well as title – of any agreement may not only be an important but also a controversial element in a negotiation. It will be important because some kinds of packaging will be better than others at disguising or at least minimising as much as possible the concessions which have had to be made. It is also likely to be controversial because it will commonly happen that what one side wants to disguise the other will want to highlight. Failure to agree on the form of an agreement following agreement on substance – which certainly happens (Cohen, 1991, pp. 140–1) – can vitiate a negotiation altogether. Settlement of the Iran hostages crisis was helped by using a form of agreement – a declaration by a third party – which suggested that the Ayatollah Khomeini had made his gesture to the Algerian mediators rather than to 'the Great Satan' (see chapter 5 above; Grenville and Wasserstein, 1987, p. 11). In what other ways can agreements be packaged in order to save face and thus ease a settlement?

Both languages – or more

It should first be noted, even though it may seem obvious, that diplomatic agreements in the contemporary world must be sensitive to the issue of language, such is the latter's centrality to nationality. Of course, this has not always been the case. Until the seventeenth century most treaties were written in Latin, thereafter in French, and in the twentieth century chiefly in English (Grenville and Wasserstein, 1987, p. 10). However, since the end of the Second World War it has become much more common for copies of agreements made between parties speaking different languages to be translated into the language of each. Furthermore, as might be imagined and as was confirmed by the Vienna Convention on the Law of Treaties, each version is typically described as 'equally authentic' or 'equally authoritative'.

The diplomatic advantage of drafting agreements in the language of each party is that it fosters the impression – whether true or not – that negotiated agreements reflect relationships of equality and provide for an exchange of concessions on an equal basis. After 1945, to take some examples, agreements between the United States and the Soviet Union were written in English and Russian, and between the United States and South American countries in English and Spanish. The Paris Peace Accords of 1973, which ended the Vietnam War, were drawn up in English and Vietnamese. The agreement concluded between Cuba and Angola in 1988 on the withdrawal of the forces of the former from the territory of the latter was written in Spanish and Portuguese. In each of these cases there were good political reasons for doing everything possible to suggest equality of status.

It should be added, though, that while there may be a clear diplomatic advantage to having equally authoritative agreements in different languages, there is a clear diplomatic disadvantage as well. This is because in the course of implementation of any agreement, which could – either by accident or design – be vague or loose at certain points, it may well transpire that the language of one text lends itself more to one interpretation than the language of the other. Where there are only two languages, this is a recipe for trouble, and it is for this reason that states sometimes wisely agree to have the text drawn up in a third language – usually English – and agree that this shall prevail in the event of a divergence of interpretation between the other two. This is what happened in the Geneva Accords on Afghanistan of 1988. The two which formally involved only the Pakistanis and the Afghans were drawn up in Urdu and Pashtu, while that which formally involved the Soviet Union as well was also written in Russian. In addition, all three agreements had an English version and it was agreed that this text would prevail in the event of 'any divergence of interpetation' (Berridge, 1991, app. 5). It is even more likely that this arrangement, provision for which was in fact also made in the Vienna Convention on the Law of Treaties, will be employed in agreements where an English-speaking state has been employed as a mediator. A case in point is the Egypt–Israel Peace Treaty of March 1979. This was written in Arabic, Hebrew and English and provided that the English text would prevail in the event of 'any divergence of interpretation'.

It remains the case, however, that many – probably most – agreements have no master text, thereby underlining the greater importance which is generally attached to saving face compared to avoiding possible future misunderstandings. To take but one example, the first of the two 'Angola/Namibia Accords', signed in December 1988, to which South Africa, Cuba and Angola were each a party, was signed in English, Spanish, and Portuguese versions, 'each language being equally authentic'. No text was nominated as the one which would prevail in the event of disagreement.

Small print

Sensitivity to language only addresses the question of face in the most general way, of course, and negotiators must needs turn to other devices when they are faced with the problem of disguising a sensitive concession in the text of an agreement. Perhaps the most common way of doing this is to say very little about it, tuck it away in some obscure recess, and ensure that the rest of the agreement is padded out with relatively trivial detail. A good example of this strategy can be found in the UN-brokered agreements of 1988 between the Soviet-backed Afghan Communist government and the American-backed Pakistanis, one of the most important provisions of which concerned the withdrawal of Soviet troops from Afghanistan. The Soviet Union, of course, was extremely sensitive to any suggestion that it was being forced into a military retreat which would leave its clients in Kabul exposed to a final onslaught from the ferocious if disorganised mujahidin. The trouble was that the Soviet concession – troop withdrawals – was the sort of thing which was considerably more attractive to television news editors than the American quid pro quo which Moscow hoped would enable the Afghan Communist regime to survive, that is, the termination of material support to the mujahidin. As a result, in the three agreements and one declaration which made up what were popularly known as the Geneva Accords on Afghanistan, only two short sentences were devoted to the Soviet troop withdrawal. Further-more, they were tacked onto the end of a paragraph (number 5) which gave no signpost at the beginning to what was to come at the end. And the agreement itself of which these two sentences were the most pregnant part was padded out, rather in the manner of a 'final act', with a resumé of the history of the negotiations, the titles of the other agreements reached, and general principles of international law (Berridge, 1991, pp. 148–51).

Another 'small print' technique for saving face is to place embarrassing concessions in documentary appendages to the main text. These take many forms: side letters, interpretive notes, appendices, additional protocols, and so on. Whatever their title, the point remains to make the concessions binding by putting them in a written, public agreement but to do so in such a way as to make them less likely to attract attention and easier to play down for those obliged to grant them. Numerous side letters – exchanges of correspondence which are figuratively speaking placed at the 'side' of the main documents – were published to accompany the two main agreements in the Camp David 'Accords' of September 1978 and the Egypt–Israel Peace Treaty of the following March. While most of these served purposes other than face-saving,[7] some existed for precisely this reason. These included the anodyne restatements of existing positions on the incendiary question of the status of Jerusalem. The Egyptians wanted the matter dealt with in side letters to obscure the fact that they had made no progress on the issue, while the Israelis happily concurred in order to obscure the fact that they had been prepared to talk about it at all (Carter, 1982, pp. 395, 397–9; Vance, 1983, pp. 225–6). The latter even persuaded the Americans not to restate the substance of their position on East Jerusalem, which was that it was occupied territory, and merely to state in their own letter that their position remained that outlined in statements by two former American ambassadors to the United Nations (Quandt, 1986, p. 252).

It should be added, though, that tucking sensitive matters away in documentary appendages to the main agreement has at least two disadvantages. First, in a complex and tense negotiation under great pressure of time, there is more chance of a slip-up. It is, for example, inconceivable that the damaging failure of the Americans in September 1978 to secure unambiguous written Israeli agreement to a freeze on new settlements in the West Bank and Gaza until the autonomy negotiations had been concluded could have occurred had this issue been addressed in the general framework accord rather than by means of a side letter which, in the event, the Israelis never signed (Vance, 1983, p. 228). Secondly, it can subsequently be claimed that ancillary documents do not have 'the same value' as the main text of an agreement, which is what in March 1979 Israeli premier, Menachem Begin, alleged of the side letter of 17 September 1978 from Sadat to Carter in which the Egyptian president indicated his readiness to negotiate on the West Bank and Gaza on behalf of the Palestinians in the event of a refusal by Jordan to assume this responsibility (Quandt, 1986, pp. 299, 386–7).[8]

Euphemisms

It is notorious that politicians who live by the vote also live by the euphemism, and that the more difficult the position in which they find themselves the more inventive in this regard they become. This is rarely an edifying spectacle. In diplomacy, however, the use of euphemisms is more defensible. Indeed, in the description of concessions, the use of words or expressions which are more palatable to the party which has made them is another face-saving feature of almost all politically sensitive international agreements, though at some price in terms of accuracy.

For example, in the Geneva Accords on Afghanistan referred to earlier, in which Soviet sensitivities on the issue of the withdrawal of their troops were so solicitously addressed by confining the relevant provisions to the small print, the risk of humiliating the Kremlin was further reduced by the complete absence of any reference whatever to the withdrawal of 'Soviet' troops. What were to be withdrawn instead were 'foreign' troops. It might be added, too, that the agreement containing the provisions on 'foreign troop' withdrawals was headed by a title which was itself a masterpiece of obscurity: 'Agreement on the Interrelationships for the Settlement of the Situation relating to Afghanistan' (Berridge, 1991, app. 5).

If this example illustrates the fact that euphemistic language can help states to sign agreements providing for the withdrawal of their military forces from situations where their prestige is at stake, others can be found to demonstrate its usefulness where they are being bought off, that is, induced to surrender some principled position by cash or payment in kind. It is, for example, perfectly obvious that rich states negotiating with poorer ones often find it possible to smooth the road to an agreement by discreetly handing over extremely large amounts of money. Since, however, it would be humiliating to the poorer state if this were to be too obvious, and not present the richer one in an especially flattering light either, these large amounts of money are never called 'large amounts of money'. Instead, they are called 'reconstruction aid', for example, which is what the Americans called the large amounts of money which they repeatedly offered to the North Vietnamese from as early as April 1965 to encourage them to negotiate an end to the Vietnam War and which were finally referred to – coyly and briefly – in Article 21 of the peace settlement of January 1973. The North Vietnamese, of course, wanted to call them 'reparations' (Kissinger, 1982, pp. 37–43).

'Separate but related' agreements

Where an agreement is based on linkage, it may be necessary to obscure this as much as possible, especially if one party has for years prior to the settlement insisted that it would have nothing to do with any such deal. This had been the position of the Angolans and their supporters (more the latter) in regard to the proposal that South Africa would withdraw from Namibia if Cuba would withdraw from Angola. Linkage is deeply offensive to those who believe that issues should be resolved 'on their merits'. It is thus significant that when a settlement of the south-west African imbroglio was achieved at the end of 1988 – which was, of course, based on this linkage – it was embodied not in one but in two agreements: one on Namibian independence and one on the withdrawal of Cuban troops from

Angola. Moreover, South Africa was not even presented as a party to the latter and so, obviously, did not sign it (Berridge, 1989).

The same device had been employed in the Camp David Accords a decade earlier, in which the draft Egypt–Israel peace treaty was presented as one of two 'Accords' published simultaneously, the other being a much more general 'Framework for Peace in the Middle East', the nub of which dealt with the West Bank and Gaza. Having the two 'related' in this way satisfied the Egyptian president, who was anxious to preserve his position that progress on the Egypt–Israel front was linked to progress on the Palestinian question. Having them nevertheless 'separated' in the text satisfied the Israeli prime minister, who was even more anxious to avoid the suggestion that progress in bilateral relations was conditional on any such thing (Quandt, 1986, pp. 211, 230).

SUMMARY

The form taken by diplomatic agreements, especially those giving expession to settlements of great political sensitivity, is often of considerable significance. When creating an international legal obligation is at a premium, the parties to an agreement will want to package it as a 'treaty', that is, write it out and give a copy to the UN. If they want to draw attention to it as well, they may go so far as to call it a 'Treaty'. If the press of business is great and their agreement is not so important, they will readily settle for an informal agreement such as an Exchange of Notes, which may or may not be published and which, therefore, may or may not be a treaty. If saving face is at a premium, the parties to an agreement can resort to any number of expedients, the tactical purposes of which are to obscure and minimise the most sensitive concessions. This is not disreputable; it is a significant part of the honourable art of negotiation.

NOTES

1. For detailed treatment of these generally, see Gore-Booth, 1979, Book IV.
2. However, it should be noted that, as the Foreign Relations Committee of the US Senate has complained, 'trivial agreements', including one to

regulate shrimp fishing off the coast of Brazil, have been sent to the Senate as treaties while much more important ones have been classified as executive agreements and thus withheld (Franck and Weisband, 1979, p. 145). This has been done presumably in an (extremely transparent) attempt to make the Senate feel that its constitutional prerogatives in foreign policy-making have not been entirely ignored; see the discussion of executive agreements below.

3. The characteristic treaty has a descriptive title; a preamble, including the names and titles of the High Contracting Parties (if in heads of state form), the general purpose of the agreement, the names and official designations of the plenipotentiaries, and an affirmation that the latter have produced their full powers, etc.; the various substantive articles, which are numbered I, II, etc., commonly begin with definitions, and usually lead from the general to the more specific; the final clauses, which deal with matters such as the extent of application of the treaty, signature, ratification, accession by other parties, entry into force, duration and provision for renewal; a clause stating 'in witness whereof' the undersigned plenipotentiaries have signed this treaty; indication of the place where the treaty is signed, together with the authentic language or languages of the text, and date of signature; and finally the seals and signatures of the plenipotentiaries (Gore-Booth, 1979, pp. 240–1; Grenville and Wasserstein, 1987, p. 13).

4. It is no doubt in part because they did not intend to provide genuine guarantees of the Geneva Accords on Afghanistan of 14 April 1988 that the United States and the Soviet Union styled their agreement of the same date on this subject as a '*Declaration* on International Guarantees' (Berridge, 1991, pp. 65, 66, 146).

5. Generally speaking, 'Final Acts' consist of summaries of the proceedings of an international conference (Gore-Booth, 1979, pp. 260–2). This means, incidentally, that a conference will often produce a treaty or other form of agreement *in addition* to a 'Final Act'. For example, the 1961 Vienna Conference which was the subject of chapter 1 of this book produced not only the 'Vienna Convention on Diplomatic Relations', together with two optional 'protocols', but also a 'Final Act'. As well as summarising the proceedings, this contained the texts of four 'Resolutions Adopted by the Conference', one of which was on special missions.

6. The British view, by contrast, is that a treaty only requires ratification if it is clear that this is the intention of the parties (Shaw, 1991, p. 569), which means that British governments can be more relaxed about using treaties. It should be added, however, that British governments can afford to be more relaxed about this than American governments anyway, since the former exist only to the extent that they command a majority in the ratifying body, namely the House of Commons.

7. Most were designed to reinforce observance of the agreements either by recording key commitments by the main parties (together and singly) in the shape of promises to the American president, or by recording undertakings to one or both of the main parties by the American president, e.g. the US promise to Israel to fund construction of new airfields in the Negev in order to compensate it for surrender of those in Sinai. Since these agreements all involved the United States, which did not wish to be seen as a main party to either the Camp David Accords or the subsequent peace treaty, side letters were clearly appropriate.

8. Begin hoped to persuade the Americans that there was no point in discussing the West Bank at all if the Jordanians refused to take part.

FURTHER READING

Barston, R. P. (1988), *Modern Diplomacy* (Longman: London and New York), ch. 10

Cohen, R. (1991), *Negotiating Across Cultures: Communication Obstacles in International Diplomacy* (US Institute of Peace Press: Washington, D. C.) ch. 9

Franck, T. M. and E. Weisband (1979), *Foreign Policy by Congress* (Oxford University Press: New York and Oxford)

Glennon, M. J. (1983), 'The Senate role in treaty ratification', *American Journal of International Law*, vol. 77

Gore-Booth, Lord (ed) (1979), *Satow's Guide To Diplomatic Practice*, 5th ed (Longman: London and New York)

Grenville, J. A. S. and B. Wasserstein (1987), *The Major International Treaties since 1945: A History and Guide with Texts* (Methuen: London and New York)

Shaw, M. N. (1991), *International Law*, 3rd ed (Grotius: Cambridge)

Wood, J. R. and J. Serres (1970), *Diplomatic Ceremonial and Protocol: Principles, Procedures and Practices* (Macmillan: London), ch. 13

CONCLUSION

Diplomacy consists chiefly of the conduct of international relations by negotiation rather than by force, propaganda or recourse to law. It is an essentially political activity which is itself regulated by custom and international law; it is, in other words, an institution of the system of states. The institutionalisation of diplomacy occurred because of the enduring significance of the balance of power in the European states-system, a balance of power which both instigated and required the reflex of international negotiation.

It is easy to lose sight of the essential character of diplomacy because of the multiplication of channels through which the activity is now conducted and the even greater multiplication in the kinds of people, including political leaders, which it now involves. The present world diplomatic system, which is the term I employ to describe the full panoply of channels and people, has its most recognisable origins in the states-system of the Italian cities of the fifteenth century. During this period the intensification of diplomatic activity made it increasingly obvious that the *nuncii* and plenipotentiaries of the Middle Ages (temporary envoys with more or less limited briefs) would have to be either replaced or supplemented by the establishment of resident embassies at important courts. Developing in Italy, the use of the resident embassy then spread northwards over the Alps and became the key mode of diplomatic activity until the beginning of the twentieth century, during which it was increasingly described as 'bilateral diplomacy' in order to distinguish it from the mode of diplomacy which now presented it with its most serious challenge: 'multilateral diplomacy'.

177

Indeed, multilateral diplomacy, diplomacy conducted in a conference of three or more states, became the hallmark of the world diplomatic system of the twentieth century, even though its own origins go back much earlier and it was already important – at least in Europe – in the nineteenth. It blossomed in the twentieth century under the press of events, the steady increase in the number of states and, among other things, the growing popularity of the liberal-democratic notion that power should rest on consent. The interwar League of Nations and the postwar United Nations, with their crowded assemblies and (in the latter case) majority voting procedures, are the most eloquent testimonies to the twentieth century faith in multilateral diplomacy. Over recent decades, however, against a background in which bilateral diplomacy in the shape of the resident embassy has displayed remarkable tenacity, this faith has been severely tested and there has been evidence of a 'crisis of multilateralism'. Third world states have expressed disillusionment with its results, especially in the economic sphere; the United States, finally reacting savagely to years of having to finance programmes to which it was opposed, began to withhold funds from the UN system; and the number of international organisations began to drop. Nevertheless, there remains little doubt that multilateral diplomacy, which is so valuable when urgent attention has to be given by many parties to a particular question, and when it is important to advertise the fact that this is being done, is here to stay. What has helped to guarantee this is now widespread acceptance that important decisions must be based on consensus.

Summitry, diplomacy conducted with the personal involvement of heads of state or government, often assumes multilateral form. Nevertheless, it has been considered under a separate heading in this book because it is diplomacy of a special kind and because, in any case, much summit diplomacy is also conducted on a bilateral basis. Professional diplomats have traditionally loathed summitry, and not without reason. The involvement of political leaders in diplomacy tends too often to inject sloppiness where there should be precision, publicity where there should be discretion, ignorance where there should be intimate acquaintance with detail, and personal considerations where there should only be objective consideration of the requirements of the national interest. Nevertheless, summits – especially serial summits – can make a broad contribution to diplomacy as well, not least because of their ability to revive the momentum of a flagging negotiation. Among other examples, the European Council – a serial summit – and the Camp David summit on the Middle East in 1978 – an *ad hoc* summit – provide evidence on just how useful this mode of diplomacy can be.

If summitry can be multilateral, mediation can be conducted at the summit and it is multilateral by definition, as in the Camp David summit just mentioned. There is, in other words, a minimum of three parties involved in a mediation and often many more, both in the ranks of the rival sides and in the ranks of the 'third parties'. (The last is the phenomenon of what I have called 'multiple mediation'.) Mediation, nevertheless, whether conducted at or below the summit, is a distinctive form of multilateral diplomacy, ranging along a continuum from the relatively passive provision of 'good offices' to the parties to a conflict to the relatively active attempt to cajole them to a settlement. Passive mediation, as in the case of Algeria's role in the Iran hostages crisis in 1980–1, requires little power relative to the parties, active mediation, as in the case of the United States in the Angola/Namibia negotiations of 1988, a great deal – though this power need not necessarily, as in the case of the Vatican, be material. The impartiality of the mediator on the issues dividing the parties is normally essential. Mediators, of course, are not always prompted by high-minded considerations and it is not least for this reason that the parties to a conflict are inclined, rather more often than is commonly supposed, to negotiate directly at the first opportunity which they find politically expedient.

The second and final Part of this book dealt with the art of negotiation because, although this is not by any means the only function of diplomacy, it is without doubt the most important. Most negotiations proceed through three stages: pre-negotiations, the formula stage and the details stage. In pre-negotiations it is necessary to agree on the need to negotiate, the agenda, and procedural questions such as the venue of the talks. In pre-negotiations between recently or still warring parties these matters are often so difficult to conclude that it is testimony not only to the pressure generated by a 'hurting stalemate' but also to the sheer professionalism of modern diplomacy that the substantive stages of negotiations are ever reached at all. In the formula stage the broad principles of a settlement are agreed and in the details stage these are fleshed out. The first and last stages are generally the most difficult, though it would seem (this is an area in which more research needs to be done) that this varies significantly with the kind of negotiation and the kind of parties involved. If the momentum of a negotiation falters, even though the parties remain keen to press on, deadlines and other techniques (also generally ignored by modern research) may be employed with some reasonable hope of reviving it. If the momentum is maintained, or – if lost – regained, and if agreement is finally reached, this agreement remains to be 'packaged'. Saving face is often an important consideration here and how this should be achieved is not always straightforward, as noted in the last chapter. As a result, the presentation of any agreement itself provides considerable scope for negotiation.

There is room for optimism about the future of diplomacy. What are the reasons for making this suggestion? For one thing, 'open diplomacy', always a contradiction in terms, is a dead slogan. For another, there is at last broad understanding that majority voting in multilateral meetings is incompatible with a radically unequal distribution of power. There is also now a more accurate appreciation of the enduring value of resident missions for those states which can afford them, and the legal regime under which these missions function has, under the Vienna Convention on Diplomatic Relations, been firmly secured since 1961. Finally, the revolution in telecommunications is making diplomacy a vastly more flexible instrument. It is at least in part against this background that the new states which have emerged from the former Soviet Union have lost no time in creating their own diplomatic services, and that severing diplomatic relations is no longer the crisis reflex which it was in the 1960s and 1970s.

It is as well that there are grounds for optimism about the future of diplomacy because while power remains dispersed between states, while there remains, in other words, a states-system, international diplomacy – bilateral, multilateral, direct or indirect, at the summit or below – remains essential. Only this activity can produce the enormous advantages obtainable from the cooperative pursuit of common interests and prevent violence from being employed to settle remaining arguments over conflicting ones. When violence breaks out nevertheless, diplomacy remains essential if the worst excesses are to be limited and if, in addition, the ground is to be prepared against the inevitable day of exhaustion and revised ambition.

APPENDIX:
THE VIENNA CONVENTION ON
DIPLOMATIC RELATIONS, 1961*

The States Parties to the present Convention,
Recalling that peoples of all nations from ancient times have recognized the status of diplomatic agents,

Having in mind the purposes and principles of the Charter of the United Nations concerning the sovereign equality of States, the maintenance of international peace and security, and the promotion of friendly relations among nations,

Believing that an international convention on diplomatic intercourse, privileges and immunities would contribute to the development of friendly relations among nations, irrespective of their differing constitutional and social systems,

Realizing that the purpose of such privileges and immunities is not to benefit individuals but to ensure the efficient performance of the functions of diplomatic missions as representing States,

Affirming that the rules of customary international law should continue to govern questions not expressly regulated by the provisions of the present Convention,

Have agreed as follows:

Article 1
For the purpose of the present Convention, the following expressions shall have the meanings hereunder assigned to them:
(a) the "head of the mission" is the person charged by the sending State with the duty of acting in that capacity;
(b) the "members of the mission" are the head of the mission and the members of the staff of the mission;

* *United Nations Treaty Series*, vol. 500, p. 96ff.

(c) the "members of the staff of the mission" are the members of the diplomatic staff, of the administrative and technical staff and of the service staff of the mission;

(d) the "members of the diplomatic staff" are the members of the staff of the mission having diplomatic rank;

(e) a "diplomatic agent" is the head of the mission or a member of the diplomatic staff of the mission;

(f) the "members of the administrative and technical staff" are the members of the staff of the mission employed in the administrative and technical service of the mission;

(g) the "members of the service staff" are the members of the staff of the mission in the domestic service of the mission;

(h) a "private servant" is a person who is in the domestic service of a member of the mission and who is not an employee of the sending State;

(i) the "premises of the mission" are the buildings or parts of buildings and the land ancillary thereto, irrespective of ownership, used for the purposes of the mission including the residence of the head of the mission.

Article 2

The establishment of diplomatic relations between States, and of permanent diplomatic missions, takes place by mutual consent.

Article 3

1. The functions of a diplomatic mission consist *inter alia* in:

(a) representing the sending State in the receiving State;

(b) protecting in the receiving State the interests of the sending State and of its nationals, within the limits permitted by international law;

(c) negotiating with the Government of the receiving State;

(d) ascertaining by all lawful means conditions and developments in the receiving state, and reporting thereon to the Government of the sending State;

(e) promoting friendly relations between the sending State and the receiving State, and developing their economic, cultural and scientific relations.

2. Nothing in the present Convention shall be construed as preventing the performance of consular functions by a diplomatic mission.

Article 4

1. The sending State must make certain that the *agrément* of the receiving State has been given for the person it proposes to accredit as head of the mission to that State.

2. The receiving State is not obliged to give reasons to the sending State for a refusal of *agrément*.

Article 5

1. The sending State may, after it has given due notification to the receiving State concerned, accredit a head of mission or assign any member of the diplomatic staff, as the case may be, to more than one State, unless there is express objection by any of the receiving States.

2. If the sending State accredits a head of mission to one or more other States it may establish a diplomatic mission headed by a chargé d'affaires ad interim in each State where the head of mission has not his permanent seat.

3. A head of mission or any member of the diplomatic staff of the mission may act as representative of the sending State to any international organization.

Article 6

Two or more States may accredit the same person as head of mission to another State, unless objection is offered by the receiving State.

Article 7

Subject to the provisions of Articles 5, 8, 9 and 11, the sending State may freely appoint the members of the staff of the mission. In the case of military, naval or air attachés, the receiving State may require their names to be submitted beforehand, for its approval.

Article 8

1. Members of the diplomatic staff of the mission should in principle be of the nationality of the sending State.

2. Members of the diplomatic staff of the mission may not be appointed from among persons having the nationality of the receiving State, except with the consent of that State which may be withdrawn at any time.

3. The receiving State may reserve the same right with regard to nationals of a third State who are not also nationals of the sending State.

Article 9

1. The receiving State may at any time and without having to explain its decision, notify the sending State that the head of the mission or any member of the diplomatic staff of the mission is *persona non grata* or that any other member of the staff of the mission is not acceptable. In any such case, the sending State shall, as appropriate, either recall the person concerned or terminate his functions with the mission. A person may be declared *non grata* or not acceptable before arriving in the territory of the receiving State.

2. If the sending State refuses or fails within a reasonable period to carry out its obligations under paragraph 1 of this Article, the receiving State may refuse to recognize the person concerned as a member of the mission.

Article 10

1. The Ministry for Foreign Affairs of the receiving State, or such other ministry as may be agreed, shall be notified of:

(a) the appointment of members of the mission, their arrival and their final departure or the termination of their functions with the mission;

(b) the arrival and final departure of a person belonging to the family of a member of the mission and, where appropriate, the fact that a person becomes or ceases to be a member of the family of a member of the mission;

(c) the arrival and final departure of private servants in the employ of persons referred to in sub-paragraph (a) of this paragraph and, where appropriate, the fact that they are leaving the employ of such persons;

(d) the engagement and discharge of persons resident in the receiving State as members of the mission or private servants entitled to privileges and immunities.

2. Where possible, prior notification of arrival and final departure shall also be given.

Article 11

1. In the absence of specific agreement as to the size of the mission, the receiving State may require that the size of a mission be kept within limits considered by it to be reasonable and normal, having regard to circumstances and conditions in the receiving State and to the needs of the particular mission.

2. The receiving State may equally, within similar bounds and on a non-discriminatory basis, refuse to accept officials of a particular category.

Article 12

The sending State may not, without the prior express consent of the receiving State, establish offices forming part of the mission in localities other than those in which the mission itself is established.

Article 13

1. The head of the mission is considered as having taken up his functions in the receiving State either when he has presented his credentials or when he has notified his arrival and a true copy of his credentials has been presented to the Ministry for Foreign Affairs of the receiving State, or such other ministry as may be agreed, in accordance with the practice prevailing in the receiving State which shall be applied in a uniform manner.

2. The order of presentation of credentials or of a true copy thereof will be determined by the date and time of the arrival of the head of the mission.

Article 14

1. Heads of mission are divided into three classes, namely:
(a) that of ambassadors or nuncios accredited to Heads of State, and other heads of mission of equivalent rank;
(b) that of envoys, ministers and internuncios accredited to Heads of State;
(c) that of chargé d'affairs accredited to Ministers of Foreign Affairs.

2. Except as concerns precedence and etiquette, there shall be no differentiation between heads of mission by reason of their class.

Article 15

The class to which the heads of their missions are to be assigned shall be agreed between States.

Article 16

1. Heads of mission shall take precedence in their respective classes in the order of the date and time of taking up their functions in accordance with Article 13.

2. Alterations in the credentials of a head of mission not involving any change of class shall not affect his precedence.

3. This article is without prejudice to any practice accepted by the receiving State regarding the precedence of the representative of the Holy See.

Article 17

The precedence of the members of the diplomatic staff of the mission shall be notified by the head of the mission to the Ministry for Foreign Affairs or such other ministry as may be agreed.

Article 18

The procedure to be observed in each State for the reception of heads of mission shall be uniform in respect of each class.

Article 19

1. If the post of head of the mission is vacant, or if the head of the mission is unable to perform his functions, a chargé d'affaires ad interim shall act provisionally as head of the mission. The name of the chargé d'affaires ad interim shall be notified, either by the head of the mission or, in case he is unable to do so, by the Ministry for Foreign Affairs of the sending State to the Ministry for Foreign Affairs of the receiving State or such other ministry as may be agreed.

2. In cases where no member of the diplomatic staff of the mission is present in the receiving State, a member of the administrative and technical staff may, with the consent of the receiving State, be designated by the sending State to be in charge of the current administrative affairs of the mission.

Article 20

The mission and its head shall have the right to use the flag and emblem of the sending State on the premises of the mission, including the residence of the head of the mission, and on his means of transport.

Article 21

1. The receiving State shall either facilitate the acquisition on its territory, in accordance with its laws, by the sending State of premises necessary for its mission or assist the latter in obtaining accommodation in some other way.

2. It shall also, where necessary, assist missions in obtaining suitable accommodation for their members.

Article 22

1. The premises of the mission shall be inviolable. The agents of the receiving State may not enter them, except with the consent of the head of the mission.

2. The receiving State is under a special duty to take all appropriate steps to protect the premises of the mission against any intrusion or damage and to prevent any disturbance of the peace of the mission or impairment of its dignity.

3. The premises of the mission, their furnishings and other property thereon and the means of transport of the mission shall be immune from search, requisition, attachment or execution.

Article 23

1. The sending State and the head of the mission shall be exempt from all national, regional or municipal dues and taxes in respect of the premises of the mission, whether owned or leased, other than such as represent payment for specific services rendered.

2. The exemption from taxation referred to in this Article shall not apply to such dues and taxes payable under the law of the receiving State by persons contracting with the sending State or the head of the mission.

Article 24

The archives and documents of the mission shall be inviolable at any time and wherever they may be.

Article 25

The receiving State shall accord full facilities for the performance of the functions of the mission.

Article 26

Subject to its laws and regulations concerning zones entry into which is prohibited or regulated for reasons of national security, the receiving State shall ensure to all members of the mission freedom of movement and travel in its territory.

Article 27

1. The receiving State shall permit and protect free communication on the part of the mission for all official purposes. In communicating with the Government and the other missions and consulates of the sending State, wherever situated, the mission may employ all appropriate means, including diplomatic couriers and messages in code or cipher. However, the mission may install and use a wireless transmitter only with the consent of the receiving State.

2. The official correspondence of the mission shall be inviolable. Official correspondence means all correspondence relating to the mission and its functions.

3. The diplomatic bag shall not be opened or detained.

4. The packages constituting the diplomatic bag must bear visible external marks of their character and may contain only diplomatic documents or articles intended for official use.

5. The diplomatic courier, who shall be provided with an official document indicating his status and the number of packages constituting the diplomatic bag, shall be protected by the receiving State in the performance of his functions. He shall enjoy personal inviolability and shall not be liable to any form of arrest or detention.

6. The sending State or the mission may designate diplomatic couriers *ad hoc*. In such cases the provisions of paragraph 5 of this Article shall also apply, except that the immunities therein mentioned shall cease to apply when such a courier has delivered to the consignee the diplomatic bag in his charge.

7. A diplomatic bag may be entrusted to the captain of a commercial aircraft scheduled to land at an authorized port of entry. He shall be provided with an official document indicating the number of packages constituting the bag but he shall not be considered to be a diplomatic courier. The mission may send one of its members to take possession of the diplomatic bag directly and freely from the captain of the aircraft.

Article 28

The fees and charges levied by the mission in the course of its official duties shall be exempt from all dues and taxes.

Article 29

The person of a diplomatic agent shall be inviolable. He shall not be liable to any form of arrest or detention. The receiving State shall treat him with due respect and shall take all appropriate steps to prevent any attack on his person, freedom or dignity.

Article 30

1. The private residence of a diplomatic agent shall enjoy the same inviolability and protection as the premises of the mission.

2. His papers, correspondence and, except as provided in paragraph 3 of Article 31, his property, shall likewise enjoy inviolability.

Article 31

1. A diplomatic agent shall enjoy immunity from the criminal jurisdiction of the receiving State. He shall also enjoy immunity from its civil and administrative jurisdiction, except in the case of:

(a) a real action relating to private immovable property situated in the territory of the receiving State, unless he holds it on behalf of the sending State for the purposes of the mission;

(b) an action relating to succession in which the diplomatic agent is involved as executor, administrator, heir or legatee as a private person and not on behalf of the sending State;

(c) an action relating to any professional or commercial activity exercised by the diplomatic agent in the receiving State outside his official functions.

2. A diplomatic agent is not obliged to give evidence as a witness.

3. No measures of execution may be taken in respect of a diplomatic agent except in the cases coming under sub-paragraphs (a), (b) and (c) of paragraph 1 of this Article, and provided that the measures concerned can be taken without infringing the inviolability of his person or of his residence.

4. The immunity of a diplomatic agent from the jurisdiction of the receiving State does not exempt him from the jurisdiction of the sending State.

Article 32

1. The immunity from jurisdiction of diplomatic agents and of persons enjoying immunity under Article 37 may be waived by the sending State.

2. Waiver must always be express.

3. The initiation of proceedings by a diplomatic agent or by a person enjoying immunity from jurisdiction under Article 37 shall

preclude him from invoking immunity from jurisdiction in respect of any counter-claim directly connected with the principal claim.

4. Waiver of immunity from jurisdiction in respect of civil or administrative proceedings shall not be held to imply waiver of immunity in respect of the execution of the judgement, for which a separate waiver shall be necessary.

Article 33

1. Subject to the provisions of paragraph 3 of this Article, a diplomatic agent shall with respect to services rendered for the sending State be exempt from social security provisions which may be in force in the receiving State.

2. The exception provided for in paragraph 1 of this Article shall also apply to private servants who are in the sole employ of a diplomatic agent, on condition:

(a) that they are not nationals of or permanently resident in the receiving State; and

(b) that they are covered by the social security provisions which may be in force in the sending State or a third State.

3. A diplomatic agent who employs persons to whom the exemption provided for in paragraph 2 of this Article does not apply shall observe the obligations which the social security provisions of the receiving State impose upon employers.

4. The exemption provided for in paragraphs 1 and 2 of this Article shall not preclude voluntary participation in the social security system of the receiving State provided that such participation is permitted by that State.

5. The provisions of this Article shall not affect bilateral or multilateral agreements concerning social security concluded previously and shall not prevent the conclusion of such agreements in the future.

Article 34

A diplomatic agent shall be exempt from all dues and taxes, personal or real, national, regional or municipal, except:

(a) indirect taxes of a kind which are normally incorporated in the price of the goods or services;

(b) dues and taxes on private immovable property situated in the territory of the receiving State, unless he holds it on behalf of the sending State for the purpose of the mission;

(c) estate, succession or inheritance duties levied by the receiving State, subject to the provisions of paragraph 4 of Article 39;

(d) dues and taxes on private income having its source in the receiving State and capital taxes on investments made in commercial undertakings in the receiving State;

(e) charges levied for specific services rendered;

(f) registration, court or record fees, mortgage dues and stamp duty, with respect to immovable property, subject to the provisions of Article 23.

Article 35

The receiving State shall exempt diplomatic agents from all personal services, from all public service of any kind whatsoever, and from military obligations such as those connected with requisitioning, military contributions and billeting.

Article 36

1. The receiving State shall, in accordance with such laws and regulations as it may adopt, permit entry of and grant exemption from all customs duties, taxes, and related charges other than charges for storage, cartage and similar services, on:

(a) articles for the official use of the mission;

(b) articles for the personal use of a diplomatic agent or members of his family forming part of his household, including articles intended for his establishment.

2. The personal baggage of a diplomatic agent shall be exempt from inspection, unless there are serious grounds for presuming that it contains articles not covered by the exemptions mentioned in paragraph 1 of this Article, or articles the import or export of which is prohibited by the law or controlled by the quarantine regulations of the receiving State. Such inspection shall be conducted only in the presence of the diplomatic agent or of his authorized representative.

Article 37

1. The members of the family of a diplomatic agent forming part of his household staff, if they are not nationals of the receiving State, enjoy the privileges and immunities specified in Articles 29 to 36.

2. Members of the administrative and technical staff of the mission, together with members of their families forming part of their respective households, shall, if they are not nationals of or

permanently resident in the receiving State, enjoy the privileges and immunities specified in Articles 29 to 35, except that the immunity from civil and administrative jurisdiction of the receiving State specified in paragraph 1 of Article 31 shall not extend to acts performed outside the course of their duties. They shall also enjoy the privileges specified in Article 31, paragraph 1, in respect of articles imported at the time of first installation.

3. Members of the service staff of the mission who are not nationals of or permanently resident in the receiving State shall enjoy immunity in respect of acts performed in the course of their duties, exemption from dues and taxes on the emoluments they receive by reason of their employment and the exemption contained in Article 33.

4. Private servants of members of the mission shall, if they are not nationals of or permanently resident in the receiving State, be exempt from dues and taxes on the emoluments they receive by reason of their employment. In other respects, they may enjoy privileges and immunities only to the extent admitted by the receiving State. However, the receiving State must exercise its jurisdiction over those persons in such manner as not to interfere unduly with the performance of the functions of the mission.

Article 38

1. Except insofar as additional privileges and immunities may be granted by the receiving State, a diplomatic agent who is a national of or permanently resident in that State shall enjoy only immunity from jurisdiction, and inviolability, in respect of official acts performed in the exercise of his functions.

2. Other members of the staff of the mission and private servants who are nationals of or permanently resident in the receiving State shall enjoy privileges and immunities only to the extent admitted by the receiving State. However, the receiving State must exercise its jurisdiction over those persons in such a manner as not to interfere unduly with the performance of the functions of the mission.

Article 39

1. Every person entitled to privileges and immunities shall enjoy them from the moment he enters the territory of the receiving State on proceeding to take up his post or, if already in its territory, from

the moment when his appointment is notified to the Ministry for Foreign Affairs or such other ministry as may be agreed.

2. When functions of a person enjoying privileges and immunities have come to an end, such privileges and immunities shall normally cease at the moment when he leaves the country, or on expiry of a reasonable period in which to do so, but shall subsist until that time, even in case of armed conflict. However, with respect to acts performed by such a person in the exercise of his functions as a member of the mission, immunity shall continue to subsist.

3. In case of death of a member of the mission, the members of his family shall continue to enjoy the privileges and immunities to which they are entitled until the expiry of a reasonable period in which to leave the country.

4. In the event of the death of a member of the mission not a national of or permanently resident in the receiving State or a member of his family forming part of his household, the receiving State shall permit the withdrawal of the movable property of the deceased, with the exception of any property acquired in the country the export of which was prohibited at the time of his death. Estate, succession and inheritance duties shall not be levied on movable property the presence of which in the receiving State was due solely to the presence there of the deceased as a member of the mission or as a member of the family of a member of the mission.

Article 40

1. If a diplomatic agent passes through or is in the territory of a third State, which has granted him a passport visa if such visa was necessary, while proceeding to take up or return to his post, or when returning to his own country, the third State shall accord him inviolability and such other immunities as may be required to ensure his transit or return. The same shall apply in the case of any members of his family enjoying privileges or immunities who are accompanying the diplomatic agent, or travelling separately to join him or return to their country.

2. In circumstances similar to those specified in paragraph 1 of this Article, third States shall not hinder the passage of members of the administrative and technical or service staff of a mission, and of members of their families, through their territories.

3. Third States shall accord to official correspondence and other official communications in transit, including messages in code or

cipher, the same freedom and protection as is accorded by the receiving State. They shall accord to diplomatic couriers, who have been granted a passport visa if such visa was necessary, and diplomatic bags in transit the same inviolability and protection as the receiving State is bound to accord.

4. The obligations of third States under paragraphs 1, 2 and 3 of this Article shall also apply to the persons mentioned respectively in those paragraphs, and to official communications and diplomatic bags, whose presence in the territory of the third State is due to *force majeur*.

Article 41

1. Without prejudice to their privileges and immunities, it is the duty of all persons enjoying such privileges and immunities to respect the laws and regulations of the receiving State. They also have a duty not to interfere in the internal affairs of that State.

2. All official business with the receiving State entrusted to the mission by the sending State shall be conducted with or through the Ministry for Foreign Affairs of the receiving State or such other ministry as may be agreed.

3. The premises of the mission must not be used in any manner incompatible with the functions of the mission as laid down in the present Convention or by other rules of general international law or by any special agreements in force between the sending and the receiving State.

Article 42

A diplomatic agent shall not in the receiving State practise for personal profit any professional or commercial activity.

Article 43

The function of a diplomatic agent comes to an end, *inter alia*:
(a) on notification by the sending State to the receiving State that the function of the diplomatic agent has come to an end;
(b) on notification by the receiving State to the sending State that, in accordance with paragraph 2 of Article 9, it refuses to recognize the diplomatic agent as a member of the mission.

Article 44

The receiving State must, even in case of armed conflict, grant facilities in order to enable persons enjoying privileges and immunities, other than nationals of the receiving State, and members of the families of such persons irrespective of their nationality, to leave at the earliest possible moment. It must, in particular, in case of need, place at their disposal the necessary means of transport for themselves and their property.

Article 45

If diplomatic relations are broken off between two States, or if a mission is permanently or temporarily recalled:
(a) the receiving State must, even in case of armed conflict, respect and protect the premises of the mission, together with its property and archives;
(b) the sending State may entrust the custody of the premises of the mission, together with its property and archives, to a third State acceptable to the receiving State;
(c) the sending State may entrust the protection of its interests and those of its nationals to a third State acceptable to the receiving State.

Article 46

A sending State may with the prior consent of a receiving State, and at the request of a third State not represented in the receiving State, undertake the temporary protection of the interests of the third State and of its nationals.

Article 47

1. In the application of the provisions of the present Convention, the receiving State shall not discriminate as between States.

2. However, discrimination shall not be regarded as taking place:
(a) where the receiving State applies any of the provisions of the present Convention restrictively because of a restrictive application of that provision to its mission in the sending State;
(b) where by custom or agreement States extend to each other more favourable treatment than is required by the provisions of the present Convention.

Article 48

The present Convention shall be open for signature by all States Members of the United Nations or of any of the specialized agencies or Parties to the Statute of the International Court of Justice, and by any other State invited by the General Assembly of the United Nations to become a Party to the Convention, as follows: until 31 October 1961 at the Federal Ministry for Foreign Affairs of Austria and subsequently, until 31 March 1962, at the United Nations Headquarters in New York.

Article 49

The present Convention is subject to ratification. The instruments of ratification shall be deposited with the Secretary-General of the United Nations.

Article 50

The present Convention shall remain open for accession by any State belonging to any of the four categories mentioned in Article 48. The instruments of accession shall be deposited with the Secretary-General of the United Nations.

Article 51

1. The present Convention shall enter into force on the thirtieth day following the date of deposit of the twenty-second instrument of ratification or accession with the Secretary-General of the United Nations.

2. For each State ratifying or acceding to the Convention after the deposit of the twenty-second instrument of ratification or accession, the Convention shall enter into force on the thirtieth day after deposit by such State of its instrument of ratification or accession.

Article 52

The Secretary-General of the United Nations shall inform all States belonging to any of the four categories mentioned in Article 48:

(a) of signatures to the present Convention and of the deposit of instruments of ratification or accession, in accordance with Articles 48, 49 and 50;

(b) of the date on which the present Convention will enter into force, in accordance with Article 51.

Article 53

The original of the present Convention, of which the Chinese, English, French, Russian and Spanish texts are equally authentic, shall be deposited with the Secretary-General of the United Nations, who shall send certified copies thereof to all States belonging to any of the four categories mentioned in Article 48.

IN WITNESS WHEREOF the undersigned Plenipotentiaries, being duly authorized thereto by their respective Governments, have signed the present Convention.

DONE at Vienna, this eighteenth day of April one thousand nine hundred and sixty-one.

REFERENCES

Acheson, D. (1969), *Present at the Creation: My Years in the State Department* (Norton: New York)

Adelman, K. L. (1989), *The Great Universal Embrace: Arms Summitry – A Skeptic's View* (Simon and Schuster: New York)

Anderson, M. S. (1993), *The Rise of Modern Diplomacy* (Longman: London and New York)

Armstrong, D. (1982), *The Rise of the International Organization: A Short History* (Macmillan: London)

Aurisch, K. L. (1989), 'The art of preparing a multilateral conference', *Negotiation Journal*, vol. 5, no. 3

Bailey, S. D. (1988), *The Procedure of the UN Security Council*, 2nd ed (Clarendon Press: Oxford)

Ball, G. (1976), *Diplomacy for a Crowded World* (Bodley Head: London)

Ball, G. (1982), *The Past has Another Pattern* (Norton: New York)

Barston, R. P. (1988), *Modern Diplomacy* (Longman: London and New York)

Berridge, G. R. and A. Jennings (eds) (1985), *Diplomacy at the UN* (Macmillan: London)

Berridge, G. R. (1987), *The Politics of the South Africa Run: European Shipping and Pretoria* (Clarendon Press: Oxford)

Berridge, G. R. (1989), 'Diplomacy and the Angola/Namibia Accords, December 1988', *International Affairs*, vol. 65, no. 3

Berridge, G. R. (1991), *Return to the UN: UN Diplomacy in Regional Conflicts* (Macmillan: London)

Berridge, G. R. (1992a), *South Africa, the Colonial Powers and 'African Defence': The Rise and Fall of the White Entente, 1948–60* (Macmillan: London)

Berridge, G. R. (1992b), *International Politics: States, Power and Conflict since 1945*, 2nd ed (Harvester Wheatsheaf: Hemel Hempstead)

198

Berridge, G. R. (1992c), 'The Cyprus negotiations: divided responsibility and other problems', *Leicester Discussion Papers in Politics*, no. P92/7

Berridge, G. R. (1994), *Talking to the Enemy: How States without 'Diplomatic Relations' Communicate* (Macmillan: London)

Binnendijk, H. (ed) (1987), *National Negotiating Styles* (Center for the Study of Foreign Affairs, Foreign Service Institute, US Department of State: Washington, D.C.)

Blancké, W. W. (1969), *The Foreign Service of the United States* (Praeger: New York)

Blumay, C. and H. Edwards (1992), *The Dark Side of Power* (Simon and Schuster: New York)

Boutros-Ghali, B. (1992), *An Agenda for Peace: Preventive Diplomacy, Peacemaking and Peacekeeping* (United Nations: New York)

Bower, D. (1994), 'Summit and symbol: Franco-German relations and diplomacy at the top', unpubl. dissertation (University of Leicester)

Bradshaw, K. and D. Pring (1973), *Parliament and Congress* (Quartet: London)

Brown, J. (1988), 'Diplomatic immunity – state practice under the Vienna Convention', *International and Comparative Law Quarterly*, vol. 37

Brzezinski, Z. (1970), 'The diplomat is an anachronism', *The Washington Post*, 5 July

Brzezinski, Z. (1983), *Power and Principle: Memoirs of the National Security Advisor 1977–1981* (Farrar, Straus, Giroux: New York)

Bull, H. (1977), *The Anarchical Society: A Study of Order in World Politics* (Macmillan: London)

Bulmer, S. and W. Wessels (1987), *The European Council: Decision-making in European Politics* (Macmillan: London)

Buzan, B. (1981), 'Negotiating by consensus: developments in technique at the United Nations Conference on the Law of the Sea', *American Journal of International Law*, vol. 72, no. 2

Cahier, P. (1961), 'Vienna Convention on Diplomatic Relations', *International Conciliation*, no. 571

Callaghan, J. (1987), *Time and Chance* (Collins: London)

Callières, F. de (1983), *The Art of Diplomacy*, ed by H. M. A. Keens-Soper and K. Schweizer (Leicester University Press: Leicester)

Carter, J. (1982), *Keeping Faith: Memoirs of a President* (Bantam: New York and London)

Central Policy Review Staff (1977), *Review of Overseas Representation* ['The Berrill Report'] (HMSO: London)

Christopher, W. and others (1985), *American Hostages in Iran: The Conduct of a Crisis* (Yale University Press: New Haven and London)

Cohen, R. (1987), *Theatre of Power: The Art of Diplomatic Signalling* (Longman: London and New York)

Cohen, R. (1991), *Negotiating across Cultures: Communication Obstacles in International Diplomacy* (US Institute of Peace Press: Washington, D.C.)

Cradock, P. (1994), *Experiences of China* (Murray: London)

Crocker, C. A. (1992), *High Noon in Southern Africa: Making Peace in a Rough Neighbourhood* (Norton: New York and London)

De Magalhães, J. C. (1988), trsl. by B. F. Pereira, *The Pure Concept of Diplomacy* (Greenwood: New York)

Denza, E. (1976), *Diplomatic Law: Commentary on the Vienna Convention on Diplomatic Relations* (Oceana: Dobbs Ferry, New York; The British Institute of International and Comparative Law: London)

Department of State Bulletin (1981), 'Presidents abroad', vol. 81, no. 2054

Dickie, J. (1992), *Inside the Foreign Office* (Chapmans: London)

Dimbleby, D. and D. Reynolds (1988), *An Ocean Apart: The Relationship between Britain and America in the Twentieth Century* (Hodder and Stoughton: London)

Donelan, M. (1969), 'The trade of diplomacy', *International Affairs*, vol. 45, no. 4

Ducci, R. (1980), 'Bidding a Fond Farewell to The Career', *The Times*, 14 January

Eban, A. (1977), *Abba Eban: An Autobiography* (Random House: New York)

Eban, A. (1983), *The New Diplomacy: International Affairs in the Modern Age* (Weidenfeld and Nicolson: London)

Edwards, R. D. (1994), *True Brits: Inside the Foreign Office* (BBC Books: London)

Eubank, K. (1966), *The Summit Conferences, 1919–1960* (University of Oklahoma Press: Norman, Oklahoma)

Far Eastern Economic Review (1989), 12 January

Fennessy, J. G. (1976), 'The 1975 Convention on the Representation of States in their Relations with International Organizations of a Universal Character', *American Journal of International Law*, vol. 70, no. 1

Financial Times (1994), 20 September

Fleming, P. (1959), *The Siege at Peking* (Rupert Hart-Davis: London)

Foreign & Commonwealth Office (1994), *The Diplomatic Service List 1994* (HMSO: London)

Franck, T. M. and E. Weisband (1979), *Foreign Policy by Congress* (Oxford University Press: New York and Oxford)

Gilbert, F. (1953), 'Two British Ambassadors: Perth and Henderson', in Craig, G. and F. Gilbert (eds), *The Diplomats, 1919–1939* (Princeton University Press: Princeton, New Jersey)

Gladwyn, Lord (1972), *The Memoirs of Lord Gladwyn* (Weidenfeld and Nicolson: London)

Glennon, M. J. (1983), 'The Senate role in treaty ratification' *American Journal of International Law*, vol. 77

Golan, M. (1976), *The Secret Conversations of Henry Kissinger: Step-by-Step Diplomacy in the Middle East* (Quadrangle: New York)

Gore-Booth, P. (1974), *With Great Truth and Respect* (Constable: London)

Gore-Booth, Lord (ed) (1979), *Satow's Guide to Diplomatic Practice*, 5th ed (Longman: London and New York)

Grenville, J. A. S. and B. Wasserstein (1987), *The Major International Treaties Since 1945: A History and Guide with Texts* (Methuen: London and New York)

Gross-Stein, J. (ed) (1989), *Getting to the Table: The Process of International Pre-negotiation* (Johns Hopkins University Press: Baltimore)

Haass, R. N. (1988), 'Ripeness and the settlement of international disputes', *Survival*, May/June

Hale, J. B. (1957), 'International relations in the West: diplomacy and war', in Potter, G. R. (ed), *The New Cambridge Modern History*, I (Cambridge University Press: Cambridge)

Hall, R. (1987), *My Life with Tiny: A Biography of Tiny Rowland* (Faber: London)

Hall, R. (1992), 'Private Diplomats: Tiny in Africa', *The Economist*, 26 September

Hammer, A. with N. Lyndon (1987), *Hammer: Witness to History* (Simon and Schuster: London)

Hankey, Lord (1946), *Diplomacy by Conference: Studies in Public Affairs, 1920–1946* (Benn: London)

Hardy, M. (1968), *Modern Diplomatic Law* (Manchester University Press: Manchester; Oceana: Dobbs Ferry, New York)

Harrison, S. (1988), 'Inside the Afghan talks', *Foreign Policy*

Hayter, Sir W. (1960), *The Diplomacy of the Great Powers* (Hamilton: London)

Heinrichs, W. H. (1986), *American Ambassador: Joseph C. Grew and the Development of the United States Diplomatic Tradition* (Oxford University Press: New York)

Henderson, N. (1994), *Mandarin: The Diaries of an Ambassador, 1969–1982* (Weidenfeld and Nicolson: London)

Henkin, L. (1979), *How Nations Behave: Law and Foreign Policy*, 2nd ed (Columbia University Press: New York)

Hersh, S. M. (1983), *Kissinger: The Price of Power* (Faber: London)

Hersh, S. M. (1991), *The Samson Option: Israel, America and the Bomb* (Faber: London and Boston)

Herz, F. M. (ed) (1983), *The Consular Dimension of Diplomacy* (Institute for the Study of Diplomacy: Washington)

Hoffmann, S. (1978), *Primacy or World Order: American Foreign Policy since the Cold War* (McGraw-Hill: New York)

The Independent (1988), 17 November

The Independent (1991), 11 October

The Independent (1992a), 18 June

The Independent (1992b), 27 July

The Independent (1994), 11 February

International Legal Materials (1981), vol. 20, p. 224ff

Jackson, G. (1981), *Concorde Diplomacy: The Ambassador's Role in the World Today* (Hamilton: London)

James, A. M. (1980), 'Diplomacy and international society', *International Relations*, vol. 6, no. 6

James, A. M. (1992), 'Diplomatic relations and contacts', *The British Yearbook of International Law 1991* (Clarendon Press: Oxford)

Jenkins, R. (1989), *European Diary, 1977–1981* (Collins: London)

Jenks, C. W. (1965), 'Unanimity, the veto, weighted voting, special and simple majorities and consensus as modes of decision in international organisations', *Cambridge Essays in International Law: Essays in honour of Lord McNair* (Stevens: London; Oceana: Dobbs Ferry, New York)

Keens-Soper, M. (1985), 'The General Assembly reconsidered', in Berridge, G. R. and A. Jennings (eds), *Diplomacy at the UN* (Macmillan: London)

Kennedy, R. T. (1982), 'Role of the U.S. Ambassador', *Department of State Bulletin*, vol. 82, no. 2067

Kerley, E. L. (1962), 'Some aspects of the Vienna Conference on Diplomatic Intercourse and Immunities', *American Journal of International Law*, vol. 56

Kirton, J. J. (1989), 'The significance of the Seven Power Summit', in Hajnal, P. I. (ed), *The Seven Power Summit: Documents from the Summits of the Industrialized Countries 1975–1989* (Kraus: Millwood, New York)

Kirton, J. J. (1991), 'The significance of the Houston Summit', in Hajnal, P. I. (ed), *The Seven Power Summit: Documents from the Summits of the Industrialized Countries. Supplement: Documents from the 1990 Summit* (Kraus: Millwood, New York)

Kissinger, H. A. (1979), *The White House Years* (Weidenfeld and Nicolson and Michael Joseph: London)

Kissinger, H. A. (1982), *Years of Upheaval* (Weidenfeld and Nicolson and Michael Joseph: London)

Langhorne, R. (1981), 'The development of international conferences, 1648–1830', *Studies in History and Politics*, vol. 11, part 2

Langhorne, R. (1992), 'The regulation of diplomatic practice: the beginnings to the Vienna Convention on Diplomatic Relations, 1961', *Review of International Studies*, vol. 18, no. 1

Lawford, V. (1963), *Bound for Diplomacy* (Murray: London)

Lindsley, L. (1987), 'The Beagle Channel settlement: Vatican mediation resolves a century-old dispute', *Journal of Church and State*, vol. 29, no. 3

Lowe, P. (1986), *The Origins of the Korean War* (Longman: London and New York)

Luard, E. (1994), *The United Nations: How It Works and What It Does*, 2nd ed rev. by D. Heater (Macmillan: London)

Lukacs, Y. (ed) (1992), *The Israeli–Palestinian Conflict: A Documentary Record* (Cambridge University Press: Cambridge)

Mattingly, G. (1965), *Renaissance Diplomacy* (Penguin: Harmondsworth)

McGee, G. (1983), *Envoy to the Middle World: Adventures in Diplomacy* (Harper and Row: New York)

Miller, M. (1976), *Plain Speaking: An Oral Biography of Harry S. Truman* (Coronet: London)

Monroe, E. (1963), *Britain's Moment in the Middle East, 1914–1956* (Methuen: London)

Morgenthau, H. J. (1978), *Politics Among Nations: The Struggle for Power and Peace*, 5th ed (Knopf: New York)

Moser, M. J. and Y. W.-C. Moser (1993), *Foreigners within the Gates: The Legations at Peking* (Oxford University Press: Hong Kong, Oxford and New York)

Multilateral Treaties Deposited with the Secretary-General (1993) (UN: New York)

Murphy, R. (1986), *Foreign Relations of the United States, 1955–1957, Vol. II, China* (US Government Printing Office: Washington, D.C.)

Nicholas, H. G. (1975), *The United Nations as a Political Institution*, 2nd ed (Oxford University Press: London and New York)

Nicol, D. (1982), *The United Nations Security Council: Towards Greater Effectiveness* (UNITAR: New York)

Nicolson, H. (1933), *Peacemaking 1919* (Constable: London)

Nicolson, H. (1954), *The Evolution of Diplomatic Method* (Constable: London)

Nicolson, H. (1963), *Diplomacy*, 3rd ed (Oxford University Press: London)

Nixon, R. M. (1979), *The Memoirs of Richard Nixon* (Arrow: London)

Parsons, A. (1984), *The Pride and the Fall: Iran 1974–1979* (Cape: London)

Peters, J. (1994), *Building Bridges: The Arab–Israeli Multilateral Talks* (RIIA: London)

Peterson, M. J. (1986), *The General Assembly in World Politics* (Allen and Unwin: Boston)

Peyrefitte, A. (1993), trsl. by J. Rothschild, *The Collision of Two Civilizations: The British Expedition to China in 1792–4* (Harvill: London)

Platt, D. C. M. (1968), *Finance, Trade and Politics in British Foreign Policy, 1815–1914* (Clarendon Press: Oxford)

Platt, D. C. M. (1971), *The Cinderella Service: British Consuls since 1825* (Longman: London)

Plischke, E. (1974), *Summit Diplomacy: Personal Diplomacy of the United States' Presidents* (Greenwood Press: New York)

Princen, T. (1992), *Intermediaries in International Conflict* (Princeton University Press: Princeton, New Jersey)

Putnam, R. (1984), 'The Western Economic Summits: a political interpretation', in Merlini, C. (ed), *Economic Summits and Western Decision-making* (Croom Helm: London; St. Martin's Press: New York)

Putnam, R. and N. Bayne (1988), *Hanging Together: Cooperation and Conflict in the Seven Power Summits*, 2nd ed (Sage: London)

Quandt, W. B. (1986), *Camp David: Peacemaking and Politics* (Brookings: Washington, D.C.)

Queller, D. E. (1967), *The Office of Ambassador in the Middle Ages* (Princeton University Press: Princeton, New Jersey)

Ragsdale, L. (1993), *Presidential Politics* (Houghton Mifflin: Boston)

Randle, R. F. (1969), *Geneva 1954: The Settlement of the Indochinese War* (Princeton University Press: Princeton, New Jersey)

Review Committee on Overseas Representation (1969), *Report of the Review Commitee on Overseas Representation 1968–1969* ['The Duncan Report'] (HMSO: London)

Roberts, A. and B. Kingsbury (eds) (1993), *United Nations, Divided World* (Clarendon Press: Oxford)

Roosen, W. (1985), 'How good were Louis XIV's diplomats?' in Schweizer, K. and J. Black (eds), *Studies in History and Politics*, no. 4

Safire, W. (1975), *Before the Fall: An Inside View of the Pre-Watergate White House* (Doubleday; New York)

Satow, Sir E. (1922), *A Guide to Diplomatic Practice*, 2nd ed (Longmans: London)

Saunders, H. (1985), 'We need a larger theory of negotiation: the importance of pre-negotiating phases', *Negotiation Journal*, vol. 1

Schlesinger, A. M. Jr. (1965), *A Thousand Days: John F. Kennedy in the White House* (Deutsch: London)

Schmidt, D. L. (1993), 'Members only: authority, efficiency and reform at the UN Security Council', *Leicester Discussion Papers in Politics*, no. P93/1

Scott, J. B. (ed) (1931), *The International Conference of American States 1889–1928* (Oxford University Press: New York)

Seale, P. and M. McConville (1978), *Philby: The Long Road to Moscow*, rev. ed (Penguin: Harmondsworth)

Shaw, M. N. (1991), *International Law*, 3rd ed (Grotius: Cambridge)

Sick, G. (1985), *All Fall Down: America's Fateful Encounter with Iran* (Random House: New York)

Sofer, S. (1988), 'Old and new diplomacy: a debate revisited', *Review of International Studies*, vol. 14

Stadler, K. R. (1981), 'The Kreisky phenomenon', *West European Politics*, vol. 4, no. 1

Stein, J. G. (1989), 'Getting to the table: the triggers, stages, functions, and consequences of pre-negotiations', *International Journal*, vol. 44, no. 2

Sullivan, W. H. (1981), *Mission to Iran* (Norton: New York)

Taylor, P. M. (1992), *War and the Media: Propaganda and Persuasion in the Gulf War* (Manchester University Press: Manchester and New York)

Thant, U. (1977), *View from the UN* (David and Charles: London)

Thompson, K. W. (1965), 'The new diplomacy and the quest for peace', *International Organization*, vol. 19

Touval, S. (1982), *The Peace Brokers: Mediators in the Arab–Israeli Conflict, 1948–1979* (Princeton University Press: Princeton, New Jersey)

Touval, S. (1989), 'Multilateral negotiation: an analytic approach', *Negotiation Journal*, vol. 5, no. 2

Trask, D. T. (1981), 'A short history of the U.S. Department of State, 1781–1981', *Department of State Bulletin*, vol. 81, no. 2046

Trevelyan, H. (1971), *Living with the Communists* (Gambit: Boston)

Trevelyan, H. (1973), *Diplomatic Channels* (Macmillan: London)

Vance, C. (1983), *Hard Choices: Critical Years in America's Foreign Policy* (Simon and Schuster: New York)

Ware, R. (1990), 'Treaties and the House of Commons', *Factsheet*, FS.57 (Public Information Office, House of Commons: London)

Watson, A. (1982), *Diplomacy: The Dialogue between States* (Eyre Methuen: London)

Watt, D. (1981), 'Do summits only lead to trouble at the top?' *Financial Times*, 3 July

Webster, Sir C. (1961), *The Art and Practice of Diplomacy* (Chatto and Windus: London)

Weihmiller, G. R. and D. Doder (1986), *US–Soviet Summits* (University Press of America: Lanham, New York, and London)

Weinberg, S. (1989), *Armand Hammer: The Untold Story* (Little, Brown: Boston)

Weizman, E. (1981), *The Battle for Peace* (Bantam: Toronto, New York and London)

Werts, J. (1992), *The European Council* (North-Holland: Amsterdam)

Whelan, J. G. (1990), *The Moscow Summit 1988* (Westview Press: Boulder)

Wilenski, P. (1993), 'The structure of the UN in the post-Cold War period', in Roberts A. and B. Kingsbury (eds), *United Nations, Divided World*, 2nd ed (Clarendon Press: Oxford)

Wood, J. R. and J. Serres (1970), *Diplomatic Ceremonial and Protocol: Principles, Procedures and Practices* (Macmillan: London)

Yearbook of the International Law Commission, 1956, vol. II; 1957, vols. I and II; 1958, vols. I and II; 1960, vol. II

Yearbook of International Organizations (1994), vol. 1

Young, J. W. (1986), 'Churchill, the Russians and the Western Alliance: the three-power conference at Bermuda, December 1953', *English Historical Review*

Zamora, S. (1980), 'Voting in international economic organizations', *American Journal of International Law*, vol. 74

Zartman, I. W. and M. Berman, (1982), *The Practical Negotiator* (Yale University Press: New Haven and London)

Zartman, I. W. and S. Touval (1985), 'International mediation: conflict resolution and power politics', *Journal of Social Issues*, vol. 41, no. 2

INDEX

207